Soviet Perspectives
on African Socialism

Soviet Perspectives
on African Socialism

Arthur Jay Klinghoffer

Rutherford ● *Madison* ● *Teaneck*
Fairleigh Dickinson University Press

Associated University Presses, Inc.
Cranbury, New Jersey 08512

SBN
8386-6907-7
Printed in the United States of America

Preface

THIS STUDY IS CONCERNED WITH THE SOVIET VIEW OF SOCIALISM in sub-Saharan Africa during the years 1955-1964. It is geographically limited, partly as a response to considerations of length, but also because the area under consideration presents a general pattern which, although not necessarily homogeneous in most respects, is predominantly Negroid, tribal, and economically underdeveloped. The countries of Northern Africa are excluded from this analysis because their basic culture has little in common with that of the nations of sub-Saharan Africa, aside from a common colonial heritage and geographical proximity. While Northern Africa is also largely underdeveloped economically, as a whole, it is more highly industrialized than sub-Saharan Africa. In addition, the countries of Northern Africa have close ties to the Arab states of the Near East, are embroiled in the affairs of the Mediterranean region, and their societies are basically non-tribal, greatly influenced by Islam, and Arab rather than Negroid. The political dynamics of this region are also at variance with those of the sub-Saharan nations, particularly in regard to the politization of the army. Since the socialist principles practised by African leaders are a prime component of this analysis, the white-dominated, non-socialist regime of the Republic of South Africa will also be excluded, as will the African territories still under Portuguese control.

In regard to time span, this study is limited to the years of Khrushchev's ascendancy in the Soviet Union. This period was marked by a strikingly new Soviet approach to the nations of Asia and Africa as the basic Soviet tenets on underdeveloped and colonial areas began to change radically during the years 1955 and 1956 and continued on this course throughout the Khrushchevian era. The end of 1964 presents an excellent point for terminating this study since Khrushchev was ousted in October, 1964, and his successors have either not yet had time, have been unable in the face of opposition, or possibly do not wish, to formulate a radically new approach to the Asian and African nations, replacing that of the fallen Nikita Sergeevich.

This study is primarily ideological but also attempts to relate the theoretical evolution of Soviet writings on sub-Saharan Africa to the Soviet Union's foreign policy vis-à-vis the states in this area. The basic Soviet view on each issue will be analyzed and differences of opinion which have important political implications will be discussed. However, minor disagreements between authors and Kreminological dissections of the pronouncements made by leading governmental and party officials will be de-emphasized since the main concern of this study is the effect of doctrinal evolution, not the ideological spectrum of Soviet politicians and ideologues on the subject of socialism in sub-Saharan Africa.

A reader of Uri Ra'anan's article on "The Third World in Soviet Perspective," which appeared in the January-February, 1965 issue of *Problems of Communism,* or the transcript of the 1964 Moscow conference on underdeveloped areas, which appeared as a special supplement to the November, 1964, issue of the *Mizan Newsletter,* probably realizes that the attitudes of Soviet Africanists toward socialism in sub-Saharan Africa are not monolithic. However, there is generally a Soviet "line" on each fundamental issue, which sets up certain guidelines for analysis, and the scholars and political ideologues all adhere to it, expressing their own concepts only through the filling in of minor details. It is to this basic "line" that the following study is primarily addressed.

During the period under study, Ivan Potekhin was the leading Soviet expert on African political developments. When the African Institute was founded in 1959, he was made its Director and this institute eventually became affiliated with the Department of Economic Sciences of the Soviet Academy of Sciences. Two rather technical journals, *Sovetskaia Etnografiia* and *Narody Azii i Afriki,* and a more popularized journal, *Aziia i Afrika Segodnia,* contained many articles on Africa and other studies on Africa frequently appeared in *Mirovaia Ekonomika i Mezhdunarodnye Otnosheniia, International Affairs* and *New Times.* Many "liberal" specialists on underdeveloped countries, such as Georgii Mirskii, favored more cordial Soviet ties with the African nationalist leaders and were optimistic about the "progressive" steps taken in certain African countries. These "liberal" writers tended to concentrate around the journal *Mirovaia Ekonomika i Mezhdunarodnye Otnosheniia* and helped bring about many revisions in Soviet theoretical concepts.

The Library of Congress system of transliteration will be used throughout this report, with the exception of the name Mikoyan, which has acquired a generally accepted spelling in English not in accord with the Library of Congress system. Soviet names of Western origin will not be transliterated in strict accordance with the Library of Congress system and it must also be pointed out that the names of the authors in some Soviet English-language journals may not be transliterated exactly since the transliteration used in these journals seems to have a logic all its own and attempting to transliterate back to the Russian language and then back to English in the proper manner often proved to be a trying task.

Acknowledgments

I would like to extend my sincere appreciation to Professor John Hazard of the Russian Institute of Columbia University and to Professor L. Gray Cowan, Director of the Institute of African Studies, Columbia University for the valuable comments and suggestions which they contributed during the preparation of this book. Special gratitude is also due to Megan John Thomas and Susann Hill for their secretarial assistance and to the editors of *African Affairs* for their permission to reprint certain passages from an article of mine which appeared in their journal.

A.J.K.

Contents

Preface   5
1. *The Basic Tenets of African Socialism*   15
2. *The Changing Soviet Outlook on Africa: From Stalinism to Khrushchevism*   40
3. *The Soviet View of Contemporary African Socialism*   60
    The Roads to Socialism   65
    Is Africa Unique?   69
    African Socialism as an Ideology   78
    Progressive and Reactionary Forms of African Socialism   103
4. *Socialism, the Class Struggle, and African Society: The Soviet Analysis*   119
    Traditional African Society   120
    The Class Struggle in Africa   126
    The African Proletariat   134
    The African Peasantry   142
    The African National Bourgeoisie   147
    Other African Social Groups   151
    Roles of the Classes in the National-Liberation Movement   156
    Nationalism and Internationalism   168
5. *The Soviet View of Africa's Future Transition to Scientific Socialism*   181
    The Non-Capitalist Path and the Evolution of African Socialism   181
    Models for the Bypassing of Capitalism   200
    The National Democratic State as a Transition to Socialism   208
    The Role of State Capitalism   215
    The Role of Agricultural Cooperatives   220
6. *Retrospect and Prospect*   226
Bibliography   249
Index   269

Soviet Perspectives
on African Socialism

1 *The Basic Tenets of African Socialism* *

AFRICAN SOCIALISM IS A CURIOUS BLEND OF MARXISM, TRADITIONAL African attitudes, and contemporary ideas of rapid modernization and social transformation. It serves both as a philosophical and as a practical guide for most African leaders and is presented by African theorists as that continent's answer to its search for a political and spiritual identity. The disintegration of the colonial empires and the emergence of numerous independent African states has led African statesmen to seek a path which will ensure the unification of their nations, promote extensive economic development, and avoid making Africa another field of battle in the Cold War. African socialism, with its frequently found concomitant policy of neutralism in East-West political affairs, has emerged as the solution to these problems as the basic socialist precepts are adapted to the African environment. Africans, stressing their cultural and socio-economic heritage, seek a path unique to their continent. They are willing to borrow ideas and methods from other non-African countries but as Leopold Senghor

---

* Since this book deals only with sub-Saharan Africa, this chapter will concentrate upon African socialism in this region and will not include references to African socialists from Northern Africa such as Ben Bella and Nasser.

15

has often warned, "we must assimilate, not be assimilated."[1]

The doctrine of African socialism is still in its period of crystallization and encompasses many diverse viewpoints.[2] An attempt to distinguish some of its main adherents would produce a broad spectrum, running from pro-Moscow and pro-Peking communists to pro-Western humanistic socialists.[3] One group, consisting of the ruling elites of Guinea and Mali (and the former Convention Peoples Party leaders of Ghana) could be termed "Afro-Marxists." These people emphasize Marxist-Leninist ideas of economic development and political structure; link socialist construction with a desire for Pan-African unity; and take a generally anti-Western posture on international issues, while still professing their "positive neutralism."

Another category might include "radical socialists" such as those in power in the Congo (Brazzaville). This country has recently been moving further to the left, both domestically and internationally, but is still in a state of great flux and has not yet developed clear and consistent political and economic programs. Thugh similar to the "Afro-Marxists," the leaders of the Congo (Brazzaville) are in the process of developing ideologically based plans of action and there is no one dominant spokesman. This contrasts greatly with Guinea and Mali where Touré and Keita respectively are recognized as the supreme theorists and where these men, who have been in

---

[1] Léopold Senghor, *On African Socialism* (New York and London, 1964, Praeger) , p. 165.

[2] The Dakar Colloquium, held in Dakar, Senegal from December 3 to 8, 1962, sought a definition of the basic precepts of African socialism. See *Africa Report,* Vol. VIII, No. 5 (May, 1963) , pp. 15–18.

[3] Fenner Brockway outlined four types of socialism in Africa. *See* Fenner Brockway, *African Socialism* (Chester Springs, Pennsylvania, 1963) , pp. 19–24. It should be made clear that this introductory chapter on African socialism includes reference to African socialist movements not in power in their respective countries. However, later chapters describing the Soviet view of African socialism deal almost exclusively with the African socialist regimes in power.

power for many years, have had the time and experience to develop viable socio-political ideologies and action programs.

A third classification of "moderate socialists" could include Kenyatta of Kenya and Kaunda of Zambia. These men appear truly non-aligned and neutral in Cold War politics and are willing to cooperate with both the Eastern and Western blocs. Domestically, they favor a state-controlled socialist economy but are willing to condone some forms of private enterprise and are anxious to attract foreign investment capital.

A fourth group, labelled "social democrats," may include Senghor of Senegal and Tom Mboya, Minister of Economic Planning and Development in Kenya. These men have been closely connected with European socialism, are generally pro-Western in their outlooks, and are more parliamentarian than revolutionary. Senghor emphasizes the humanistic aspect of Marxist thought while Mboya sees socialism as a method for rapid economic development.

Besides the communists, who have not been in power in any African country, there are communist-oriented revolutionary groups which could be called "militant extremist." They include the Union des Populations Camerounaises in Cameroun, some of the leaders of the 1964 revolution in Zanzibar (Babu and Hanga), the Mulele movement in the Congo (Kinshasa) and, to a lesser extent, the Gbenye movement in the Congo (Kinshasa). Although their ideologies are often not too profound, these "militant extremists" use a communist vocabulary, receive support from communist countries, and favor campaigns of revolution and terrorism.

Mention should also be made of the underground Parti Africain de l'Indépendance in Senegal, which is a communist party in all but name. It should also be reiterated that not all African leaders and parties are socialist. Notable exceptions are the late Léon M'ba of Gabon and William Tubman of Liberia.

African socialism is thus comprised of many diverse strands, but, as William Friedland and Carl Rosberg, Jr. have correctly pointed out:

> The many tendencies that exist today in African Socialism make it appear as a potpourri of ideas having little coherence. However, it must be seen in the light of an ideology struggling to meet a vast and formidable range of problems. In time, as some tendencies prove more viable than others, their acceptance, and the discarding of the nonsuccessful, will give to the ideology a clearer direction.[4]

*   *   *

Socialist ideas started to become widespread in Africa during World War II and by the late forties socialism was the ideology of most of the rising African political leaders. The French Communists and Socialists disseminated their respective doctrines throughout the French colonial empire in Africa, and in 1942 and 1943 communist-sponsored Marxist study groups, called Groupes d'Études Communistes, were established in five of the major cities of French Africa. Many future African leaders living in Great Britain were influenced by the British Communists and Labourites and socialist ideas were prominent at the Fifth Pan-African Congress, held in Manchester, England in 1945. Nkrumah, Kenyatta, Banda and Azikiwe were among the participants at this congress. Another important factor is that at the end of World War II socialism was extremely popular in Europe, particularly in France, and many of Africa's future leaders were then students in Paris and London and came under its influence.

After the war, there was very close cooperation between some of the leading African politicians in French Africa and the French Communists and Socialists. There were African representatives in the French National Assembly and the new interterritorial French-African political organization, the Rassemblement Démocratique Africain, was pervaded with

---

[4] William Friedland and Carl Rosberg, Jr., "The Anatomy of African Socialism," in William Friedland and Carl Rosberg, Jr., eds., *African Socialism* (Stanford, Stanford University Press, 1964), p. 2.

socialist and communist ideas. Among the leading figures in British Africa were Nkrumah and Kenyatta, who were influenced by socialism during their period of education abroad and who were active in the socialist-influenced Pan-African movement.

By the time that the African nations were ready to receive their independence, some form of socialist ideas was dominant among the majority of the new African political elite. Probably the first person actually to use the term "African socialism" was Léopold Senghor, during the late forties.

*   *   *

Although there are many conflicting schools of African socialism, there are certain basic tenets which are accepted by most adherents.

African socialists stress the need for rapid economic development and believe that the industrially backward countries of Africa cannot afford to follow the long capitalist path taken by the Western countries. Socialism promises a more dynamic and less anarchic path, but for the African socialists, socialism is a method and a means for achieving a prosperous society, not a step forward toward communism.

The Africans associate capitalism with the colonialists who dominated them and they also give great credence to Lenin's theory of imperialism, which avers that there is a causal relationship between capitalist development and the initiation of imperialist expansion. They also assert that capitalism has no place in Africa because traditional African society is socialist.[5] Julius Nyerere charges that the colonialists brought the capitalist idea of individual ownership of land to Africa and that this concept must be rejected. He opposes landlords who do no work themselves and claims that they are parasites. A man is entitled only to the land which he is able to use.[6] Nyerere believes that under capitalism, wealth is used for

[5] For a further discussion on this point, see below, pp. 27–29.
[6] Julius Nyerere, "Ujamaa: The Basis of African Socialism," in Friedland and Rosberg, *op. cit.,* pp. 242–243.

power and prestige, when it should be used only to satisfy man's basic needs and to abolish poverty.[7] He concludes: "I believe that no underdeveloped country can afford to be anything but socialist."[8]

Kwame Nkrumah is in agreement with Nyerere on this point. He has written: "Capitalism would be a betrayal of the personality and conscience of Africa."[9] "My assertion is that socialism is the only pattern that can within the shortest possible time bring the good life to the people. For socialism assumes the public ownership of the means of production—the land and its resources—and the use of those means for production that will bring benefit to the people."[10]

A terse and logical evaluation of the role of capitalism in Africa has been given by Seydou Badian Kouyate, former Minister of Planning and Rural Economy in Mali: "You cannot be a capitalist when you have no capital."[11]

The African socialists seek to adapt socialism to singularly African conditions and to avoid inroads of ideologies which have no relevance to African society. Tom Mboya has written:

It will be a difficult task keeping Africa clear of ideologies. There will be the Cold War growling its thunder around us. There will be professional communists and professional capitalists finding their way into Africa and preaching their irrelevant ideologies. This is why the newly independent states here are battling to define the African goal without being drawn into the Cold War, why they demand that

---

[7] Speech by Nyerere, August 5, 1961 at World Assembly of Youth's Second Pan-African Youth Seminar. See "Special Issue on African Socialism," *Africa Report*, Vol. VIII, No. 5 (May, 1963), p. 22.

[8] See Paul Sigmund, Jr., ed., *The Ideologies of the Developing Nations* (New York and London, Praeger, 1963), p. 207.

[9] Kwame Nkrumah, *Consciencism* (London, Heinemann, 1964), p. 74.

[10] Kwame Nkrumah, "Some Aspects of Socialism in Africa," in Friedland and Rosberg, *op. cit.*, pp. 259–260.

[11] Cited by Kenneth Grundy, "Mali: The Prospects of 'Planned Socialism,'" in Friedland and Rosberg, *op. cit.*, p. 176.

Africa be left alone in these formative years to develop her own personality and her own brand of socialism.[12]

Great emphasis is placed on traditional African spiritual and cultural values and there is constant reference to what Senghor calls "Négritude" and what Nkrumah and Mboya call "the African personality." Mboya, in discussing the "African personality," has explained: "The phrase represents all the feelings and aspirations the African people have, and especially their resolve to create an African 'image,' as opposed to the image of Africa created by the colonial powers."[13] Senghor sees African culture as a vessel for the "Négritude" of the African peoples and for him, "Culture is the very texture of society."[14] "Culture is inside and outside, above and beneath all human activities: It is the spirit that animates them, that gives a civilization its unique style."[15]

A closely related concept is that of dignity. As expressed by Sékou Touré, the Africans must have dignity in order to assert their identity and personality. For him, there is no dignity without liberty and liberty is a natural right.[16] When de Gaulle came to Guinea in August, 1958 to campaign for a "yes" vote in the referendum on the French Community Touré stressed the dignity of the Guinean people and even used a capital "D." He went on to avow: "We prefer poverty in liberty to riches in servitude."[17] In the September referendum, Guinea opted for independence and did not join the French Community.

* * *

In political terms, African socialism derives many of its

---

[12] Tom Mboya, *Freedom and After* (Boston, Little, Brown, 1963), p. 169.
[13] *Ibid.*, p. 230.
[14] Senghor, *op. cit.*, p. 49.
[15] *Ibid.*, p. 80.
[16] Sékou Touré, *Expérience Guinéenne et Unité Africaine* (Paris, Présence Africaine, 1961), p. 81.
[17] *Ibid.*, p. 81.

precepts from Marxism-Leninism. Besides the use of Marxist-Leninist terminology, African socialism also features centralized one-party rule, the principle of democratic centralism within this ruling party, state control of the basic sectors of the economy, and a belief in Lenin's theory of imperialism. The dominant political party is the hub of all facets of the organized social, economic and political life of the community as it extends its radiating influence into all mass organizations. William Friedland calls this type of structure "monism" and writes that "monism" exists when "all institutions have a central institutional focus."[18] This principle of central coordination is reflected in the concluding resolutions of the Parti Démocratique Guinéen adopted at a congress in Kankan in April, 1960: "The Guinean revolution is not a multi-revolutionary action whose interventions in the various sectors of national activities each has its specific internal logic. On the contrary, ours is a single political revolution, and thus each action must be coordinated with all other actions both as to its nature and objectives."[19] The ruling party always serves as the instrument of coordination. Writing in *I Speak of Freedom*, Kwame Nkrumah declared: "The Convention People's Party is Ghana. Our party not only provides the government but is also the custodian which stands guard over the welfare of the people."[20]

In *The Communist Manifesto*, Marx and Engels discussed ten features of development once the proletariat gains power. The African socialists, although not proletarians, are carrying out many aspects of this program set forth by Marx and Engels. They have opposed the concept of private property in land, have created national banks which control all credit, have established state control over transportation and communication, have extended state control over the means of production, and have attempted to provide free public educa-

---

[18] William Friedland, "Four Sociological Trends in African Socialism," in *Africa Report, op. cit.*, p. 10.
[19] *Africa Report, op. cit.*, p. 27.
[20] Kwame Nkrumah, *I Speak of Freedom* (New York, Praeger, 1961), p. 161.

tion for all. In addition, they believe in the equal obligation of all to work and have established agricultural labor armies (as in the rural programs in Guinea and Mali). *The Communist Manifesto* calls for the abolition of the distinction between town and country and this has been aided inadvertently in Africa as many peasants work for part of the year as industrial workers in the cities.

All the facets of African socialism just cited point out the many similarities between African socialism and both Marxism and Soviet communism. However, African socialism differs from both of these schools of thought in many respects. For the Africans, socialism is not considered to be a step toward communism. It is cited as a programmatic response to the needs of the African peoples and is actually viewed as a return to the supposed socialist structure of Africa which existed before the arrival of the colonialists. Also, Africa is believed to be unique and therefore not subject to any universal laws of development. African socialism is regarded as different from socialism in any other environment. This idea is opposed by Marxist-Leninists, who believe that there are universal objective laws of history and that there can be only one variety of socialism.

African socialists also differ from Marxist-Leninists in that they usually do not recognize the existence of a class struggle on the African continent. They also have dominant parties which claim to represent the masses, not specific classes. Broad national people's fronts govern the African countries and there is no dictatorship of the proletariat. Furthermore, the parties in power, although often having the duty of serving as the vanguard of the people, have more of a mass than an elitist composition.

Although many African socialists are Pan-Africanists, the dynamic force of nationalism plays a vital role in the formulation of the concepts of African socialism. The regimes in power are usually the political cores of the national independence movements, placed in control of their nations for the first time. The task of national unification is among the most important. This emphasis on nationalism is opposed to Marx's condemnation of nationalism as "bourgeois." It is also opposed to the Soviet concept of "proletarian internationalism" but the Soviets have taken a more favourable attitude toward nationalism during the last few years.[21]

African socialism also differs from Soviet communism in the obvious respect that no African nation has yet joined the Soviet bloc (or "socialist commonwealth"). Admiration for many of the methods used in the Soviet Union does not lead the Africans to seek a political alliance with a potential dominating partner. And, as has already been pointed out, some African socialists are actually pro-Western.

Léopold Senghor has thoughtfully analyzed the relationship between his brand of African socialism and the ideas of Karl Marx. His approach is: "We shall take Marx's ideas, theory and theories as a starting point."[22] He stresses Marx's humanistic philosophy and considers Marx to be primarily a sociologist and philosopher, not an economist.[23] "Humanism, the philosophy of humanism, rather than economics, is the basic character and positive contribution of Marxian thought."[24] Senghor is also attracted by other aspects of Marx's philosophy: "Let us recapitulate Marx's positive contributions. They are: the philosophy of humanism, economic theory, dialectical method. To these we may add trade unionism, planning, and also federalism and cooperation, . . ."[25]

Senghor believes that Marx was too deterministic and underestimated man's freedom. He also opposes many of Marx's economic theories. He points out that socialism has not triumphed in the industrialized countries of Western Europe, that economic crises are occurring less often, and that Marx's theory of capitalistic concentration has not come

---

[21] This point is discussed below, pp. 175–180.
[22] Senghor, *op. cit.*, p. 27.
[23] *Ibid.*, p. 33.
[24] *Ibid.*, p. 34.
[25] *Ibid.*, p. 45.

true as the number of small and medium-sized firms has grown. He also charges Marx with underestimating the importance of the peasantry and with not realizing the complexity of class relationships.[26]

Senghor is cited here just as an example of the way one African socialist views Marxism. Of course, many other African leaders have different conceptions of the relevancy of Marxism to Africa. While Senghor emphasizes Marx's philosophical humanism, others, such as Nkrumah, stress the application of Marx's economic theories to the African scene. Nkrumah advocates rapid industrialization and often speaks about state ownership of the means of production. For him, economics, not culture, is the basis of society: "Above all, our economic advancement must be the foundation upon which to erect an equitable and happy society."[27]

Although African socialists avow the importance of socialist theory, they are generally more pragmatic than doctrinaire in their approaches to practical problems. Theory is a guide to action but one must not be dogmatic in its application. As Sékou Touré has said, "To adopt socialism for the sake of socialism is to try to harvest with nothing but the handle of the sickle."[28]

African socialists usually stress practice, not theory. Tom Mboya has written: "African socialism consists in practice, not in theory, and one cannot argue its merits in terms of communism or British or Italian socialism."[29] Léopold Senghor rejects "prefabricated models" such as the Russian, Chinese and Scandinavian. Much can be learned from them but applying methods dogmatically leads to failure.[30] His former prime minister, Mamadou Dia, said while visiting Moscow in 1962:

---

[26] *Ibid.,* p. 32.
[27] Nkrumah, "Some Aspects of Socialism in Africa," *op. cit.,* p. 262.
[28] *Africa Report, op. cit.,* p. 27.
[29] Mboya, *op. cit.,* p. 169.
[30] Senghor, *op. cit.,* p. 157.

Our choice is to build socialism in our country, to build it not in an abstract but in a concrete manner, not according to theoretical schemes but proceeding from the natural economic and social condtions in our country. We say at the same time that we do not wish to be dogmatists. And I wish to tell you, since I am bound to be frank here, that we do not pretend to be Marxist-Leninists. We are only people of good will, concerned about our country's failure and determined to learn the lessons of history.[31]

Sékou Touré has been the chief exponent of the primacy of practice over theory. He claims: "Practice is superior to thought, superior to theory."[32] He has said:

Society is not made for principles, for a philosophy, for a doctrine, for a given science, but, on the contrary, science, philosophy and principles of action must be determined by the people in the light of the realities of the people. Instead of applying society to science, science must be applied to society. Thus the Marxism which served to mobilise the African populations, and in particular the working class, and to lead that class to success, has been amputated of those of its characteristics which did not correspond to the African realities.[33]

Touré expresses his belief in Marxism but accepts only those tenets of Marxism which are applicable to Africa.[34] He says that failure results if one completely accepts an abstract philosophy. "I say that Philosophy does not interest us. We have concrete needs."[35]

This emphasis by African socialists on the need to adapt socialist theory to specific conditions leads to the establishment of various national socialisms and is one of the reasons for the existence of many varieties of African socialism, not one unified body of thought and practice.

---

[31] *Pravda,* June 6, 1962, p. 1.
[32] Touré, *op. cit.,* p. 468.
[33] Aimé Césaire, "The Political Thought of Sékou Touré," *Présence Africaine* (English edition), Vol. I ,1960, p. 69.
[34] Touré, *op. cit.,* p. 420.
[35] Césaire, *op. cit.,* p. 69.

In regard to the role of theory, Kwame Nkrumah takes a more doctrinaire approach than do most other African socialists. He believes that "the ideology of a society is total." It is manifested in all aspects of society and "embraces the whole life of a people."[36] Following an orthodox Marxist line of reasoning, Nkrumah has written:

> In societies where there are competing ideologies, it is still usual for one ideology to be dominant. This ideology is that of the ruling group. Though the ideology is the key to the inward identity of its group, it is in intent solidarist. For an ideology does not seek merely to unite a section of the people; it seeks to unite the whole of the society in which it finds itself. In its effects, it certainly reaches the whole society, when it is dominant. For, besides seeking to establish common attitudes and purposes for the society, the dominant ideology is that which in the light of circumstances decides what forms institutions shall take, and in what channels the common effort is to be directed.[37]

Despite his analysis of the role of ideology, Nkrumah realizes practical needs. He welcomed certain foreign investments and also permitted the functioning of a private sector in the Ghanaian economy. Neither act was in accord with his ideological convictions.

*   *   *

Most African socialists claim that even before the arrival of the colonialists, traditional African society was socialist or communalist. Julius Nyerere has said: "We in Africa have no more need of being 'converted' to socialism than we have of being 'taught' democracy. Both are rooted in our own past —in the traditional society which produced us."[38] Tom Mboya has described some of the aspects of traditional African socialism:

> When I talk of "African Socialism" I refer to those proved codes of conduct in the African societies which have, over

---

[36] Nkrumah, *Consciencism, op. cit.,* p. 59.
[37] *Ibid.,* p. 57.
[38] Nyerere, *op. cit.,* p. 246.

the ages, conferred dignity on our people and afforded them security regardless of their station in life. I refer to universal charity which characterized our societies and I refer to the African's thought processes and cosmological ideas which regard man not as a social means, but as an end and entity in the society.[39]

Nkrumah and Senghor have similar interpretations.[40]

Ruth Schachter Morgenthau has written that one of the main features of African socialism is the "solidarity of the kinship group."[41] Africans can express themselves and attain a personal identity only when they are part of a larger group. All men are considered brothers. Mamadou Dia said at the Dakar Colloquium in 1962: "As you know, African development is characterized by an underlying conception of man. Not individualistic man, but l'homme personnaliste, who finds his full blossoming in the coherence of a living society, of an organic community."[42]

Julius Nyerere supports this view and has avowed his intention to spread the principles of kinship solidarity to the national level, and then to the international level: "The foundation, and the objective, of African Socialism is the extended family. The true African Socialist does not look on one class of men as his brethren and another as his natural enemies. . . . He rather regards all men as his brethren—as members of his ever extending family." Nyerere went on to say: " 'Ujamaa,' then, or 'familyhood,' describes our Socialism."[43]

Touré differs somewhat with Nyerere on the issue of kinship solidarity. Although he agrees that man expresses him-

---

[39] Tom Mboya, "African Socialism," in Friedland and Rosberg, *op. cit.,* p. 251.

[40] See Nkrumah, *Consciencism, op. cit.,* p. 68 and Senghor, *op. cit.,* p. 49.

[41] Ruth Schachter Morgenthau, "African Socialism: Declaration of Ideological Independence," in *Africa Report, op. cit.,* p. 3.

[42] *Africa Report, op. cit.,* p. 18.

[43] Nyerere, *op. cit.,* p. 246.

self only when part of a community, he finds this community more on the state level than in the traditional culture.[44]

Another feature of traditional African society, which is pointed to by Nyerere as a manifestation of socialism, is the concept that all people must work. Everyone must contribute to the economic welfare of the community. "There is no such thing as socialism without work."[45]

The communal system of agriculture is still another socialistic aspect of traditional African society, according to the African socialists. Tom Mboya has explained how the communes can be modernized and become a part of the present socialist structure. He advocates a cooperative system: "Through cooperatives, a clan can translate the old tribal structure into the modern money economy. Its members can live and work together as they did before, but organize a better accounting system and introduce a money market without surrendering their sense of communal obligation and security."[46]

The African socialists assert their desire to return to the socialist values and practices of traditional African society, many of which were disrupted during the lengthy period of colonial rule. However, they expect to integrate these traditional elements with knowledge gained during the past centuries and to produce a modern variety of socialism which is singularly adapted to the African environment. Nkrumah has pointed out that present African society differs from the traditional society because of the additional influences of Islam and Euro-Christianity. He calls for an ideology which will combine the humanism of traditional African society with the Islamic and Euro-Christian influences.[47]

African socialists generally deny the existence of either

---

[44] See Charles Andrain, "Guinea and Senegal: Contrasting Types of African Socialism," in Friedland and Rosberg, op. cit., p. 161.
[45] Nyerere, op. cit., p. 241.
[46] Mboya, Freedom and After, op. cit., p. 172.
[47] Nkrumah, Consciencism, op. cit., p. 70.

classes or a class struggle in African society. Senghor writes about "social groups" competing for influence but denies that they are classes. He claims that there is no exploitation of others in Africa: "Thus, in the working out of our African mode of Socialism, the problem is not how to put an end to the exploitation of man by his fellow, but to prevent it ever happening. . . ."[48]

Nkrumah recognizes the existence of some classes and thus is in disagreement with most other African socialists. He believes that the coming of the colonialists brought about the formation of classes. However, he concurs with other African theorists when he writes that there were no classes, in the Marxist sense of horizontal stratification, nor was there exploitation, in traditional African society. Among the African socialist leaders who have held power, Nkrumah's views most closely approach those of the Soviet communists in regard to the subject of classes. In the communist vein, he has written: "The history of a nation is, unfortunately, too easily written as the history of its dominant class."[49]

Since most African socialists deny the existence of classes in Africa, they certainly oppose the Marxist idea that class determines consciousness. They believe that any member of society can become a socialist. Nyerere stated in his "Ujamaa" speech: "Socialism—like democracy—is an attitude of mind. . . . In the individual, as in the society, it is an attitude of mind which distinguishes the socialist from the nonsocialist. It has nothing to do with the possession or nonpossession of wealth."[50] He believes that even a millionaire can become a socialist.

In contrast with the views of Karl Marx and the Soviet communists, the African socialists are usually not atheists and see no incompatibility between religion and socialism.

---

[48] Léopold Senghor, "African-Style Socialism," in Friedland and Rosberg, op. cit., p. 265.
[49] Nkrumah, Consciencism, op. cit., p. 63.
[50] Nyerere, op. cit., p. 238.

Kofi Baako, a former Ghanaian spokesman, has written: "In fact, atheism is foreign to Africa, and religion is the basis of all our culture."[51] Leading adherents of African socialism, such as Nkrumah, Touré, Senghor and Keita, have all recognized the role of religion under African socialism. Senghor has queried: "Can we integrate Negro-African cultural values, especially religious values, into socialism? We must answer that question once and for all with an unequivocal yes."[52] Modibo Keita of Mali declared in a speech at Bamako: "I am convinced that the republic and people of Mali will (prove) the socialist concept and also will remain good Moslems, Christians and animists."[53]

* * *

At least in their theoretical pronouncements, African socialists emphasize the importance of the masses and generally think of society as a collective rather than as a community of individuals. This is in accordance with the concept of the extended kinship group and the stress is on national unity and on an interpretation of the function of the ruling party as the depository of the general will of the people. According to Touré, the Parti Démocratique Guinéen represents all of the people, gives important assignments to common people, and has confidence in the masses. The leaders must know and respect the masses and the level of democracy is dependent upon the degree of intimacy between the masses and the leaders.[54] The guiding party must not become over-intellectualized and divorce itself from the realities of Guinean life. It is preeminent but strives to carry out the will of the people it represents. The views of Touré appear to have much in common with those of Jean Jacques Rousseau.

Senghor's approach is less collectivist than that of Touré and most other African socialists as he asserts his belief in the

---

[51] Sigmund, *op. cit.*, p. 190.
[52] Senghor, *On African Socialism, op. cit.*, p. 26.
[53] *Africa Report, op. cit.*, p. 29.
[54] See Touré, *op. cit.*, pp. 352–368 and pp. 386–387.

importance of individual expression and identity. However, he points to the party as the consciousness of the masses and avers that the party must raise the masses to political consciousness.[55] This idea that the party is a political vanguard of the masses is strongly supported by Nkrumah. The 1957 Constitution of the Convention People's Party stated that the aim of the C.P.P. is, "to serve as the vigorous conscious political vanguard for removing all forms of oppression and for the establishment of a democratic government."[56]

African socialists claim both practical and theoretical grounds for the establishment of one-party regimes. They assert that their nations were united in the struggle for independence and that once this independence has been achieved, the national unity must be maintained during the period of nation-building and extensive economic development. Central direction is needed to promote rapid technological progress and to unify the diverse elements of the society. A multi-party system can only create divisions among the population and slow down economic and social advancement. African socialists also point to a traditional African practice of gaining unanimity of decision through persuasion. The majority convinces the minority of the correctness of its decisions and no final solution can be reached until all are in agreement. On the theoretical side, they cite the Marxist concepts that one party must always be dominant and that the party of the workers (which in Africa has been extended to include the whole nation) must serve as the political vanguard.

The African socialist parties have a mass, rather than an elitist, nature and usually do not grant the workers a special status as the vanguard. There is no belief that the state must wither but Leninist concepts of party organization are predominant. Sékou Touré has said that organization is the

---

[55] Senghor, On African Socialism, op. cit., p. 159.
[56] Kwame Nkrumah, Ghana: The Autobiography of Kwame Nkrumah (New York, Thomas Nelson and Sons, 1957), p. 289.

most important aspect of politics.[57] In general, the parties have a rigid structure of command, in accordance with the principle of "democratic centralism," and they are highly disciplined, centralized, and engaged in almost all facets of the life of the community and state.

The African socialist approach to trade unions is similar to that of the Soviet communists. There should be no conflict between the state, which is a major employer, and the unions since they have the same purposes: to increase production and raise the standard of living of the workers. The unions should be constructive rather than destructive and should emphasize production rather than the material prosperity of their members. Any opposition to the state is viewed as ambivalent since the state represents all citizens and opposing it is really opposing one's own interests. The general pattern is to favor one large union in each country and, in some countries, the union is part of the party-state apparatus.

Rapid economic development is one of the prime targets of the African socialists. They no longer want to be dependent upon the industrially advanced countries, many of which were colonial powers, for their necessities. While it is recognized that most African countries are primarily agricultural, industrialization is stressed. Senghor is an exception as he wants Senegal to remain predominantly agricultural.

In African socialist economies, the state usually controls the basic sectors of the economy such as heavy industry, foreign trade, transportation and communication. Other features are comprehensive economic planning and, in some countries such as Guinea and Mali, labor armies for special projects ("investissement humain" programs). The state also has great control over agricultural developments and supports communal and cooperative landholding.

*   *   *

Although many aspects of African socialism are quite sim-

---

[57] See his Political Report at the Second National Conference of the P.D.G. Cadres, November 27, 1958 in Touré, *op. cit.*, pp. 352–368.

ilar to Soviet communism, most African socialists follow a policy of non-alignment and do not desire to join the communist camp. Julius Nyerere has said: "The people who anxiously watch to see whether we will become 'Communist' or 'Western democrats' will both be disconcerted. We do not have to be either . . . but we have the lessons of the East and West before us, and we have our own traditions to contribute to mankind's pool of knowledge."[58]

African socialists generally support the Soviet stands on colonialism, neo-colonialism, and imperialism. However, these anti-Western positions should not be misconstrued as being pro-communist. In the presence of Leonid Brezhnev, then Chairman of the Presidium of the Supreme Soviet of the U.S.S.R., Sékou Touré bluntly expressed his views on both communism and colonialism:

> Though we courageously expressed the feelings of the Guinean people by declaring that Guineans are not Communists, that the Guinean Democratic Party is not a Communist Party and that the state of Guinea is not an organizational subsidiary of any other people or a branch of any military of financial coalition, we are also firmly convinced that we expressed the political and moral views of our people when we made the historical choice of a relentless struggle against all phenomena connected with imperialism and colonialism, a struggle for the most comprehensive democratization of our society and for the establishment of a system based exclusively on the common interests of the Guinean people and the other peoples of the world.[59]

African socialists usually associate imperialism with the Western powers but Jomo Kenyatta has warned that imperialism from the East is as great a threat as that from the West. He went on to say: "Kenya shall not exchange one master for

---

[58] Cited by Colin Legum, *Pan-Africanism: A Short Political Guide* (London and Dunmow, Pall Mall Press, 1962), p. 114.
[59] *Sovetskii Soiuz—iskrennyi drug narodov Afriki* (Moscow, Gosudarstvennoe Izdatel'stvo Politicheskoi Literatury, 1961), p. 53.

a new master. We intend to remain our own masters forever.
Let every nation in the East or West take heed of this warn-
ing."[60] In a similar vein, Mamadou Dia, former Prime Minister of Senegal, has questioned the sincerity and motives behind the Soviet support for African independence movements:

> What we should point out particularly to the apologists of
> Marxism-Leninism, who pose at the same time as champions
> of African nationalism, is that their ideological support of
> the liberation movement is in reality motivated by tactical
> and strategic considerations. As a matter of fact, in Marxism-
> Leninism there could be no absolute right to indepen-
> dence.[61]

For the Africans, the Soviet system serves as a model which
should not be completely imitated, but from which certain
ideas should be borrowed. Many elements of the Soviet system
such as the atheistic policy of the government and the re-
stricted membership of the ruling party, are considered to be
irrelevant to the African setting. Modibo Keita said, while
visiting Moscow, that he hopes to borrow from the Soviet experience, even though Mali's conditions of life and socialist
methods differ from those of the Soviet Union.[62] Léopold
Senghor has a harsher evaluation of Soviet communism:

> We are not Communists for a practical reason: the anxiety
> for human dignity and the need for freedom—man's free-
> doms and freedoms of collectivities—that animate Marx's
> thought and provide its revolutionary ferment, this anxiety
> and this need are unknown to Communism whose major
> deviation is Stalinism. The 'dictatorship of the proletariat,'
> which was to be only temporary, becomes the dictatorship
> of the Party and State in self-perpetuation.[63]

Kwame Nkrumah has expressed admiration for the Soviet
Union's consolidation of many nationalities into one state.

---

[60] New York Times, June 2, 1965, p. 5.
[61] Mamadou Dia, The African Nations and World Solidarity (New
York, Praeger, 1961), p. 15.
[62] Modibo Keita, Pravda, May 23, 1962, p. 1.
[63] Senghor, On African Socialism, op. cit., p. 46.

He cites the Soviet Union as an example of effective political union and he claims that the Soviet experience has great relevance to the ideal of African unity and should therefore be emulated.[64]

African socialists are in the process of creating a uniquely African variety of socialism which takes into account many of the features of traditional African society and includes non-Marxist elements. They seek to overcome economic underdevelopment and it should be kept in mind that the institution of the Soviet system was also, in many respects, an answer to the very same need. Some similarities are therefore bound to exist.

* * *

The African socialist leaders derive many of their concepts from the West but their ideologies are, to a great extent, directed against the West. Accepting the validity of many Western socialist views and being influenced by Western ideas of equality, consent of the governed, and national self-determination, they nevertheless use these ideas to attack the colonial practices of the Western powers and to denigrate the basic human values of capitalist society. Attempting to master the technological skills of the West, they strive to modernize their countries but this modernization is more a response to underdevelopment than a conscious effort to imitate Western life and it is therefore inaccurate to apply the term "Westernization" to this process. Almost every underdeveloped nation must eventually cope with the problems of the Industrial Revolution and despite the fact that this stage of development was first manifested in the Western world, it was not a peculiarly Western phenomenon. African socialists borrow methods and ideas from both the East and West but they attempt to integrate them into African life and not be drawn into the arena of world conflict, in which both their values and political independence would soon be overwhelmed. In this respect, African socialism has an element of isolationism.

---

[64] Kwame Nkrumah, *Pravda,* July 25, 1961, p. 3.

The emphasis upon African history and traditional African values is partly a response to the humiliating colonial experience but, to a great degree, it is a myth around which to rally the African peoples and help raise their self esteem. The names Ghana and Mali were selected purely to show that Africa has a long historical heritage and the study of African history has been accelerated for the very same purpose. Great attention is devoted to the supposedly unique African personality and traditional African society is idealized beyond reasonable bounds. Although there is some basis for the views that African man expresses himself only within a community and that Africans always arrive at unanimity after discussions, these are definitely over-simplifications and true African society is not quite this idyllic.

The socialist programs and one-party structures adopted by most African leaders are largely aimed at helping the African peoples but they also serve as instruments for absolute rule by the educated elite. As the self-appointed vanguard of the people, this elite creates a centralized party through which it controls almost all aspects of national life and suppresses all opposition. Since there are so few trained administrators, the party elite considers itself the only group capable of effectively conducting national affairs and it concentrates all authority in itself. Although actions are performed in the name of the people, the people are not trusted to decide their own actions. Central direction is the keynote as the African socialist elite considers itself superior to the masses. It usually disdains manual labor and yet it exhorts the people to work hard for their nation. Palace politics, attention paid mainly to the needs of the elite, and a wide gap between the leadership and the masses is often the result and it therefore is not surprising that the African military has increasingly been stepping in to end the rule of this elite "new class."

The one-party systems set up in many African countries are structured in accordance with the Leninist principle of "democratic centralism." As in the Soviet Union, the centralist aspect predominates, despite the avowals of African socialist leaders that their parties are truly democratic. Although these parties have large memberships, mass participation does not denote that these masses are free to exercise their will. Strong central control is dominant, even in those parties which permit a degree of internal democratic discussion. The fact that no opposition parties are permitted to run rival candidates in elections belies the democratic professions of the leaders, at least democracy as we know it in the Western world. The limitations placed upon trade union activity and the concept that there should be no contradictions between the trade unions and the party-state apparatus are also restrictions upon free democratic activity. However, this system of rule, although undemocratic in many respects, may be most appropriate to the developing African countries. Practices of Western democracy may be irrelevant to the present African experience as decisive governmental action is needed to weld peoples together into nations and to forge the available resources into viable national economies. In such a context, Western democracy may be a luxury which can not be afforded, rather than a necessity.

Although the trend toward autocratic methods may be part of a passing phase, the African socialist regimes may be sowing the seeds of totalitarianism. Carl Friedrich and Zbigniew Brzezinski have outlined six major facets of totalitarianism which, reduced to their simplest form, include an ideology which encompasses all aspects of society: a single party; terroristic police control; party control of the means of communication; state control of the means for armed combat, and central control and direction of the economy.[65] The relevance of this description to certain African countries (and particularly to the former Ghanaian government of Nkrumah) must not be dismissed.

African socialists usually aim at economic self-sufficiency

---

[65] Carl Friedrich and Zbigniew Brzezinski, *Totalitarian Dictatorship and Autocracy* (New York and London, Praeger, 1961), pp. 9–10.

for their countries and at abolition of the capitalist exploitation evident in private industry. They stress industrialization so that the African nations will no longer have to rely upon others for their industrial needs and they seek Pan-African economic cooperation for the same reason. In these respects, African socialism breeds isolationism. However, the African leaders recognize the weakness of their economies and realize that it is presently in their interest to encourage both foreign trade and aid and some domestic private enterprise. Pragmatism has therefore proved to be a stronger force than ideological commitment.

* * *

The theory of African socialism blends the past with the future as traditional African values are believed to be compatible with modern industrial society. It is questionable whether these values truly existed and it is also questionable whether the African nations will be able to master the industrial process and overcome economic retardation. However, the African leaders are seeking their own continental synthesis to this seemingly paradoxical situation and only time will tell the future evolution of African life.

2 The Changing Soviet Outlook on Africa: From Stalinism to Khrushchevism

DURING THE YEARS 1955 AND 1956, THE SOVIET UNION DEVELOPED a fresh approach toward Africa as the Stalinist concepts regarding the African scene were discarded for a new Khrushchevian analysis. The Stalinist outlook had featured a rigid dualistic view of the world and the African countries had been considered reserves of the imperialist camp. The Soviet Union paid little attention to Africa and therefore missed an opportunity to gain influence within the nationalist movements. Emphasis was placed upon the revolutionary potential of the African proletariat and this tiny group was far from being either politically influential or well organized.

The new Khrushchevian analysis was evolved during the period of the Bandung Conference (April, 1955) and the Twentieth Congress of the Communist Party of the Soviet Union (February, 1956). It contained a strikingly different evaluation of the political independence of former colonies; replaced the two camp concept with a recognition of neutralism; considered most African countries as being anti-imperialist rather than reserves of imperialism; and stressed the theme of peace, with the concomitant adoption of a line which was less revolutionary. Extremely significant was the more favorable attitude adopted toward the national bourgeois leaders. This change in viewpoint may have been brought about because of the communists' failure to gain mass support in the colonial areas; because the national bourgeois leaders were firmly in control and the possibilities for proletarian seizures of power were negligible; because many national bourgeois leaders were adopting progressive social and economic programs; and because the Soviets saw a chance to channel the anti-Western views of the national bourgeois leaders into diplomatic support for the Soviet Union's foreign policy pronouncements and acts.

The flexible "creative Marxist" approach of the Khrushchevian era featured a realization that all African countries did not possess the same economic and social conditions and that different Soviet policies were thus needed for different countries. The Soviet Union greatly stepped up both its trade and aid programs with African states and attempted to encourage these states to take a non-capitalist path of development. It aligned with many of them on the issues of colonialism, peace, and disarmament and tried to spread Soviet influence throughout Africa. Richard Lowenthal has ably described the Soviet Union's intentions in Africa: "Generally, it will try step by step to replace Western political, economic and cultural influence in these countries, while respecting their military neutrality and ideological independence."[66]

It must be pointed out that although cooperation with national bourgeois governments was a main facet of the Khrushchevian approach to Africa, Soviet foreign policy also had another side, that of working against non-communist governments from behind the scenes. African communist parties helped in this process, as did communist agents who worked within the ruling, and other, parties.

*   *   *

In the Stalinist view of Africa, both the colonial and newly

---

[66] Richard Lowenthal, "The Prospects for Pluralistic Communism," *Dissent,* Vol. XII, No. 1 (winter, 1965), p. 141.

independent countries were considered to be reserves of the imperialist camp. The independence of the latter nations was thought to be a sham since the colonialists still maintained control of the economies of these areas and dictated the policies of their governments. The African countries were considered relatively unimportant as Stalin focused his attention upon the industrial nations of the West. What significance Africa had was due to its role as an appendage of the imperialist camp. Colonial independence movements were therefore of consequence since they weakened the power of the imperialists and hastened the advent of the proletarian revolutions in the mother countries. Ivan Potekhin, the leading Soviet authority on Africa from the end of World War II until his death late in 1964, wrote in 1950:

> The struggle of the oppressed peoples in the colonies and dependent countries likewise coalesces with the struggle of the proletariat against imperialism in the metropoles of all advanced capitalist countries—for the dictatorship of the proletariat, for socialism. On the other hand, since the colonies are the rear forces, the reserve of imperialism, the proletariat of the advanced capitalist countries cannot attain a durable victory over imperialism without liberating the colonies.[67]

Soviet writers during the Stalinist period had blanket theories which attempted to cover events in all African countries. Hardly any differentiation was made between various parts of Africa and, as Potekhin has pointed out, Soviet research had definite aims and did not strive for objectivity: "The Soviet ethnographer cannot study the ethnography of the peoples in the colonies apart from the national liberation movement of these peoples. He cannot do this, first of all, because he feels it the duty of the Soviet scientist to use his

---

[67] Ivan Potekhin, "Stalin's Theory of Colonial Revolution and the National Liberation Movement in Tropical and South Africa," *Sovetskaia Etnografiia*, No. 1, 1950. (See translation in Thomas Thornton, ed., *The Third World in Soviet Perspective* (Princeton, Princeton University Press, 1964), p. 34.)

research to aid the struggle of the forces of progress against the forces of imperialist reaction."[68]

Great emphasis was placed upon the African proletariat. It was considered to be the only force capable of achieving true independence for the African nations. According to the two-stage theory of colonial revolution, the bourgeois-democratic revolution would be followed by a socialist revolution, led by the proletariat. As has already been mentioned, the independence achieved under national bourgeois leadership, as a result of the bourgeois-democratic revolution, was considered by the Soviets to be a sham. Potekhin averred: "Stalin's theory of colonial revolution proceeds from the fact that the solution of the colonial question, the liberation of oppressed peoples from colonial slavery, is impossible without a proletarian revolution and the overthrow of imperialism."[69] He claimed that the national bourgeoisie wanted independence but it sought to follow the capitalist path and avoided democratic reforms.[70] "Comrade Stalin warned, and the past quarter-century has completely confirmed, that complete and final victory of the colonial revolution is possible only when the proletariat has the leading role."[71] Writing in 1953, Potekhin asserted that the national-liberation movement was moving into its second stage and that national bourgeois leadership was being replaced by that of the proletariat. The peasantry and petty bourgeoisie were allied with the proletariat in this venture.[72]

The idea that the national bourgeoisie was prone to compromise with the imperialists was one of the fundamental aspects of the Stalinist view of Africa. The national bourgeoisie was actually considered to have two parts: a fairly progressive petty bourgeoisie, which would sometimes support

---

[68] *Ibid.,* p. 38.
[69] *Ibid.,* p. 32.
[70] *Ibid.,* p. 33.
[71] *Ibid.,* p. 37.
[72] Ivan Potekhin, "Etnicheskii i klassovoi sostav naseleniia Zolotogo Berega," *Sovetskaia Etnografiia,* No. 3, 1953, p. 113.

the program of the proletariat, and a big bourgeoisie, which cooperated with the imperialists. However, the former group was believed to be incapable of completing the task of national liberation and was more interested in constitutional reform than in revolution. National bourgeois governments were deemed to be fronts for rule by the colonial powers. Writing in 1953 about the Gold Coast (now Ghana), which was then still a colony but which was governed by Nkrumah's Convention People's Party, Potekhin declared: "The government of the People's Party is basically a screen concealing the actual rule of English imperialism. . . . The People's Party, representing the interests of the big national bourgeoisie of the Gold Coast, deceived the confidence of the people. Coming to power because of the support of the people, the leaders of the party made a sharp turn to the right, to the side of the collaboration with English imperialism. . . ."[73]

A quite different analysis of the nature of the Convention People's Party was to be put forth during the Khrushchevian era.

*   *   *

The new Khrushchevian approach to African affairs began to crystallize at about the time of the Bandung Conference of Asian and African leaders (April, 1955). It is significant that the beginning of this new attitude came immediately after the resignation of Georgii Malenkov as Chairman of the Council of Ministers of the U.S.S.R. (February, 1955) and his replacement by Nikolai Bulganin. As First Secretary of the Central Committee of the Communist Party of the Soviet Union, Nikita Khrushchev formed a ruling combination with Bulganin, with Khrushchev being the senior partner. In March, 1958, Khrushchev emerged as the sole leader as he replaced Bulganin as Chairman of the Council of Ministers, while still retaining his post as First Secretary of the Communist Party.

Soviet writers showed enthusiasm for the Bandung Confer-

---

[73] *Ibid.,* p. 113.

ence, even though most of the delegates present were representatives, at least in Soviet eyes, of the national bourgeoisie.
E. Zhukov, writing in the Soviet journal *International Affairs*, declared that the solidarity of the peoples of Asia and
Africa was the greatest threat to the interests of the imperialists.[74]

The Bandung Conference ushered in a revised analysis of
the nature of the national bourgeoisie. Political independence
was seen in a new light and Soviet writers recognized that the
national bourgeoisie could lead the national-liberation movements. Most nationalist parties, which were led by the national bourgeoisie, were no longer the subject of accusations
that they were fronts for the imperialists and Potekhin, writing at the beginning of 1956, asserted: "Not all bourgeois
parties were attached to the progressive camp but the very fact
of the creation in a short period of time in all colonies of mass
political organizations signifies the beginning of a new historical stage in the life of the peoples of Africa."[75]

The Stalinist dictum that only proletarian leadership of the
liberation struggle could produce true national independence
in the African nations was rejected in accordance with the
new Soviet policy line. An article signed by "Commentator,"
which appeared in the April, 1955 issue of *International Affairs*,[76] still reflected the old Stalinist line on this subject but
an editorial in *Sovetskoe Vostokovedenie* in 1956, immediately following the Twentieth Party Congress, attacked the
Stalinist view:

The Marxist-Leninist thesis is well known that during the
general crisis of capitalism the proletariat in colonial and
dependent countries—where capitalism is relatively highly

[74] See E. Zhukov, "The Bandung Conference of African and Asian
Countries and its Historic Significance," *International Affairs*, No. 5
(May, 1955), pp. 18–32.
[75] Ivan Potekhin, "Politicheskoe polozhenie v stranakh Afriki,"
Sovetskoe Vostokovedenie, No. 1, 1956, p. 25.
[76] Commentator, "The National-Liberation Movement," *International Affairs*, No. 4 (April, 1955), p. 21.

developed—can achieve hegemony of the national liberation and anti-feudal revolution. . . . From this absolutely
correct thesis, however, was drawn the incorrect conclusion
that only the leadership of the proletariat can assure victory
in the struggle for national independence.[77]

The new Soviet attitude recognized that the gaining of
political independence by the African countries was a progressive step. Early in 1956, Potekhin wrote:

> The gaining of political independence is only the first step
> on the road to attaining real independence, but it is a very
> important step. A sovereign state is the most powerful
> means of developing the national economy and of attaining
> economic independence by such a path. Already, the very
> fact of the formation of a sovereign state limits the power
> of the imperialist powers and ties their hands.[78]

He had a much stronger position by 1960: "The gaining
of political independence is the most important precondition
for resolving all other tasks of the national revolution."[79] He
cited the fact that sixteen African states became independent
during the year 1960.

Although political independence was now considered to be
an extremely important factor affecting the future evolution
of the African states, Soviet writers repeatedly warned that
it was only the first step toward full independence from the
colonialists. Also, the significance of achieving independence
was not to be exaggerated. K. Ivanov, writing in 1962, reflected this view:

> The liberation of the peoples from the fetters of colonial-
> ism only begins with political independence, which in many

---

[77] "The Twentieth Congress of the C.P.S.U. and the Problems of
Studying the Contemporary East," *Sovetskoe Vostokovedenie,* No. 1,
1956. See Thornton, *op. cit.,* p. 82.

[78] Potekhin, "Politicheskoe polozhenie v stranakh Afriki," *op. cit.,*
p. 32.

[79] Ivan Potekhin, "1960 god—reshaiushchii god natsional'noi revoliutsii v Afrike," *Sovremennyi Vostok,* No. 12 (December, 1960),
p. 5.

African countries, for example, is for various reasons far from complete and is often confined to the granting of a national anthem, flag and a seat in the United Nations. The peoples are forced to continue their struggle if they are to cast off the political and other colonial fetters.[80]

Political independence, according to Soviet writers, must be followed by economic and social reforms. These reforms form an integral part of the struggle for national liberation. The 1961 Program of the C.P.S.U. declared: "A national-liberation revolution does not end with the winning of political independence. Independence will be unstable and will become fictitious unless the revolution brings about radical changes in the social and economic spheres and solves the pressing problems of national rebirth."[81]

Soviet works on Africa continually stressed the theme that the Western powers are pursuing a policy of neo-colonialism and are trying to keep the African countries in a position of economic subservience. The Soviet view was that "economic dependence restricts a country's freedom in choosing its path of further development."[82] This means that continued economic dependence upon the Western capitalist countries will delay Africa's transition to socialism and this dependence is therefore strongly denounced.

The Khrushchevian approach to Africa had a flexibility which was definitely missing during the years of Stalin's rule. Theory was often changed to keep up with the fluid political situations in the African countries and Soviet experts were not as greatly entwined in their own dogmas, as they were in the Stalinist period. This more realistic outlook was often called "creative Marxism." The main theoretical guide of the

---

[80] K. Ivanov, "Present-Day Colonialism and International Relations," *International Affairs,* No. 4 (April, 1962), p. 43.

[81] *Program of the Communist Party of the Soviet Union* (Moscow, Foreign Languages Publishing House, 1961), pp. 44–45. Also see this argument in Iu. Popov, "Zhizhn' oprovergaet," *Aziia i Afrika Segodnia,* No. 12 (December, 1961), p. 11.

[82] Ivan Potekhin, *Africa: Ways of Development* (Moscow, Nauka Publishing House, 1964), p. 13.

Khrushchevian era, *Fundamentals of Marxism-Leninism* asserted: "But the Marxist-Leninist theory is not a dogma, it is a guide to action. Like life itself, this theory does not stand still but develops and becomes richer as the historical conditions alter and new tasks arise in the struggle of the progressive forces of mankind. Genuine Marxism-Leninism is always living, creative Marxism-Leninism."[83]

Strongly reflecting the "creative Marxist" outlook was a statement made by Ul'ianovskii at the conference on "Socialism, Capitalism and the Underdeveloped Countries," held in Moscow in 1964. He made a plea for objectivity and for recognizing differences between countries:

> In studying the situation in the developing countries, we must remember that Marxism cannot and does not pretend to give ready made answers applicable to all circumstances. There must be profound study of social and economic processes in each country, related always to the processes of international affairs. Conclusions drawn in one situation must not be mechanically applied to another superficially similar.[84]

The adoption by the Soviet Union of this more flexible policy brought Soviet actions into greater accord with the political realities and therefore presented the West with a more formidable challenge in Africa.

* * *

Jawaharlal Nehru visited Moscow in June, 1955 and the new Soviet approach to the underdeveloped countries was put into full swing by November, when Khrushchev and Bulganin took off on a tour of India, Burma and Afghanistan. They recognized the importance of political independence and attempted to gain the diplomatic support of these countries by stressing the issues of peace and colonialism. Differences in ideology

---

[83] *Fundamentals of Marxism-Leninism,* second revised edition (Moscow, Foreign Languages Publishing House, 1963), p. 18.
[84] "The U.S.S.R. and the Developing Countries," *Mizan Newsletter* special issue, Vol. VI, No. 10, 1964, p. 21.

were played down and similarities in view were emphasized. In a speech on November 19, Bulganin stated: "India and the Soviet Union have different social and political systems, but our people have much in common and this community strengthens our friendship and makes it more solid and fruitful not only for India and the Soviet Union but for the whole world."[85] He claimed that the Indian and Soviet peoples were similar since both were peace-loving, industrious and opposed to racism and colonialism.[86]

Khrushchev attached great significance to the fact that India was an independent country. Speaking before the Indian parliament on November 21, he declared: "India's conquest of state sovereignty and national independence is a momentous thing."[87] He went on to call for the strengthening of India's economic independence. Speaking in Bombay on November 23, Khrushchev touched upon the same theme: "We see how brightly sparkle the eyes of the free men who have won their country's independence and who want to be the masters of their state, of their destinies. . . . We rejoice that the peoples of great India have won national independence."[88]

Khrushchev and Bulganin kept to the theme of friendship between the Soviet and Indian peoples and minimized the hostile politics of the Cold War. They referred to peaceful coexistence between socialist and capitalist nations and, in reference to India, Khrushchev asserted: "We say, perhaps there is something in our practical experience that may suit you. If so, use it; if not, don't. We do not force anything upon anyone; we are not seeking to impose any political obligations."[89]

---

[85] "Speeches by Khrushchev and Bulganin During Trip to India, Burma and Afghanistan, November–December, 1955," supplement to *International Affairs*, No. 1, 1956, p. 172.
[86] *Ibid.*, p. 173.
[87] *Ibid.*, p. 182.
[88] *Ibid.*, p. 191.
[89] Khrushchev in a speech in Bangalore, November 26, 1955. *See Ibid.*, p. 198.

The Twentieth Congress of the C.P.S.U. was held in February, 1956 and it brought a new emphasis on peaceful coexistence, noninevitability of war, parliamentary means of achieving socialism, and the initiation of a new "peace zone" concept, which linked the national-liberation movements with the world struggle for peace. According to this concept, the socialist countries were aligned with the underdeveloped countries of Asia, Africa and Latin America on the issue of peace. Also, these countries were no longer considered to be reserves of the imperialists, but were now deemed to be allies of the progressive and anti-imperialist socialist forces.

The preoccupation with peace, manifested by Soviet theorists during the Khrushchevian era, had a great effect upon Soviet doctrines concerning Africa. It came to be accepted that national independence could be achieved by peaceful means, that socialism could be ushered in without revolution, and that wars of national liberation were serious threats to world peace as they could escalate into atomic holocausts. I. Sokolov wrote in 1963: "The events of the present day are such that the struggle for peace has become the most important prerequisite of a struggle for socialism. . . . Not a single revolutionary or national liberation problem can be viewed today apart from the struggle for peace and the prevention of a thermonuclear war."[90] Despite their preference for peaceful methods, the Soviets also recognized that armed struggle was not excluded as a means for achieving either national independence or socialism.[91]

Of course, the Soviets used the peace theme as part of their propaganda barrage but many of the views which they ex-

---

[90] I. Sokolov, "The Principle Problems of the Present Age," *Mirovaia Ekonomika i Mezhdunarodnye Otnosheniia*, No. 2 (March–April, 1963). See JPRS 19821, p. 6.
[91] See V. Solodovnikov, "Africa on the Path of Freedom," *Pravda,* December 1, 1964, p. 5 and Iu. Iudin, "Some Problems of the Establishment of National States in the Independent African Countries," *Sovetskoe Gosudarstvo i Pravo*, No. 2, 1961 (see Thornton, *op. cit.*, p. 254).

pressed had elements of truthfulness and cannot be dismissed as sheer verbosity. Attempts to avoid armed confrontation with the Western powers were in evidence and Soviet aid to national-liberation fighters was negligible. In fact, the Chinese have accused the Soviets of turning their backs on those fighting for national liberation, a term, which in communist parlance, can be applied to countries which have already received their political independence.

Beginning at the time of the Twentieth Party Congress, there were vitriolic attacks on the Stalinist attitudes toward Africa. The initial broadside appeared as an editorial in the first 1956 issue of *Sovetskoe Vostokovedenie*. Without ever specifically mentioning Stalin, it included a call for the revitalization of the Institute of Orientology of the Academy of Sciences (for the Soviets, the Orient at that time included Africa) [92] because there had been too much ideological stagnation and "dogmatism and blind acceptance were widespread."[93] Not enough attention had been paid to the contributions of Lenin and, in an obvious reference to Stalin, the editorial stated: "The Congress pointed to the need to struggle against the remnants of subjectivist-idealist views on the role of personality in history."[94]

The editorial went on to declare:

We cannot reconcile ourselves to the fact that many of the most vital and important problems in studying the East have been either avoided completely or considered from erroneous positions. Dogmatism and blind acceptance are

---

[92] In the late fifties, the term Orient included the countries of both Asia and Africa. Starting in about 1960, Africa was usually considered to be a separate entity and was not classified as part of the Orient. In March, 1961, the name of the journal *Sovremennyi Vostok* (Contemporary East) was changed to *Aziia i Afrika Segodnia* (Asia and Africa Today) and that of *Problemy Vostokovedeniia* (Problems of Oriental Studies) was changed to *Narody Azii i Afriki* (Peoples of Asia and Africa).

[93] "The Twentieth Congress of the C.P.S.U. and the Problems of Studying the Contemporary East," *op. cit.*, p. 80.

[94] *Ibid.*, p. 80.

still being encountered in the handling of many economic and historical problems of the contemporary East. Criticism of imperialism, colonialism, and bourgeois ideology has not always rested on convincing examples and facts.[95]

It was claimed that the development of capitalism in the underdeveloped countries had been ignored as Soviet writers had focused only upon the role of foreign capital. The evaluation of the nature of the national bourgeoisie was charged with containing "sectarian errors" and the editorial asserted: "Underestimation of the contradictions between the national bourgeoisie and imperialism led to groundless negation of the indisputable fact that, in certain stages of the anti-imperialist struggle, the interests of the bourgeoisie have coincided with the interests of the popular majority."[96] The editorial also claimed that the possibility of achieving independence through peaceful means had been ignored.[97]

The attacks on Stalinist ideas continued during the Khrushchevian era and one month before the ouster of Khrushchev, K. Ivanov wrote in *International Affairs*:

> Part of the fight against the personality cult is to exterminate the prejudices it has born, prejudices that prevent us seeing things in their true light, without dead patterns and simplifications. Dead patterns and simplifications were the soil that nourished the former conception which erroneously classed several important fighters for national liberation as puppets of American, British and French capital, and later as 'representatives' of the large, medium or petty bourgeoisie.[98]

One aim of the Khrushchevian approach to Africa was to gain the diplomatic support of the African countries on certain international political issues. Khrushchev tried to forge an

---

[95] *Ibid.,* p. 80.
[96] *Ibid.,* p. 82.
[97] *Ibid.,* p. 84.
[98] K. Ivanov, "The National-Liberation Movement and the Non-Capitalist Path of Development," *International Affairs,* No. 9, 1964, pp. 39–40.

anti-imperialist alliance between the socialist camp and the countries of Asia and Africa and he attempted to minimize the differences in ideologies. One of his remarks at the Twenty-first Party Congress in 1959 was particularly revealing:

> We do not conceal the fact that we and some of the leaders of the United Arab Republic have divergent views in the sphere of ideology. But our position coincides with theirs in questions of the struggle against imperialism, of strengthening the political and economic independence of countries that have freed themselves from colonialism, and of the struggle against the war danger. The differences in ideological views should not impede the development of friendly relations between our countries and the cause of joint struggle against imperialism.[99]

Some of the issues on which the Soviet Union and many of the African states have reached a community of interests include support for peaceful coexistence, the Moscow agreement on nuclear testing, the cause of the revolutionaries in the Portuguese colonies of Africa, and opposition to the U.S. and Belgian actions in the Congo, the apartheid policies of the South African government and the policies of the U.S. in Vietnam and Cuba.

In 1961, the Soviet Union took the unprecedented step of inviting delegates from the ruling parties of Guinea, Ghana and Mali to the Twenty-second Congress of the C.P.S.U. These delegates even made speeches on the floor of the Congress. Ivan Potekhin explained in an article in *Narody Azii i Afriki* that although these African parties were non-communist, they were "democratic" and "anti-imperialist."[100] The rulers of these three countries were all to receive Lenin Peace Prizes: Touré of Guinea in 1961, Nkrumah of Ghana in 1962, and Keita of Mali in 1963.

---

[99] Nikita Khrushchev, "Speech to Twenty-first Congress," *Pravda*, January 28, 1959, pp. 2–10. See *CDSP*, Vol. XI, No. 4 (March 4, 1959), p. 21.
[100] Ivan Potekhin, "Nekotorye problemy Afrikanistiki v svete reshenii XXII s"ezda KPSS," *Narody Azii i Afriki*, No. 1, 1962, p. 6.

Khrushchev succeeded in gaining the good will of many African countries and in rallying them behind the Soviet Union in an anti-Western, anti-colonialist crusade, but so far not one African country has joined the socialist (communist) camp.

* * *

Although Soviet analysts of the Khrushchevian era replaced the rigid Stalinist formulations with more flexible interpretations of events in the developing nations, many of these interpretations were an outgrowth of previous communist views on the national and colonial questions and many aspects of the ideological erosion manifested during the Khrushchevian period were actually foreshadowed in the writings of Lenin and Mao.

Marx and Engels concentrated upon the revolutionary potential of the proletariat in the advanced industrial nations and paid little attention to the colonial areas of the world. They expected proletarian revolutions in the mother countries to precede the rise of insurrections against colonial rule and they failed to link the question of nationalism with that of colonialism. Lenin accomplished this latter task as his theory of imperialism related the capitalist countries to their colonies and recognized the role of colonies in the struggle against imperialism. Lenin discussed a world anti-imperialist process which included the workers' movements in the advanced countries and also stressed the point that an imperialist country would be greatly weakened by the loss of its colonies.

Folowing their seizure of power in Russia, the Bolsheviks were optimistic about the prospects for proletarian revolutions in Europe, particularly in Germany. However, such revolutions failed to materialize and by 1920, the Bolsheviks and the Comintern started to look eastward for murmurs of insurrection against imperialism and feudalism. The Second Comintern Congress (1920) featured a debate on the colonial question between Lenin and Roy and the Baku Congress of

1920 aimed at fomenting revolutions against colonial and traditionalist Asiatic rulers.

Communist tactics in the colonial and semi-colonial areas hinged upon the critical questions of revolutionary stages, the juxtaposition of class forces, the role to be assumed by the proletariat and the alliance strategy to be pursued by the communists. Similar problems were faced by communist tacticians throughout the Leninist, Stalinist and Khrushchevian periods and as new interpretations were proffered, some of the basic Marxist tenets became diluted. Doctrinal analyses had to keep abreast of changing circumstances and a certain amount of ideological erosion was the result. Prior to Khrushchev, two of the chief communist innovators who greatly modified Marxist thought were Lenin and Mao.

One major erea of analysis which these men helped make quite flexible concerned the problem of revolutionary stages. Marx and Engels had outlined a progression from feudalism to capitalism to socialism and had differentiated between "bourgeois-democratic" and "socialist" revolutions. Lenin, while ostensibly adhering to the guideline of these two phases of revolution, helped blur the distinctions with some of his additions to revolutionary theory. In his *Two Tactics of Social-Democracy in the Democratic Revolution* (1905), Lenin maintained that the Russian bourgeoisie was incapable of completing its own "bourgeois-democratic" revolution and he therefore called upon the proletariat and peasantry to help bring this revolution to completion through a "revolutionary-democratic dictatorship of the proletariat and peasantry." Further modifying some Marxist concepts, Lenin prepared a communist take-over before "objective conditions" seemed to favor a "socialist" revolution. Russia was not highly industrialized, nor did it have a huge proletariat, and Lenin's arguments with the Mensheviks over these points appeared to run counter to the spirit of Marx. Lenin also developed the theory that the capitalist chain could be broken at its weakest link (i.e., in backward Russia). These views cast some doubt upon the Marxist dictums that a "socialist" revolution takes place in an advanced capitalist country and that a "socialist" revolution is preceded by a "bourgeois-democratic" revolution led by the bourgeoisie. Mao Tse-tung's concept of "new democracy" also helped erode the two-stage concept of revolution as he considered his communist-led revolution to be of a new type which was neither "bourgois-democratic" nor "socialist." Another argument which modified the Marxist concept of historical progression was Lenin's belief that with the aid of the proletariat of advanced nations, certain underdeveloped countries could bypass the capitalist stage of development.[101]

The idea that a "socialist" revolution must be conducted by the proletariat and that a communist party is proletarian in nature was greatly altered by Lenin's theory that a vanguard is needed to raise the proletarian masses to the proper level of consciousness. Communist parties served as this vanguard and the leaders of these parties often were not of proletarian origin. Therefore, the equation of communist party with proletariat became a myth. Communist parties became centralized, authoritarian organizations aimed at creating totalitarian regimes, rather than organizations aimed at expressing the interests of the proletarian class. In addition, Lenin and Mao recognized the important revolutionary role of the peasantry, called for alliances between the proletariat and peasantry, and carried out their revolutions in primarily agrarian countries. Therefore, their communist movements were at least as agrarian in nature as they were proletarian.

The issue of class consciousness also underwent considerable ideological revision as a result of the views of Lenin and Mao. Lenin lacked faith in the spontaneity of the proletarian masses and believed that the supposed ideology of the proletariat must be introduced to this class from outside, by the

---

[101] See Gene Overstreet, "Soviet and Indian Communist Policy in India, 1935–1952," doctoral dissertation, Columbia University, 1959, pp. 31–32.

communist leadership. Since many members of this elite were not proletarians, the ideology of this class was actually being formulated by non-workers, while the working class was ostensibly unable to develop its own revolutionary consciousness and ideology. Therefore, the questions of class and consciousness were somewhat divorced. Mao Tse-tung added to this estrangement by contending that the consciousness of men may be changed through indoctrination and propaganda. He attempted to win class enemies over to the communist position, rather than have them liquidated.[102]

Lenin and Mao altered Marx's views on many issues but Stalin showed less originality in his political interpretations. Although initiating many tactical changes for the international communist movement, including the great shift between the Sixth and Seventh Comintern Congresses (1928 and 1935), Stalin did not contribute much in the theoretical vein. Particularly in regard to underdeveloped countries, Stalin's analyses were rather rigid and unimaginative as he concentrated his attention upon the developed European countries and the United States. It is true that even after the suppression of Varga in the late forties, Soviet attitudes toward African and Asian nations were somewhat altered. Stalin came to recognize the importance of the peace theme and attempted to improve relations with certain Afro-Asian nations, particularly those in the Middle East. He strengthened diplomatic, cultural and economic ties between the Soviet Union and many underdeveloped nations and also began to perceive some of the contradictions inherent in the motherland-colonial relationship. However, Stalin and his Soviet academicians continued to denigrate the political independence achieved by new nations. They also stressed proletarian leadership of nationalist movements and it was not until the Khrushchevian period that Soviet analyses of events in underdeveloped

---

[102] See Richard Lowenthal, *World Communism: The Disintegration of a Secular Faith* (New York, Oxford University Press, 1964), pp. 113–114 and Stuart Schram, *The Political Thought of Mao Tse-tung* (New York and London, Praeger, 1963), pp. 220–221.

countries were radically changed. Stalin's bipolar view of the world remained predominant while he lived, despite some modest overtures toward recognition of the emerging "third world."

Nikita Khrushchev was faced with the dynamics of rapid political evolution in the Afro-Asian world. Independence movements were gaining great momentum, colonial empires were reaching the twilight of their existence, and men like Nkrumah, Nasser and Sukarno were becoming influential in the international political arena. Khrushchev quickly realized that the anti-colonialist, anti-imperialist postures of many Afro-Asian leaders could be useful in the Soviet struggle against the West and he therefore brought about a major reorientation in Soviet strategy toward the national and colonial questions. Khrushchev believed that the Afro-Asian nations were natural allies of the Soviet Union in opposing Western "imperialism" and his attempt to cooperate with the nationalist leaders and win them over to the Soviet side was the result of new, long-range Soviet strategy, rather than short-range tactics of temporary expediency. Khrushchev hoped that many African and Asian nationalist regimes would voluntarily move into the communist orbit and he therefore subordinated the activities of local communists to this end. Khrushchev's program of broad united fronts including the national bourgeoisie was not very different from Stalin's program during the thirties, as in India, but Khrushchev significantly changed communist strategy, whereas Stalin had merely changed communist tactics. Khrushchev believed in the eventual radicalization of nationalist parties and recognized the importance of the Afro-Asian nations in the communist struggle against imperialism. Stalin's tactical changes were not an integral part of any greatly revised analysis of international political forces but were just temporary measures aimed at contributing to the effectiveness of the Soviet Union's foreign policy.

Soviet ideology dealing with the underdeveloped countries

was eroded during the years of Khrushchev's rule and despite the fact that Khrushchev had precedents for many of his concepts in the writings of Lenin and Mao, he went even further than his predecessors in revising communist doctrines. Not only did Khrushchev stand out because of the sheer number of innovations he made but he even asserted that Marxism must be "creative" in order to keep abreast of changing circumstances. Probably the most startling of his revisions concerned the role of the proletariat in underdeveloped countries. Khrushchev did not stress the revolutionary mission of this class, nor did he emphasize the role of communist parties. In fact, he usually discussed a broad coalition of classes rallied around the existing nationalist parties and he expected these parties to move closer toward communism as their leaders acquired the "proper" knowledge of Marxism-Leninism.

Soviet writers of the Khrushchevian period were faced with many of the same problems as their Marxist forebears but they seemed to shed many rigid dogmas and came to grips with some of the incipient realities of twentieth century Africa and Asia.

3 The Soviet View of Contemporary African Socialism

THE LATE IVAN POTEKHIN, THE LEADING SOVIET AUTHORITY ON Africa during the Khrushchevian era, often wrote that there can be no such thing as "African socialism" but only an "African road to socialism." By this, he meant that there is only one variety of socialism, the type which Soviet writers call "scientific," "true," or "Marxist-Leninist" socialism. It has the same characteristics no matter where it is established and since the African continent is no exception to the general world pattern of development, Africa can not create a unique brand of "African socialism." The "African socialism" proclaimed by many African leaders is therefore not really socialism.

On the other hand, the paths taken to achieve socialism do differ in various places. Which path is taken is dependent upon the relationships between social classes in the given area and upon how these classes stand vis-à-vis the seat of state power. Multiple roads to socialism are possible and Potekhin recognized a specifically African road. Therefore, according to Potekhin, Africa may have unique means of achieving socialism but there is no room for an explicitly African brand of socialism. He claimed that although African socialists and scientific socialists agree on the end that the exploitation of man by man must be eliminated, they disagree as to what type of society can bring this about: a singularly African society which is ostensibly socialist or a Marxist-Leninist socialist society built under African conditions.[103]

During the years of Khrushchev's rule, Soviet doctrines regarding Africa underwent great ideological erosion. The new concepts accepted by Soviet theorists included the views that there may be different roads to socialism and that socialism may be achieved through a peaceful transition. Closely related were the new ideas that independence may be gained peacefully, political independence is a progressive step, and independence may be won despite the fact that the proletariat does not lead the independence struggle.

Another set of Khrushchevian innovations concerned the nature of nationalism and the role of the national bourgeoisie. It came to be recognized that nationalism has a democratic content and that national bourgeois leaders may carry out progressive reforms, including the initiation of the non-capitalist path of development. It was also believed that non-proletarian elements could build socialism and even adhere to scientific socialism, although the latter view seemed to contradict the basic Marxist-Leninist assumption that class determines consciousness. Soviet writers also asserted, in regard to the African context, that a dictatorship of the proletariat is no longer a required step leading to socialism and it was maintained that socialism may be built without communist parties playing the leading role. During this same period, Soviet analysts introduced the concept of national democracy and this was one of the factors contributing to the abandonment of the two-stage theory of revolution. The doctrine of class struggle within individual countries, while still maintained, was greatly revised in accordance with the new idea of an international class struggle. Also affected by the Khrushchevian analysis was the doctrine that the state is an instrument of class oppression. Soviet theorists claimed that an African state need not be an instrument of class rule

---

[103] Potekhin, *Africa: Ways of Development, op. cit.,* p. 56.

and that it may represent the interests of many classes. They even accepted the African socialist assertion that African nationalist parties may represent all of the people. Related to this subject of classes was the new interpretation given to the status of the intelligentsia. Although not specifically stated, Soviet writings definitely gave the impression that the intelligentsia was considered to be a distinct class, not just a stratum of another class.

Seen on an international scale, most African nations were deemed to be allies of the Soviet Union in the struggles for peace and against imperialism and colonialism while, according to the old Stalinist analysis, these nations were seen as reserves of the imperialist camp. Khrushchevian scholars also accepted the African policy of neutralism in international affairs and came to terms with African socialism on many other grounds. Religion was considered to be compatible with socialism, state capitalism was viewed as progressive, and African socialism was cited as a step toward scientific socialism. Another important change was the great emphasis placed upon the prospects of the African nations for skipping capitalism, while yet another was the view that Africans have a choice between capitalism and socialism. This latter interpretation seemed to negate the concept of determinism.

There were fundamental differences between the Soviet and African conceptions of socialism but the Soviet doctrine on the subject of socialism acquired greater flexibility (or, viewed in another way, there was ideological erosion from the Stalinist line). In accordance with the dynamics of this theoretical change, the Soviet Union demonstrated an increasing amount of maneuverability and political realism in its foreign policy toward the countries of sub-Saharan Africa.

More noteworthy than any single example of ideological erosion was the fact that the Soviet theses on colonial areas, which lay stagnant during the Stalinist era, were revitalized by an infusion of new ideas and doctrines during the Khrushchevian era. The ideology lost much of its rigidity and began to react to world events and evolve in accordance with changing circumstances. New concepts, such as the "national democratic state" and the category of "revolutionary democrats" were developed and one can expect more doctrinal innovations in the future as Soviet ideologists attempt to keep abreast of the swift winds of changes now hurtling across the African continent.

Although the Soviet writers adopted a more realistic view of Africa and adapted their theoretical outlooks accordingly, they also became less ideology-oriented and more policy-oriented. By this, I mean that the Soviet Union's foreign relations with the African states usually acted as catalysts to the ideological change, rather than vice-versa. There was no dearth of Soviet doctrinal pronouncements but ideology gradually lost much of its role as a foreign policy determinant and became more of a reflection of the Soviet Union's international posture. In order to reap the good will of the African states, the Soviet theorists felt that it was necessary to accept certain parts of the doctrine of African socialism. Many economic policies, recognized as being progressive when put into effect in Ghana, Guinea, or Mali, were considered to be covers for capitalist exploitation when practiced in Israel. Cuba, despite its many deviations from the theoretically proper model for the construction of a socialist society in an underdeveloped country, was accepted as a member of the socialist camp and this could possibly mean that an African socialist government which wishes to join the socialist camp will also be accepted. The concept of national democracy may even have been adopted specifically for the purpose of using the Cuban experience as a guide for the future development of African and Asian nations.[104] Therefore, one of the major criteria used by the Soviet theorists for determining advancement toward socialism was this or that country's foreign policy stance vis-à-vis the Soviet Union. Of

---

[104] This is discussed below, pp. 212–213.

course, the socialist aspects of a country's domestic policy were also carefully analyzed and no country which was openly capitalist was recognized as moving toward socialism.

At first glance, it may seem that there is some incongruity between the views that the Soviet ideology pertaining to Africa became more realistic and, at the same time, more subject to the exigencies of the Soviet Union's foreign policy. However, there is really no contradiction when one realizes that the world socialist system is no longer a monolith and that there are many national leaders who claim to have unique brands of socialism. Socialism has become almost indefinable and one of the only ways to determine who should really be classified as a Marxist-Leninist socialist is to see who vows allegiance to Moscow or Peking, each of which claims to be the true fountain of Marxist-Leninist knowledge. Therefore, as has already been mentioned, the Soviet political experts used this criterion of degree of allegiance as one of their measuring sticks for determining advancement toward socialism. At the same time, they looked at Africa in a more realistic way and recognized that the nationalist leaders could turn into Marxist-Leninist socialists (à la Castro), if, by this term, we mean those who adhere to either the Moscow or Peking camps.

For example, let's look at Kwame Nkrumah. During the Stalinist years, he was considered to be a "national-bourgois stooge of the imperialists" but, according to the analysis propounded during the latter years of Khrushchev's rule, he was deemed a "revolutionary democrat" and Soviet writings of that period often cited the fact that Nkrumah claimed adherence to the theory of scientific socialism. This latter analysis was more realistic, as it was certainly conceivable that Nkrumah's Ghana would become a member of the pro-Soviet socialist camp. And even though Ghana did not, it was certainly realistic to recognize that Nkrumah leaned more toward the views of the pro-Moscow socialist camp than he did toward those of the Western powers. In addition, this Khrushchevian analysis was also partly predicated upon the fact that Nkrumah had shown great friendship for the Soviet Union and had taken a far left position on most international issues. Also extremely relevant to this issue was the example of Sukarno.

According to Soviet theorists of the Khrushchevian era, African socialism was a deviation from true Marxism-Leninism but, as the Soviet ideology gradually eroded, African socialism came to be more and more acceptable to the Soviets and was recognized as a step toward true socialism. Certain African countries were cited as having taken the non-capitalist path of development and it was claimed that national bourgeois leaders of the African countries could come over to the scientific socialist position of the working class.[105]

THE ROADS TO SOCIALISM

The Twentieth Congress of the C.P.S.U., held in February, 1956, recognized that there may be different roads to socialism and that strict adherence to the Soviet model was no longer obligatory for all countries. Wolfgang Leonhard has suggested four possible reasons for this new turn: it could facilitate a rapprochement with Yugoslavia; appease some Eastern European countries; help forge unity with social-democratic parties, and bring closer cooperation with nationalist movements.[106]

Nikita Khrushchev declared before the Congress that the forms of transition to socialism could quite probably become "more and more varied" and that under some circumstances, this transition could be made peaceably.[107] However, he

---

[105] Ghana, Guinea, and Mali have been cited as taking the non-capitalist path. *See* below, p. 193.
[106] Wolfgang Leonhard, *The Kremlin Since Stalin* (New York, Praeger, 1962), p. 125.
[107] Nikita Khrushchev, "Report of the Central Committee of the Communist Party of the Soviet Union to the Twentieth Party Congress," *Pravda*, February 15, 1956, pp. 1–11. See *CDSP*, Vol. VIII, No. 4 (March 7, 1956), p. 11.

warned: "In all the forms of transition to socialism, an absolute and decisive requirement is political leadership of the working class, headed by its vanguard. The transition to socialism is impossible without this."[108]

Dmitri Shepilov, who was soon to become the Soviet Union's foreign minister, joined Khrushchev in acknowledging the possibility of multiple roads to socialism:

> In these circumstances only formalists and Marxist dogmatists can think that such deep upheavals as the transition from one social system to another can be carried out according to a single pattern, according to a stereotyped plan, let us say the same way in Denmark as in Brazil and the same way in Sweden as in Malaya. This is a distortion of the substance of Marxism, of its creative spirit.[109]

A similar view was expressed at the Congress by V. M. (not Mikhail) Suslov.[110]

Soviet leaders continued to stress this new concept and in September, 1956, Anastas Mikoyan declared while in Communist China:

> Chinese Communist comrades, proceeding from the fundamental principles of Marxist-Leninist theory, applied them creatively to the concrete conditions of China and were able to find distinctive new forms and methods of building socialism very suitable to the Chinese situation, including forms and methods which although they have not been tried in other countries have yielded rich fruits on Chinese soil.[111]

Mikoyan therefore recognized a Chinese road to socialism

---

[108] *Ibid.*, p. 12.

[109] "Speech by Comrade D. T. Shepilov at the Twentieth Party Congress," *Pravda,* February 17, 1956, pp. 3–5. See *CDSP,* Vol. VIII, No. 7 (March 28, 1956), p. 19.

[110] "Speech by Comrade V. M. Suslov at the Twentieth Party Congress," *Pravda,* February 18, 1956, p. 7. See *CDSP,* Vol. VIII, No. 8 (April 4, 1956), p. 23.

[111] Anastas Mikoyan, "Speech to the Eighth Congress of the Communist Party of China," *Pravda,* September 18, 1956, pp. 2–3. See *CDSP,* Vol. VIII, No. 38 (October 31, 1956), p. 7.

and he then told the Chinese: "Marxism is not a dogma; it is a living teaching which in the course of the development of human history is subjected to tests in its particulars, is supplemented, enriched and developed by the experience of the struggle of the working class and its party."[112]

Soviet writers and statesmen upheld the doctrine of different roads to socialism throughout the course of the Khrushchevian era and the Soviet Union also secured the doctrinal concurrence of the other socialist states on this issue. The Declaration of the Twelve Communist Parties in Power, issued in November, 1957, stated that there are "basic laws applicable in all countries embarking on a socialist course." These include the establishment of a dictatorship of the proletariat, "in one form or another," and the development of a proletarian revolution, "in one form or another."[113] However, the Declaration went on to claim:

> Disregard of national peculiarities by the proletarian party inevitably leads to its divorce from reality, from the masses and is bound to prejudice the cause of socialism. And, conversely, exaggeration of the role of these peculiarities, from the universal, Marxist-Leninist truth on the Socialist revolution and Socialist construction is just as harmful to the Socialist cause.[114]

The Declaration affirmed that there may be different forms of transition to socialism and that these forms depend upon the concrete conditions in each country.[115]

Khrushchev reiterated his idea of multiple paths to socialism many times during his rule and in December, 1963, replying to a group of journalists, he declared: "Life itself will introduce much that is new both in the forms of transition to socialism and in the pace of social changes. In any

[112] *Ibid.*, p. 7.
[113] Dan Jacobs, ed., *The New Communist Manifesto and Related Documents* (Evanston and Elmsford, New York, Row, Peterson, 1961), p. 176.
[114] *Ibid.*, p. 177.
[115] *Ibid.*, p. 180.

case, there is no doubt that life demands advance, and one cannot advance except by moving toward socialism."[116]

The Khrushchevian doctrine of different paths to socialism had great relevance to the Soviet analysis of African socialism. It came to be recognized that there can be a uniquely African path to socialism and this helped place the theory of African socialism in a more favorable light, as far as Soviet writers were concerned. In fact, Ivan Potekhin wrote: "There are no grounds therefore to oppose 'African Socialism' to scientific socialism if all that is meant by 'African Socialism' is the specific paths and means of proceeding to socialism that correspond to African reality."[117] But, of course, Potekhin indicated many times that "African socialism" does imply, as far as its proponents are concerned, much more than the means of proceeding to socialism. It is also concerned with the type of socialism to be constructed and in regard to this facet, Potekhin was an outspoken critic: "There is indeed much in Africa that is peculiar to it and sets it apart from the other, non-African countries. . . . What bearing has that on the question of socialism? The bearing is that it necessitates special paths of transition to socialism. But, of course, there cannot be different kinds of socialism."[118]

V. Solodovnikov, writing in *Pravda* on December 1, 1964, claimed that the African peoples are now realizing that there is only one kind of socialism and, in his view, there could not be "Arab, Ghanaian, Kenyan or Algerian socialism."[119] But at the same time, he affirmed his belief in different transitions to socialism. *Fundamentals of Marxism-Leninism,* the chief theoretical guidebook of the Khrushchevian era,

---

[116] "Replies of N. S. Khrushchev to Questions of Editors of Ghanaian Times, Alger Républicain, Le Peuple and Botataung," *Pravda* and *Izvestiia,* December 22, 1963, pp. 1–2. See *CDSP,* Vol. XV, No. 51 (January 15, 1964), p. 13.

[117] Potekhin, *Africa: Ways of Development, op. cit.,* p. 67.

[118] *Ibid.,* p. 64.

[119] V. Solodovnikov, "Afrika na puti svobody," *Pravda,* December 1, 1964, p. 5.

also supported this doctrine and predicted that the special features of the African countries would lead to the institution of "new forms of working people's political power."[120] This authoritative book cited Lenin to the effect that revolutions in Oriental countries would have more peculiarities than did the Russian Revolution.

IS AFRICA UNIQUE?

Soviet theorists of the Khrushchevian period believed that although different parts of the world have their specific characteristics, they are all nevertheless subject to certain objective laws of historical development.[121] Africa has its own individuality, which can affect its transition to socialism, but Africa can not have its own ideology and form of socialism. According to Ivan Potekhin, Africa's claim to have its own ideology and form of socialism is based upon the assumption that Africa is not developing in the same manner as did other continents. Potekhin cited the African socialist claims that Africa is classless, private ownership and exploitation are alien to African society, and that Africa was socialist before the arrival of the colonialists but that the colonialists destroyed this socialist system and it now must be rebuilt. Potekhin went on to write: "The general laws governing the development of human society are said not to extend to Africa, which apparently has its own laws and should therefore have its own ideology."[122] Of course, Potekhin opposed all of these arguments proffered by the African socialists and claimed that Marxism is applicable everywhere.

Potekhin distorted the African socialist position when he

---

[120] *Fundamentals of Marxism-Leninism, op. cit.,* p. 538 (1960 edition, pp. 661–662).
[121] See Ivan Potekhin, *Afrika smotrit v budushchee* (Moscow, 1960), p. 27.
[122] Ivan Potekhin, "Pan-Africanism and the Struggle of the Two Ideologies," *International Affairs,* No. 4, 1964, p. 53.

asserted: "Some African leaders claim that Marxism cannot be applied to their countries because the proletarian and bourgois classes are not yet fully formed there. But Marxism offers, among other things, an explanation of the most general lines governing any society, including a pre-capitalist one."[123] In fact, African socialists do not deny the applicability of Marxism to Africa. They often claim that Marxism is definitely relevant to their continent but that Marxism is not a dogma and its lessons must be put into practice in accordance with different national conditions. Potekhin's view was that although African conditions must be respected and the Soviet Union need not be copied in all respects, Marxism contains certain objective truths which are pertinent to all societies. Among the basic tenets of Marxism is the existence of a class struggle, a tenet which the African socialists generally deny.

Soviet writers recognized that Africa was unique in many respects and coupled this belief with the view that Africa must strive to gain self respect following the humiliating period of colonialism. Potekhin claimed that the Africans stress the individuality of their continent as a reaction to the treatment they suffered at the hands of the colonialists. Africans were considered to be both inferior and uncreative.[124] He also asserted that the individuality of Africa was not due to the African peoples being different from others but was a result of the interference of European imperialism in the affairs of Africa.[125] Therefore, Africa's anti-imperialist revolution brought about spiritual rebirth as well as liberation from colonialism.[126]

Potekhin also charged that the colonialists denigrated African history and instilled the belief that Africans were inferior so as to provide an ethical basis for colonial rule and the

[123] *Ibid.*, p. 54.
[124] *Ibid.*, p. 53.
[125] Potekhin, *Afrika smotrit v budushchee, op. cit.*, p. 27.
[126] *Ibid.*, p. 65.

institution of slavery. The history taught in the African colonies was not that of Africa but was the history of the European colonial powers and in these history courses, the colonial instructors described African independence fighters as "tyrants" and "bandits."[127]

Soviet writers constantly defended Africa's cultural heritage against its critics and maintained that the traditional African society which existed at the time of colonization was not indeed backward as the colonial powers have claimed. Potekhin charged that the imperialists spoke of Africa's backwardness so they could blame Africa's present underdeveloped position on the Africans, rather than upon themselves.[128]

Potekhin maintained that the development of the African peoples was uneven. During the Middle Ages, many of them lived in primitive-communal societies and were not organized into states but he stated: "On the whole the Africa of that period could not be considered a backward continent."[129] In an article written for *Kommunist* in August, 1961, Potekhin went to ridiculous lengths to emphasize his point. In order to illustrate his contention that Africa was not backward and that it actually had a rich historical experience, he cited the generally accepted anthropological theory that Africa was the birthplace of man. He then concluded that if this anthropological theory was valid, man's earliest history took place in Africa and that Africa was therefore the only continent to witness all stages of man's development from Australopithecus to homo sapien.[130]

Georgii Mirskii and Lev Stepanov concurred with Pote-

---

[127] *Ibid.*, p. 66.
[128] Ivan Potekhin, "Osnovnye problemy istorii narodov Afriki," *Kommunist*, No. 12, (August, 1961), p. 102.
[129] Ivan Potekhin, "Legacy of Colonialism," *International Affairs*, No. 3, 1964, p. 15.
[130] Potekhin, "Osnovnye problemy istorii narodov Afriki," *op. cit.*, p. 101.

khin's analysis and criticized the theory of backwardness advanced by the colonialists:

> For many long years imperialist propaganda assiduously depicted Africa as a continent populated by exceptionally backward, ignorant, almost primitive people, by savages who had no idea whatever of the fundamentals of modern society. It tried to instill in people's minds the notion that the Africans had a long way to go before they could 'grow up' to the level of the 'civilized' part of humanity, and that they could never do that by themselves. And this argument was used as a motive for establishing Western 'trusteeship.'[131]

. . . .

Soviet writers stressed that Africa was unique because of its colonial experience but they denied that race was a factor in this African exceptionalism. One reason for the adoption of this viewpoint was that Marxism-Leninism recognizes a class struggle, not racial solidarity. Another important reason, which was explicit in the Soviet exchanges with the Chinese, was the Soviet fear that the Chinese were attempting to align the nations of Asia and Africa on a racial basis. Of course, many Asian and African states had an anti-white bias before the Chinese began their campaign to set up an Afro-Asian bloc under their domination but this Chinese drive has made the Soviets even more sensitive on the question of race impeding their relations with the nations of Asia and Africa. The Soviets had to meet the Chinese challenge by continuing to deny the importance of race, since they are mostly white, and by claiming that not all white people were the colonizers of Asia and Africa. Even before the Sino-Soviet conflict had become such a critical international phenomenon, Potekhin wrote in his book, *Afrika smotrit v budushchee,* that imperialism and the white race are not synonymous and that Africans have many friends of the white race.[132]

Soviet political experts opposed the idea of "Négritude,"

---

[131] Georgii Mirskii and Lev Stepanov, *Asia and Africa: A New Era* (Moscow, Foreign Languages Publishing House, 1960), p. 8.
[132] Potekhin, *Afrika smotrit v budushchee, op. cit.,* p. 80.

which was most prominently put forth by Léopold Senghor. They were averse to this racial concept, partly because it includes only Negroes, and Potekhin indicated that white and black Africans should be united in the struggle against the remnants of colonialism.[133] Soviet writers considered "Négritude" to be "anti-racial racism"[134] and it was also attacked for its emphasis upon a uniqueness among Negroes:

> The term 'negritude' is sometimes explained by the following example: All Negroes, independent from the conditions in which they live, have a general psychological viewpoint, one world outlook and unique ideology. Out of this situation it follows that it is not the social environment and not the common existence of man but the biological peculiarities, in particular the black color of the skin, that determines the conscience of man.[135]

In his noteworthy article entitled "Pan-Africanism and the Struggle of the Two Ideologies," Ivan Potekhin discussed "Négritude" at length.[136] He believed that this theory is a reaction against the French colonial policy of assimilation, which disparaged Africa's cultural achievements. The Negro African intellectuals in Paris, such as Senghor, developed this concept to assert their identity and regain their pride, which was hurt by the humiliations suffered at the hands of the French. According to Potekhin, "Négritude" has two sides: it seeks to restore dignity to the African Negroes and is also a racist theory. He admired the former aspect but condemned the latter: "A wide range of historical experience convincingly shows that racial considerations have always been introduced into politics by reactionary forces . . . to justify their repugnant anti-popular policies."[137] He also disagreed with

---

[133] *Ibid.,* p. 78.
[134] O Vadeev, ed., *Vstrecha s Afrikoi,* (Moscow, Izdatel'stvo Politicheskoi Literatury, 1964), p. 170.
[135] Potekhin, "Pan-Africanism and the Struggle of the Two Ideologies," *op. cit.,* p. 80.
[136] See *Ibid.,* pp. 51–52.
[137] *Ibid.,* p. 52.

Senghor's idea that Negroes are "intuitive" and are therefore different from the "analytical and logical" whites.

Léopold Senghor has been the chief advocate of "Négritude" and both he and his concept were constantly attacked by Soviet writers. However, Nkrumah's idea of an "African personality" was not similarly vilified by the Soviet analysts. The probable reason is that Senghor was pictured as a reactionary while Nkrumah was considered a progressive. The concepts of these two men, although similar, were therefore viewed in different lights. It was deemed the better part of valor not to criticize Nkrumah's concept and this was accomplished by not even mentioning the "African personality." On the other hand, Potekhin wrote that the supporters of "Négritude" are not strongly anti-colonialist. They prefer to ally with imperialist France, rather than with the movement for Pan-African unity.[138] In summing up "Négritude," Potekhin asserted:

> This is the short, as yet unfinished, history of a contemporary movement founded on a racial concept: it started with anti-racialism and condemnation of French colonial policy and ended in alliance with the imperialists. One reason why the advocates of Negritude find themselves in this unnatural alliance with the oppressors is because they reject an alliance between the oppressed peoples of Africa and the European workers.[139]

"Négritude" was one of the factors involved in African uniqueness which the Soviet theorists would not accept. Two other important facets of African life which now require analysis are religion and Pan-Africanism.

*   *   *

According to the official Soviet view, religion is sheer superstition and has no basis in rationality. The Soviet government favors atheism and it is one of the tenets of the communist party. Limited practice of some religions is per-

---

[138] *Ibid.*, p. 52.
[139] *Ibid.*, p. 52.

mitted in the Soviet Union but it is believed that through education (and propaganda), the Soviet people will eventually become materialistic atheists. Marxism-Leninism sees an incompatibility between socialism and religion as the Marxist view is still maintained that religion is the "opiate of the masses." However, in their writings on Africa, Soviet theorists increasingly recognized that socialism and religion are compatible. This was a concession to the African socialists, since most of them emphasize the religious values of their cultures, and was made in order to make the Soviet model more palatable to religious African nations. Soviet writings on this topic usually coupled attacks upon religion with statements to the effect that even though religion has many negative aspects, it may nevertheless exist in a socialist society.

An article by V. Kudriavtsev in the October 1962 issue of *International Affairs* charged that the clergy often keeps people backward and illiterate by feeding them with outdated traditions. However, he cited declarations by many African leaders, including Ben Bella, to the effect that socialism and Islam are compatible. Without outwardly supporting this view, Kudriavtsev lent it support by asserting that the religious masses will "decide for themselves whether Socialist construction is compatible with religious prejudice. . . ."[140]

An unsigned article in *Narody Azii i Afriki* early in 1963 expressed a similar view.[141] It explained that the political leaders of Mali do not oppose religion and that Mali's religious people and leaders do not oppose the path taken by their government. There is religious freedom in Mali and the article even cited the report of the Sixth Congress of the Union Soudanaise (September, 1962), which mentioned that there was no incompatibility between Islam and socialism in the U.S.S.R. Despite this veiled recognition of the role of religion in African socialist societies, the article claimed that

---

[140] V. Kudriavtsev, "Fighting Africa's Daily Round," *International Affairs,* No. 10 (October, 1962), p. 54.
[141] "Respublika Mali na puti sotsial'nykh preobrazovanii," *Narody Azii i Afriki,* No. 2, 1963, p. 34.

where feudalism is strong, the religions oppose socialism. This therefore left room for the Soviet writers to accept religion in the African countries considered to be progressive and to oppose it in backward feudal countries.

Writing in *Kommunist* in March, 1963, Iurii Bochkarev explicitly recognized that Islam is not incompatible with socialism. Discussing the idea that communism is alien to Africa, Bochkarev wrote:

> No less groundless is this pretext: the Communists have no place in Moslem countries inasmuch as they are enemies of religion. The Communist outlook and philosophy is indeed atheistic. But the doors of the majestic edifice of socialism are not closed to believers. The experience of countries which have established socialism shows that in the socialist countries there exists genuine freedom of religion and there are no persecutions of the religiously inclined. Communists are convinced that religion will die out in time, but not by way of violence or decrees of any sort, rather as a result of the dissemination of scientific knowledge, the growth of literacy and culture of human beings. Consequently, Islam cannot serve as an obstacle to taking the road to socialism.[142]

* * *

Pan-Africanism is another concept which the African socialists often link to socialism and in regard to this issue, Soviet writers took an equivocal position. Historically speaking, the Soviet communists objected to any pan-national movements because they were based upon ethnic differences and they supposedly glossed over the class struggle in each country as they emphasized the unity of all peoples of a certain racial stock. Until the mid-fifties, when the Soviet outlook became more conciliatory, the Pan-Arab movement was opposed for these reasons, and also for the purported reason that it was British-inspired. Another factor which may have

---

[142] Iu. Bochkarev, "Communists are Doughtiest Fighters for National Independence," *Kommunist*, No. 5 (March, 1963). See JPRS 18768, pp. 24–25.

conditioned the Soviet stand on this issue was the fear that the Moslems in the Soviet Union might become attracted to a supra-national Islamic grouping of Arab states.

The Soviet view of Pan-Africanism, held during the Khrushchevian era, was imbued with many misgivings but, due to the anti-Western nature of this movement, the Soviet analysts decided that Pan-Africanism should be recognized as progressive in certain respects. Following the All-African People's Conference held in Accra, Ghana in 1958, Ivan Potekhin wrote:

> The ideology of Pan-Africanism pursues the aim of rallying all African peoples to fight against colonialism and imperialism for their national liberation. From this point of view Pan-Africanism deserves the support of all people of good will advocating the ideas of progress and democracy. On the other hand, one cannot sympathize with the spirit of non-resistance to violence which permcates the utterances of many leaders of this movement.[143]

Potekhin was extremely sensitive to the racial element of Pan-Africanism but he expressed the view that the racial basis of Pan-Africanism is giving way to an acceptance of unity among Africa's races in the common struggle against imperialism. He explained that Pan-Africanism was once a racial movement which included Negroes in the Western hemisphere but that it had changed into an African movement which includes white Africans: "There is little cause therefore to oppose Black Africa to Arab Africa as something united and solid. This counter-position was invented by the imperialists in their selfish interests; it is a manifestation of the well-known 'divide and rule' policy."[144] Potekhin praised the development that Pan-Africanism is no longer a Negro movement but is a movement of all African peoples, including those in the Arab north. Writing a few years later in

[143] Ivan Potekhin, "Africa Shakes Off Colonial Slavery," *International Affairs*, No. 2 (February, 1959), p. 88.
[144] *Ibid.*, p. 87.

1961, he stressed that all Africans are united in the anti-imperialist struggle and that the Pan-Negro movement of the past has turned into genuine Pan-Africanism.[145]

Discussing the same subject early in 1962, Potekhin again cited the positive role of Pan-Africanism in uniting the African peoples against imperialism and colonialism but he also pointed out three negative aspects of Pan-Africanism: it can be a source of extreme nationalism, set the black race against the white, and can be used by the exploiting classes as a cover for their class domination.[146]

Despite many reservations about the nature of the Pan-African movement, Soviet writers recognized that it is in many ways progressive. Although wary of its racial implications, they felt more secure in supporting its economic doctrine of African economic cooperation and a reduction in reliance upon the former colonial powers. Pan-Africanism is inextricably bound with African socialism, particularly in the views of Nkrumah, Keita and Touré, and the Soviet analysts sought to gain the good will of these leaders, and of most of the other African leaders, by mildly praising Pan-Africanism and de-emphasizing their belief in class struggle on the African continent.

AFRICAN SOCIALISM AS AN IDEOLOGY

Soviet theorists claimed that Africa has failed to develop true Marxist-Leninist socialism because of bourgeois and petty-bourgeois influences but African socialists are beginning to see the relevance of Marxist-Leninist teachings and African socialism is evolving into scientific socialism. According to the Soviet view, socialism is only a stepping stone to communism but Soviet writers sidestepped this point when

[145] Ivan Potekhin, "The African Peoples Forge Unity," *International Affairs*, No. 6 (June, 1961), p. 80.
[146] Potekhin, "Nekotorye problemy Afrikanistiki v svete reshenii XII s' 'ezda KPSS," *op. cit.*, p. 15.

praising the purported trend toward scientific socialism manifested in the African countries. Most African socialists seek to establish a socialist society but do not advocate building communism.

In the eyes of Soviet analysts, there is a struggle throughout the world between the socialist and bourgeois ideologies and this struggle is complicated in Africa by the influences of nationalism and tribalism.[147] In regard to this subject, *Fundamentals of Marxism-Leninism* stated: "The liberation of the non-proletarian masses—the peasantry, the petty bourgeoisie and the intelligentsia—from the influence of bourgeois ideas, and winning them over to socialist ideas, is therefore yet another important task in the workers' ideological struggle."[148]

Ivan Potekhin has described the impact of bourgeois ideas upon Africa.[149] He claimed that the bourgeois countries of Europe and the United States strongly influenced Africa and that Africa was receptive to bourgeois ideology because it contained petty commodity producers, owners of private property, a petty bourgeoisie and, in many countries, a capitalist class which exploits others. "As a result, bourgeois ideas are more widespread in Africa today than Socialist ideas which have only recently begun to filter through, although they are today spreading quickly."[150] Potekhin was trying to find a rational explanation for the fact that the ideas of Marxism-Leninism are not predominant on the African continent but his argument on this subject contradicted many points he made in relation to similar issues. According to Potekhin's view in this instance, bourgeois ideology was brought to Africa from outside and was not a result of domestic historical development. This contradicted the offi-

---

[147] Potekhin, "Pan-Africanism and the Struggle of the Two Ideologies," *op. cit.*, p. 48.
[148] *Fundamentals of Marxism-Leninism, op. cit.*, p. 168 (1960 edition, p. 207).
[149] Potekhin, "Pan-Africanism and the Struggle of the Two Ideologies," *op. cit.*, p. 53.
[150] *Ibid.*, p. 53.

cial Soviet position, which was even expounded on many occasions by Potekhin, that ideology can be neither imported nor exported. It must grow out of the environment in which it is to be applied. In still another inconsistency evident in this article, Potekhin emphasized that bourgeois ideology found "fertile soil within African society" because Africa had certain capitalist tendencies. Usually, Potekhin de-emphasized the capitalistic aspects of African society and even claimed that the weak development of capitalism in Africa was the prime reason that Africa was capable of taking a non-capitalist path, bypassing the capitalist stage of development. Potekhin therefore tried to have it two ways: he cited the existence of capitalist elements in Africa as a cause for Africa's acceptance of many aspects of bourgeois ideology but then cited the lack of capitalist development as a feature contributing to Africa's capability to take a non-capitalist path.

African socialism was considered to be just one of many special theories of socialism which, according to Soviet theorists, are not really socialism. In his book *Afrika smotrit v budushchee,* Potekhin included a section on the false theories of socialism which were criticized by Marx and Engels in *The Communist Manifesto.*[151] He pointed out that the supposed theories of socialism which existed before the advent of scientific socialism only used the guise of socialism in order to deceive the masses and keep them in a position of servitude. He outlined types of socialism attacked by Marx and Engels, which they labeled "feudal socialism," "petty-bourgeois socialism," "conservative (or bourgeois) socialism," and "critical-Utopian socialism." Potekhin cited certain elements which are characteristic of a truly socialist state. They are: control of the state by the workers, public ownership of the means of production, the absence of exploitation, and a planned economy which serves the needs of the people.

Soviet writers lavishly praised the desire of many African

---

[151] Potekhin, *Afrika smotrit v budushchee, op. cit.,* pp. 11–13.

leaders to build socialism, even though this brand of socialism was deemed to be at variance with the Marxist-Leninist Soviet model. K. Grishechkin, writing in *New Times* in October, 1963, proudly announced that "the leaders of 25 out of 32 African states favour socialist development in one or another form."[152] However, he added: "True, their motives differ widely, and not all pro-socialist pronouncements are sincere." An article by I. Beliaev, which appeared in *Pravda* on April 21, 1964, declared:

> When in September, 1960, the Sudanese Union, Mali's only political party, came out resolutely for socialism, many people were skeptical of such a bold statement. Socialism in a destitute country, until yesterday a French colony? 'Impossible!' ill-wishers shouted. But, as Modibo Keita, President of Mali, has emphasized more than once, only the building of socialism—a society without exploitation—can secure for the republic unprecedented prosperity.[153]

Soviet political experts recognized that African socialism was not a monolithic doctrine and that it has many different strands. Ivan Potekhin concluded, after studying them all, that various theories of African socialism sometimes arise because people striving for true socialism get confused and, at other times, because the African national bourgeoisie uses certain socialist methods, such as economic planning and the creation of a state economic sector, but makes sure that its own class interests are preserved intact.[154] Potekhin claimed that although there are many interpretations of African socialism, the African popular masses see it as a rejection of capitalism and as a counter to imperialist exploitation. They view it as "authentic scientific Socialism." This statement by Potekhin is rather intriguing since it seems to be opposed

---

[152] K. Grishechkin, "African Prospects," *New Times,* No. 41 (October 16, 1963), p. 7.

[153] I. Beliaev, "From Bamako to Timbuktu," *Pravda,* April 21, 1964, p. 4. See *CDSP,* Vol. XVI, No. 16 (May 13, 1964), p. 28.

[154] Potekhin, "Pan-Africanism and the Struggle of the Two Ideologies," *op. cit.,* pp. 53–54.

to the orthodox Marxist tenet that class determines consciousness. Theoretically, only the proletariat should interpret socialism as scientific socialism and the Soviet writers certainly do not claim that the African masses are basically proletarian.

In his book, *Africa: Ways of Development,* Potekhin charged that bourgeois influences are present in theories of socialism, other than Marxism-Leninism. Marxism-Leninism is the only theory which can guide the transition to socialism:

> Marxism-Leninism is a universal theory in the sense that it serves as a guide to action in all circumstances, provided one knows how to apply it correctly. It is the only scientific theory on the transformation of contemporary society into socialist society. Those who reject it are inevitably led astray by sundry bourgeois theories designed to justify the capitalist system and obstruct the transition to socialism. The question stands sharply: either socialism or capitalism; there is no third way.[155]

Because it ostensibly contains bourgeois elements, the theory of African socialism was strongly attacked by Soviet writers.

Iu. Guzevaty claimed that the ideas of national-type socialism, such as those in Africa, are disseminated by the petty bourgeoisie.[156] This class has a great ideological influence on the masses and most intellectuals and army officers are members of it. He asserted that the petty bourgeoisie joins with the patriotic forces to fight imperialism but the reforms which it brings about are bourgeois-democratic, not socialist.

In the Soviet view, the intellectuals were still another group influencing the theory of African socialism. Ivan Potekhin claimed that they are the leading force in most African countries and their position is due to the weakness of both the proletariat and bourgeoisie in these countries.

---

[155] Potekhin, *Africa: Ways of Development, op. cit.,* p. 40.
[156] Iu. Guzevaty, " 'Third Way' or Genuine Freedom?," *International Affairs,* No. 4 (April, 1963), p. 47.

He asserted that their outlook "is marked by eclecticism, an odd mixture of different and even contradictory, basically idealistic views of society, the laws of its development and man's inner world."[157]

Although Soviet writers identified many non-proletarian elements within the doctrine of African socialism, they rarely mentioned one aspect of African socialism which was probably the most important factor in conditioning the Soviet response to this uniquely African ideology. This was the attitude of the African socialists toward the Soviet Union and toward the Soviet model of socialist development. Karen Brutents brought up this subject late in 1962 in a *New Times* article. In reference to the Soviet Union serving as an example, Brutents declared:

> Many African national leaders who sincerely favour socialism are weighed down by a burden of prejudice, Utopian illusions and the muddled ideas of social reformists. Some of them seriously believe that it is possible to have as many "socialisms" as there are states and that socialism can be built without following the example and drawing on the experience of the Soviet Union and the other socialist lands. The lessons of reality should help to discard their illusions and erroneous concepts.[158]

Brutents also seemed to hint that there can't be real socialism unless it is pro-Soviet when he wrote:

> There are other African leaders, however, whose vows of dedication to socialism are merely a screen for reactionary pro-imperialist activities. Some even contrive to combine such vows with hostility towards the socialist countries. True, they are few in number but this does not mean that they are not dangerous for, after all, they mask themselves under the banner of socialism.[159]

---

[157] Potekhin, "Pan-Africanism and the Struggle of the Two Ideologies," *op. cit.*, p. 48.
[158] Karen Brutents, "The October Revolution and Africa," *New Times,* No. 45 (November 7, 1962), p. 10.
[159] *Ibid.*, p. 10.

Since Soviet writers portrayed African socialism as a mixture of ideas, many of which had little in common with scientific socialism, an important question which they had to answer was why most Africans failed to adopt the theory of scientific socialism. Of course, one of the main reasons cited by Soviet authors was the fact that most African leaders are not of proletarian origin and, since class determines consciousness, their concepts of socialism are not doctrinally pure, as are those of proletarian theorists. However, Soviet spokesmen also pointed to many other reasons. V. Tiagunenko claimed that revolutionary practice precedes ideology.[160] This is especially true, and actually inevitable, where revolutionary democrats, rather than proletarians, lead the revolutionary struggle. The ideology of the revolutionary democrats is usually eclectic. Tiagunenko cited Mali, Algeria, Burma, and the United Arab Republic as countries in which his dictum holds true (Tiagunenko expressed this view in 1964 at the Moscow conference on underdeveloped countries). He seemed to be coming to terms with African and Asian socialist doctrines by saying that the socialist programs in African and Asian countries are more progressive than the ideologies with which the leaders of these countries explain their programs.

It is curious to note that when Soviet writers specifically used the term "African socialism," they almost invariably cited Senghor and Dia in their attacks upon this doctrine and failed to mention those African socialists whom they considered more progressive. This latter group of African socialists was seen to be moving closer toward scientific socialism and the term "African socialism" was usually reserved for descriptions of the brands of socialism preached by the less progressive African leaders. An exception to this point was this statement made by Ia. Abet in the May, 1960 issue of *Mirovaia Ekonomika i Mezhdunarodnye Otnosheniia*: "Senghor, Keita and Dia are adherents of the so-called 'African

---

[160] "The U.S.S.R. and the Developing Countries," *op. cit.*, pp. 31–32.

road to socialism.' Their 'socialism' clearly bears a marked petty-bourgeois, reformist character and represents an eclectic mixture of various ideological trends."[161] Keita was included in this reference to an "African road to socialism" but it must be remembered that this assertion by Abet was made in 1960, prior to the dissolution of the Mali union. During the ensuing years, Keita was considered to be one of Africa's leading progressives and was even a recipient of a Lenin Peace Prize in 1963.

Soviet writers claimed that African leaders do not correctly interpret socialism because they do not live in advanced industrial countries and they have been brought up greatly isolated from the outside world. V. Kudriavtsev declared: "Supporters of Socialism often present it in an abstract way because, having grown up in a backward African country and being confronted with present-day African realities, their thinking must differ from that of a person in an industrial country and living in a big collective of workers."[162] Kudriavtsev's orthodox Marxist statement implied that the African leaders cannot become advocates of scientific socialism until their countries are highly industrialized but this interpretation was not in accord with the view, often expressed during the Khrushchevian era, that many African leaders are becoming scientific socialists, even though their countries are still economically backward.

The idea of isolation from the outside world was also touched upon by V. P. Verin in his book *Prezidentskie respubliki v Afrike*. Discussing the political leaders in French Africa, he stated: "But the majority of them grew up and were educated in rigorous isolation from the outside world and were subjected to heavy indoctrination by imperialist propaganda. They could not raise themselves to the level of progressive proletarian ideology and at best, came to terms with

---

[161] Ia. Abet, "Federatsiia Mali," *Mirovaia Ekonomika i Mezhdunarodnye Otnosheniia*, No. 5 (May, 1960), p. 106.
[162] Kudriavtsev, "Fighting Africa's Daily Round," *op. cit.*, p. 53.

the ideas of petty-bourgeois socialism."[163] Verin seemed to overlook the fact that many of these leaders were educated in the West and were therefore not very isolated.

Ivan Potekhin explained the impact of the imperialist propaganda barrage upon the minds of the Africans. He claimed that the main reason the Africans have not accepted scientific socialism is the effect of anti-communist propaganda.[164] He charged that the Christian missions in Africa play upon the religious feelings of the people and turn them against socialism by helping the imperialists with their anti-communist propaganda. The Africans are attracted to socialism but the effect of all this propaganda is to make them seek a supposedly socialist alternative to scientific socialism. Potekhin declared: "Imperialist agents keep drilling it into their minds that they are menaced from the East, that is, by the socialist countries, and have invented the legend of Soviet expansion. Acceptance of the ideas of scientific socialism is portrayed as the opening of ideological expansion, allegedly to be followed by political expansion."[165] Potekhin's critique of the theme of imperialist propaganda actually seems quite accurate in describing one of the prime motives of Soviet policy.

Another reason for the non-acceptance of scientific socialism by African leaders, as cited by Potekhin, is the dissemination of socialist doctrines by the British Labour Party and the French "Right-Wing" Socialists.[166] They spread their ideas throughout Africa and were aided in this process by the colonial authorities. Their varieties of socialism were acceptable even to the colonialists.

In Soviet eyes, not only do many African leaders practice brands of socialism which are not in accord with scientific socialism, there are also those who falsely masquerade under

---

[163] V. P. Verin, *Prezidentskie respubliki v Afrike* (Moscow, Izdatel'stvo Instituta Mezhdunarodnykh Otnoshenii, 1963), p. 114.
[164] Potekhin, *Africa: Ways of Development, op. cit.,* p. 59.
[165] *Ibid.,* p. 69.
[166] *Ibid.,* p. 61.

the banner of socialism in order to gain the support of the masses. According to the basic Soviet view, the masses desire socialism, even though some influences are at work which cause them to deviate somewhat from the Marxist-Leninist path. For a politician to stay in power, he must cater to the socialist aspirations of the people and, therefore, many leaders who actually favor capitalist development hide behind professions of socialism.[167] Nikita Khrushchev, in a December, 1963 interview, discussed the desire of the masses to take the socialist path and he stated in reference to this point: "This is apparently why even these statesmen of the young national states who advocate 'Western' development and are actually implanting capitalism do not dare put forward a capitalist program openly. They adapt themselves to the temper of the masses and also talk about socialism, although they fear social reforms like fire."[168]

Ivan Potekhin described those whom he called "ideologists of imperialism." He claimed that "they speak in favour of Socialism, but interpret it in such a way that Socialist ideas become a veiled apology for the capitalist way of development."[169] However, Potekhin believed that the African intelligentsia could play a positive role in this matter: "Progressive sections of the African intelligentsia oppose this kind of camouflage and help a large number of the masses to distinguish the true supporters of Socialism from all kinds of false Socialists. Herein lies the great historic task of the African intelligentsia. May we wish them success in their noble work."[170]

This statement by Potekhin is typical of Soviet pronounce-

---

[167] See Ivan Potekhin, *Afrika, 1956–1961* (Moscow, Izdatel'stvo Vostochnoi Literatury, 1961) , p. 143.
[168] "Replies of N. S. Khrushchev to Questions of Editors of Ghanaian Times, Alger Républicain, Le Peuple and Botataung," *op. cit.*, pp. 12–13.
[169] Ivan Potekhin, "On 'African Socialism'," *International Affairs*, No. 1 (January, 1963) , p. 75.
[170] *Ibid.*, pp. 75–76.

ments during the Khrushchevian era as the African intelligentsia was discussed as an entity within itself, not as a stratum of a certain class. According to the official Soviet ideology, and as explained by Stalin in his report on the 1936 constitution, the intelligentsia is not a class but is only a stratum of a class. However, Soviet writings on Africa failed to mention to which class the intelligentsia in question belongs and they therefore gave the impression that the African intelligentsia is indeed organized as its own class. This is just another example of the ideological erosion manifested during years of Khrushchev's rule.

In reference to the underdeveloped countries of Asia and Africa, the Eighty-one Party Statement of 1960 declared: "Communists expose attempts by the reactionary section of the bourgeoisie to represent its selfish, narrow class interests as those of the entire nation; they expose the demagogic use by bourgeois politicians of socialist slogans for the same purpose; . . ."[171] Soviet writers also distinguished another variety of supposed socialism in which the African leaders have kinship or economic ties to the exploiting elements. These leaders are concerned with the welfare of the people and hope to raise the standard of living in their countries but they also do not want to affect the economic positions of their friends. They therefore practice a kind of socialism which helps the people to some extent but, at the same time, preserves "the interests of the top circles."[172] This is not really socialism in either the Soviet, or any other, sense.

Of course, the Soviet idea that the African masses desire socialism is at variance with Marxist doctrine, which stipulates that class determines consciousness. Soviet writers did not claim that the African masses are basically proletarian and failed to explain their purported desire for socialism in terms of class structure.

* * *

---

[171] Jacobs, *op. cit.,* p. 34.
[172] See Potekhin, "On 'African Socialism,' " *op. cit.,* p. 77 and Potekhin, *Africa: Ways of Development, op. cit.,* pp. 61–62.

Although African socialist leaders were often flattered by the Soviet press, their policies were attacked on many issues. Of prime importance were their economic programs and K. Grishechkin claimed that the Africans do not want to abolish private property but only desire to establish a more efficient system for distributing wealth.[173] He pointed out that this will not work since the exploiters will never voluntarily relinquish their profits. Mirskii and Tiagunenko declared that some national bourgeois elements claim adherence to socialism but they really do not want to abolish capitalism, they want to improve it.[174] Potekhin noted that some African socialists believe private enterprise can exist under socialism.[175] This is impossible since, according to the tenets of scientific socialism, private ownership of the means of production must be abolished.

Avakov and Stepanov also touched upon this issue and asserted that "socialism of a national type" defends private property.[176] Mixed economies, in which both national and foreign capital play roles, supposedly contribute to the welfare of the citizens but, in reality, conceal class differentiation. Those countries with the greatest class differentiation are the least likely to be aware of its existence and their leaders speak about "class peace."

Another contributor to the Soviet position on this subject was V. Dmitriev. Writing in April, 1963, he declared: "Many seem to picture socialist society as an idyllic society of universal affluence in which each person produces for himself all that is necessary and all people help each other. But Africans, adhering to such a point of view, are very far from real actu-

---

[173] Grishechkin, *op. cit.,* p. 8.
[174] Georgii Mirskii and V. Tiagunenko, "Tendentsii i perspektivy natsional'no-osvoboditel'nykh revoliutsii," *Mirovaia Ekonomika i Mezhdunarodnye Otnosheniia,* No. 11 (November, 1961), p. 30.
[175] Potekhin, "On 'African Socialism,'" *op. cit.,* p. 76.
[176] Avakov and Stepanov, "Sotsial'nye problemy natsional'no-osvoboditel'noi revoliutsii," *Mirovaia Ekonomika i Mezhdunarodnye Otnosheniia,* No. 5, 1963, p. 48.

ality."[177] Dmitriev went on to explain that these Africans don't understand class contradictions or the role of the state in industry and agriculture. He asserted that as long as private property exists, there will be exploitation.

Since Soviet authors found fault with African socialism, they propagandized their own brand of Marxism-Leninism. V. Solodovnikov wrote in December, 1964:

> The imperialists accuse the Communists of propagandizing socialism. We are happy to accept this 'guilt,' because we indeed consider socialism the best system for contemporary society. But neither the U.S.S.R. nor any other socialist country is imposing its own system or ideology on other countries. Socialism as a system and Marxism-Leninism as a social ideology are receiving ever broader dissemination throughout the world, including Africa, through the logic of life itself and the force of historical example.[178]

Soviet political experts constantly stated that ideology can neither be imported nor exported so Solodovnikov's remarks are therefore demonstrative of an inconsistency in the Soviet position. There would be no need to propagandize if ideology can not be exported and if socialism must grow out of the economic base of a given society.

Probably one of the most powerful assaults on African socialism was that made by S. Ogurtsov in the July, 1963 issue of *Aziia i Afrika Segodnia*.[179] He started out by claiming that the concepts of "special socialism," which had become so widespread in the countries of Asia and Africa, were far from being genuine Marxism-Leninism. Some of these concepts contain a "petty-bourgeois spirit" and "Utopian conclusions." Going even further, Ogurtsov charged that many adherents of

---

[177] V. Dmitriev, "Kontinent bor'by i nadezhd," *Aziia i Afrika Segodnia*, No. 4 (April, 1963), p. 13.
[178] Solodovnikov, "Africa on the Path of Freedom," *op. cit.*, p. 18.
[179] S. Ogurtsov, "The Developing Countries and Social Progress," *Aziia i Afrika Segodnia*, No. 7 (July, 1963). See *CDSP*, Vol. XV, No. 37 (October 9, 1963), p. 10.

these concepts are really trying to promote the interests of certain national bourgeois circles and they disguise their reactionary ideas as progressive ones in order to deceive the masses. He went on:

> Still others are characterized by the circulation of purely demagogic slogans and abstract propositions, mixed in a single stack of diverse and frequently completely antithetical concepts, combining socialism with religion, placing socialism in opposition to communism, etc. The authors of the concepts of the 'special type' do much of their interpretation from idealistic positions and often grossly distort the essence of socialism.[180]

Fundamentals of Marxism-Leninism concurred in the view there is no room for any special types of Marxism-Leninism and that its doctrines need no improvement nor adaptation. Discussing enemies of the working class, it stated: "Under the pretext of 'improving' Marxism they constantly strive to distort it and make it harmless to the bourgeoisie and useless to the workers."[181]

Since there are many varieties of African socialism and most innovations made by African leaders are declared to be socialist, it was often difficult for Soviet analysts theoretically to categorize African socialism as a whole. At the 1964 Moscow conference on underdeveloped areas, Iu. Ostrovitianov pointed out some of the problems encountered by Soviet political specialists.[182] He explained that in Asia and Africa, all moves, either to the left or right, are made under professions that they are socialist. There are so many doctrines labeled as socialist that some of them are even feudal or pre-feudal.

Avakov and Stepanov wrote in 1963 that socialism of a national type often serves as a cover for capitalist development and that it is frequently supported by both feudal and reli-

---

[180] *Ibid.*, p. 10.
[181] *Fundamentals of Marxism-Leninism, op. cit.,* p. 168 (1960 edition, p. 207).
[182] "The U.S.S.R. and the Developing Countries," *op. cit.,* p. 2.

gious leaders.[183] In many instances, such theories of socialism
are the same as the West European conception of socialism.
They warned against taking an extreme view of different types
of socialism. At one extreme are views similar to those of the
European socialists. They feature a concept of a "third world"
and contain feudal and "religious-mystical variants" of socialism. At the other extreme are nihilistic views which reject any
reforms not brought about by the working class. Such reforms
can benefit the people, even though they were not made
strictly in accordance with ideology.

Soviet African specialists during the Khrushchevian era
claimed that Africans were beginning to criticize African socialism more and more and that they were recognizing the
validity of scientific socialism. This analysis became more
prominent in Soviet writings toward the end of Khrushchev's
rule but had been outlined as early as 1960 in Potekhin's book
Afrika smotrit v budushchee.[184] Writing in *International Affairs* in 1964, Potekhin returned to the same subject and
stated: "Bourgeois journals throughout the world support
'African Socialism' or, to give it its other variant, 'Pan-African
Socialism' in the belief that this theory will not lead to Socialism. For this reason those African statesmen and political
figures who really are striving for Socialism have lately begun
to use the more exact term 'scientific Socialism.' "[185] He also
discussed the trend toward scientific socialism in another of
his works in 1964, *Africa: Ways of Development*. He asserted
that the imperialists are trying to slander and vilify the theory
of scientific socialism but that the "truth of scientific socialism was attracting an increasing number of adherents. New
forces able to master the scientific theory of socialism and

---

[183] R. Avakov and L. Stepanov, "Sotsial'nye problemy natsional'no-
osvoboditel'noi revoliutsii," *Mirovaia Ekonomika i Mezhdunarodnye
Otnosheniia*, No. 5, 1963, p. 49.
[184] See Potekhin, *Afrika smotrit v budushchee, op. cit.*, pp. 5–6.
[185] Potekhin, "Pan-Africanism and the Struggle of the Two Ideologies," *op. cit.*, p. 53.

apply it to the highly concrete and specific conditions of contemporary African society are rising on that continent."[186]

Potekhin cited pronouncements in favor of scientific socialism made by the Convention People's Party of Ghana, the Union Soudanaise of Mali, and, to some extent, by Sékou Touré of the Parti Démocratique Guinéen.[187] He also declared that the Parti Africain de l'Indépendance in Senegal adheres to scientific socialism, as does the National Association of Socialist Student Organizations in Ghana.[188]

Soviet writers repeatedly mentioned the fact that Kwame Nkrumah proclaimed his adherence to scientific socialism and no longer spoke about African socialism. This is true but Soviet analysis did not point out that Nkrumah's concept of scientific socialism was not really a Marxist-Leninist one. Although Nkrumah increasingly recognized the existence of class struggle in Africa and came to think of his Convention People's Party as an elitist vanguard, he still maintained some uniquely African socialist elements in his programs, such as deference to religion and certain aspects of traditional life.

T. Kolesnichenko asserted in *Pravda* on July 1, 1964, that the Convention People's Party had exposed the doctrine of African socialism and had "stated clearly and resolutely that Ghana will follow the road of scientific socialism applied to concrete African conditions."[189] On November 6, 1963, *Pravda* proudly reported a speech made by Kwame Nkrumah in Accra in which he told a visiting delegation from the Supreme Soviet of the Soviet Union: "We in Ghana have formally chosen the socialist path and we will build a socialist society. The question is, what kind of socialism? Only scientific so-

---

[186] Potekhin, *Africa: Ways of Development, op. cit.,* p. 69.
[187] See Potekhin, "Pan-Africanism and the Struggle of the Two Ideologies," *op. cit.,* p. 53 and Potekhin, *Africa: Ways of Development, op. cit.,* p. 68.
[188] Potekhin, *Afrika smotrit v budushchee, op. cit.,* p. 6.
[189] T. Kolesnichenko, "Novaia zhizn' Gany," *Pravda,* July 1, 1964, p. 3.

cialism, of course—there is no other kind of socialism. Thus our countries, the Soviet Union and Ghana, will go forward together."[190]

Although Nkrumah and some other African leaders such as Keita, have claimed to be scientific socialists, they really retain many aspects of African socialism and, more importantly, have not joined the Soviet Union's socialist camp. Nevertheless, their transition toward a greater acceptance of the Soviet version of Marxism-Leninism could only be viewed by Soviet experts as a progressive sign.

*   *   *

Despite their frequent and bitter attacks upon African socialism, Soviet authors also perceived certain elements which they did not consider to be too negative and they warned against rejecting African socialism as a whole. They also asserted that the desire of the Africans to build socialism is a step forward, even though the African brand of socialism is not pure Marxism-Leninism. In regard to Kenya, A. M. Glukhov wrote that although many Kenyans have a rather confused conception of socialism and are quite far from the proper understanding of scientific socialism, the fact that they are attracted to socialism is extremely important. The Kenyans reject capitalism and want a socialist future.[191] This idea that the Africans reject capitalism was very significant for the Soviet theorists. Since Africa is taking a socialist path, it is therefore fertile ground for Soviet political and ideological influences.

Boris Ponomarev, in a highly authoritative article appearing in the May, 1961 issue of *Kommunist*, recognized the importance of the dissemination of socialist concepts in Asia and Africa. He declared:

The leading figures of many of the liberated countries speak of socialism. Naturally, the conception of socialism

---

[190] *Pravda*, November 6, 1963, p. 5.
[191] A. M. Glukhov, *Keniia: ul'timatum kolonializmu* (Moscow, 1964), p. 109.

held by the bourgeois and petty bourgeois leaders of the liberated countries is not identical, and is often opposed, to the Marxist-Leninist conception of socialism. But it is characteristic that already today, a leader wishing to win popular sympathy cannot but come out with a recognition of socialism as the path ensuring the development of the country to national independence. . . . This is the banner of the times.[192]

Actually, the progressive significance of the socialist ideas held by Asian and African leaders was recognized as early as the Twentieth Party Congress in 1956. In his report to the Congress, Dmitri Shepilov spoke of the unity of all anti-imperialist forces. He called for a united effort by all "downtrodden people" and specifically mentioned the African people in this regard. He then avowed:

The attractive force of the ideas of socialism has grown so much that—besides the proletarian Marxist revolutionaries —politicians, groups and parties who do not interpret socialism in accord with the principles of revolutionary Marxism, but who are ready to fight against imperialism and for the vital interests of the working class and all the working people declare themselves supporters of socialism. This is why in many instances the existing differences and viewpoints can be relegated and are relegated to the background when it is a question of common interest in fighting against the capitalist yoke, for freedom and democracy.[193]

Shepilov did not specifically claim that the socialist ideas of the Asian and African leaders were intrinsically progressive but he implied that these ideas were progressive because of the fact that they were directed against capitalism and imperialism. The underdeveloped countries and the Soviet Union had a common enemy, imperialism, and they therefore should join forces in the struggle against this world menace. According to Shepilov's analysis, the needs of Soviet foreign policy were primary, and ideology was relegated to the background.

[192] B. Ponomarev, "O gosudarstve natsional'noi demokratii," *Kommunist,* No. 8 (May, 1961), p. 47.
[193] Shepilov, *op. cit.,* p. 20.

Georgii Mirskii, one of the leading Soviet specialists on underdeveloped areas, believed that the leaders of Ghana, Guinea, and Mali, who all advocated socialism, were representatives of the progressive intelligentsia and revolutionary democrats and were not representatives of the bourgeoisie. He asserted that their type of socialism "is still far from the Marxist concept of socialism" but "the very fact of striving for socialism is a sign of our era."[194] In discussing the socialist views of Kwame Nkrumah, another Soviet writer, O. Melikian, stated: "Nkrumah's understanding of socialism, as that of many other outstanding leaders of young independent states of Asia and Africa, in the main is different from the Marxist-Leninist understanding of socialism. However, it doubtlessly reflects the powerful influential force of the ideas of scientific socialism on the national-liberation movement of the peoples of Asia and Africa."[195]

Soviet friendliness toward certain African socialist leaders and coming to terms with their avowals of socialism was best exemplified by the comments of Anastas Mikoyan during his trip to Ghana in January, 1962. He declared: "Our parties operate under different conditions; they have a different history and different tasks. What brings us nearer to each other, however, is your effort to build socialism." He went on to assert: "Your party sees its task as raising the whole people for the attainment and construction of socialism under African conditions."[196] A few days later, Mikoyan said: "Dr. Nkrumah knows how to build the new life in Ghana. He called this 'socialism in conditions of Africa'—African socialism. The programmatic part of the rules of the Convention

---

[194] Georgii Mirskii, "Creative Marxism and Problems of the National-Liberation Movement," *Mirovaia Ekonomika i Mezhdunarodnye Otnosheniia,* No. 2 (March–April, 1963). See JPRS 19821, p. 13.
[195] O. Melikian, Review of Kwame Nkrumah's "I Speak of Freedom," *Narody Azii i Afriki,* No. 6, 1962, p. 157.
[196] "Gana privetstvuet Sovetskogo gostia," *Pravda,* January 13, 1962, p. 3.

People's Party of Ghana says that this type of socialism is impossible without a broad development of industry and the development of agriculture on this basis. This correct thesis is so general that it concerns us all."[197] While on his good-will mission, Mikoyan emphasized the similarities between Ghanaian and Soviet socialisms and remained silent on the differences.

In another speech during his trip, Mikoyan stated that "socialism means equality and brotherhood without the exploitation of man by man. Your people understands this and that is why it has risen in a struggle to transform its life."[198] He claimed that Ghanaians and Russians may understand the teachings of Marx and Lenin in different ways but the fact that the Ghanaians are familiar with the works of these great men shows that they were versed in the social sciences. Mikoyan also reiterated the familiar Soviet view that the U.S.S.R. neither imports nor exports ideology. Socialism propagates itself and its advent can not be prevented.

Of course, Mikoyan's conciliatory remarks on African socialism in Ghana were made while he was serving as a foreign policy missionary of good will, but the scholarly Soviet journals also contained similar viewpoints. For example, S. Ogurtsov discussed Asian and African concepts of socialism in the July, 1963 issue of *Aziia i Afrika Segodnia*.[199] He listed Nehru, Sukarno, Ne Win, Nkrumah, Keita, and Senghor as having proclaimed socialism and he even quoted Senghor's profession of socialism without adding any critical comment. This was indeed a conciliatory gesture since Senghor was usually described by Soviet writers as an ally of the imperialists and his brand of African socialism was generally attacked more violently than that of any other African socialist leader.

---

[197] William Lewis, "Sub-Saharan Africa," in Cyril Black and Thomas Thornton, eds., *Communism and Revolution* (Princeton, Princeton University Press, 1964), p. 381. Mikoyan speech as carried by Tass, January 17, 1962.
[198] *Pravda*, January 18, 1962, p. 3.
[199] Ogurtsov, *op. cit.*, p. 10.

A similarly accommodating stand was taken by A. A. Guber as early as 1956. He declared:

> The popularity of the ideas of socialism among the broadest people's masses in all countries of the East is so great that even the national bourgeoisie in a number of non-socialist countries (India, Burma, and others) officially propose the task of constructing socialism, the creation of an economy of the socialist type, etc. The desire to make use of that rich and fruitful experience which has been amassed, not only in the Soviet Union but also in other countries of the socialist system, characterizes the contemporary learned literature in the countries of the East.[200]

Guber did not call for the rejection of the socialist ideas advocated by the national bourgeoisie, and even failed to point out any faults inherent in these ideas.

Ivan Potekhin wrote that African socialism must not be "dismissed out of hand. It embraces genuine attempts by progressive people to find ways of transition to socialism which accord to the special conditions of Africa."[201] However, Potekhin claimed that African socialism is dualistic and is sometimes used by those who favor capitalism. They deceive the working masses with their slogans of socialism.

E. Zhukov warned that the Asian and African concepts of socialism should not be viewed from dogmatic positions. Although the democratic measures carried out by Asian and African leaders are not really socialist, they must not be belittled on this account. These measures do have a "progressive importance."[202] S. Ogurtsov had a similar analysis of the subject. Writing in the July, 1963 issue of *Aziia i Afrika Segodnia*,

---

[200] A. A. Guber, "Gluboko i vsestoronne izuchat' krizis i raspad kolonial'noi sistemy imperializma," *Sovetskoe Vostokovedenie,* No. 3, 1956, p. 13.

[201] Potekhin, "Nekotorye problemy Afrikanistiki v svete reshenii XII s' 'ezda KPSS," *op. cit.,* p. 15.

[202] E. Zhukov, "Significant Factor of Our Times," *Pravda,* August 26, 1960, pp. 3-4. See *CDSP,* Vol. XII, No. 34 (September 21, 1960), p. 19.

he criticized certain aspects of national-type socialism but went on to state:

> However, it would be incorrect to reject all concepts of 'national socialism,' all the tenets and conclusions contained in them. First, one must not forget that many of these concepts, reflecting the will and aspirations of the masses, were born during the people's struggle against imperialism and colonialism. Second, it must be taken into account that, along with the erroneous, anti-scientific and reactionary tenets (denial of the class struggle, of the idea of the dictatorship of the proletariat, of the guiding role of a revolutionary party of the Marxist type, and so forth) there are individual tenets of a progressive nature in the concepts of 'Afro-Asian socialism' that do not contradict revolutionary teaching and that are directed against imperialism, toward the complete uprooting of colonialism.[203]

Ogurtsov claimed that there are "healthy democratic principles" in these concepts. However, his main point was that these theories of African and Asian socialism are directed against imperialism and colonialism. He was therefore saying that their progressivism lies not in their positive programs, but in the fact that African and Asian socialist leaders share common enemies with the Soviet Union—imperialism and colonialism.

The official Soviet position was that there is only one variety of socialism and theories of "national-type socialism" were therefore attacked. They were accused of being "verbal smoke screens" used by the feudal and bourgeois reactionaries to "alienate the masses from genuine Socialism" and of being "petty-bourgeois illusions" which mislead the masses and hinder the development of the national-liberation movement.[204] However, Soviet writers demonstrated a growing ac-

---

[203] Ogurtsov, *op. cit.*, p. 10.
[204] See Karen Brutents, "Integral Part of the World Revolutionary Process," *International Affairs*, No. 2 (February, 1964), p. 34 and "Proekt programmy KPSS i nekotorye problemy natsional 'no-osvoboditel'nogo dvizheniia narodov Azii i Afriki," *Narody Azii i Afriki* editorial, No. 5 1961, p. 11.

ceptance of the progressive value of these theories and acknowledged that they were a step toward the proper Marxist-Leninist understanding of socialism. One of the leading Soviet spokesmen on nationalism and colonialism, Karen Brutents, wrote in February, 1964, that in many instances, theories of "national-type socialism" were deeply imbued with negative aspects but, he went on to write:

> In other cases, they are Socialist concepts of revolutionary democracy and are inseparable from the new content of the national-liberation movement, from the interests of the masses. Though at times infected with nationalistic and other prejudices, they reflect the militant democratic sentiments of the masses, profound hatred of capitalism, warm sympathy with people's suffering, and a desire to give them a better life. Such theories are capable of serving not as an antipode to scientific Socialism but a step towards it.[205]

The progressive aspects of "nation-type socialism" were also evaluated at two important conferences. G. Starushenko reported early in 1963 that at a conference of communist specialists on underdeveloped areas, conducted in Prague, many speakers warned against an unfounded rejection of "national-type socialism." Such theories, although they have little in common with scientific socialism, show that capitalism is not suited to the underdeveloped nations and they also help spread socialist ideas among the masses.[206]

At the 1964 Moscow conference on "Socialism, Capitalism and the Underdeveloped Countries," both Akopian and Avakov touched upon the same subject. Akopian explained that although "national-type socialism" does not correspond to scientific socialism, it is nevertheless progressive as many economic and social reforms carried out under its aegis go beyond capitalism and "create conditions for non-capitalist development."[207] Avakov declared:

---

[205] Brutents, *Ibid.*, p. 34.
[206] G. Starushenko, "Socialism and the National-Liberation Movement," *Mirovaia Ekonomika i Mezdunarodnye Otnosheniia*, No. 2 (March-April, 1963). See JPRS 19821, p. 21.
[207] "The U.S.S.R. and the Developing Countries," *op. cit.*, p. 25.

In my opinion, there is now in progress a definite transition from the ideology of nationalism to that of national-type socialism. National-type socialism represents a breaking out from the national bourgeois framework, when the revolutions in question have not yet become socialist. It is the national democratic stage of the liberation revolution. As the revolutions develop the doctrines will become more defined and finished. One cannot exclude the possibility of these theories evolving towards merger with Marxism-Leninism. It is true that national-type socialist doctrines create illusions and incorrect ideas of socialism; but it is nevertheless important that hundreds of millions of people adhere to the idea of socialism. As their class and political awareness increases they will be able to escape these illusions and incorrect ideas, and to demand real socialism, thus strengthening and deepening the national liberation revolution.[208]

As this statement by Avakov illustrates, the Soviet view of "national-type socialism," as it exists in Africa, increasingly included acceptance of its progressive aspects and the possibility that it could develop into true Marxism-Leninism. However, Soviet analysts looked bitterly upon any manifestations of national particularism in the socialist countries of the Soviet bloc.[209]

Another Soviet theme was that the programs of national-type socialism may lay the groundwork for the future state of national democracy. A. Sobolev, writing in the *World Marxist Review*, declared: "They contain a sound democratic core, a still latent germ of the future. Indeed, they resolve into a program of national-democratic revolution, an essentially anti-imperialist agrarian revolution of a new type destined to sweep away all the remnants of feudalism and tribal relations."[210] R. Avakov concurred on this issue. Following his attack on socialists who are not Marxist-Leninists, he asserted: "But all this cannot hide the fact that in the doctrines

---

[208] *Ibid*, pp. 17–18.
[209] For a comparison between the Soviet views of nationalism in Africa and the countries of the Soviet bloc, see below, p. 178.
[210] A. Sobolev, "National Democracy—The Way to Social Progress," *World Marxist Review*, Vol. VI, No. 2 (February, 1963), p. 41.

of national-type socialism there are certain revolutionary and progressive principles, which can bring the liberation revolution forward to the national democratic stage."[211] These statements by Sobolev and Avakov illustrate the Soviet view that African socialists can inaugurate the national-democratic revolution. The state of national democracy was seen by Soviet analysts as a transition to the non-capitalist path of development and these analysts even believed that African socialist leaders could guide their countries through the state of national democracy.[212]

*   *   *

The Soviet view of African socialism was an ambivalent one: although most aspects were considered to be at variance with Marxism-Leninism, it was believed that African socialism could evolve into scientific socialism and, furthermore, that it was progressive in the respect that it was opposed to imperialism and colonialism. Nikita Khrushchev, in a speech at a Soviet-Mali Friendship meeting in Moscow on May 30, 1962, emphasized that although socialism is the wave of the future, building socialism is not an easy task. Great effort is required and just professing belief in socialism is not enough:

> The social system changes only as a result of resolute struggle by the new against everything old and outmoded, against those who cling to the old. Especially great efforts and time will be required to alter people's psychology, to make them think and build life in a new way. It would be wrong to think that it is enough to proclaim the slogan 'We are for socialism' and that one can lie down in the cool shadow of a tree and wait for everything to arrange itself. No. A people building socialism must display energy, persistence and labour.[213]

---

[211] "The U.S.S.R. and the Developing Countries," *op. cit.*, p. 16.
[212] Guinea, under the leadership of the African socialist Sékou Touré was cited by Anastas Mikoyan as building a national democratic state. See below, p. 214.
[213] Speech by Khrushchev, *Pravda*, May 31, 1962, p. 1.

Khrushchev was thus exhorting people to hasten the inevitability of socialism.

PROGRESSIVE AND REACTIONARY FORMS OF AFRICAN SOCIALISM

Soviet African specialists recognized many forms of African socialism, some of which they deemed progressive and others which they considered reactionary. One of the main criteria used in determining the nature of African socialist regimes in power seems to have been the foreign policy postures of the countries in question, especially their attitudes toward the Soviet Union. In the eyes of Soviet analysts, the Casablanca powers were usually perceived as the African nations most closely approaching Marxist-Leninist positions and the countries of former French Africa, with the exception of Guinea, Mali and the Congo (Brazzaville), were generally viewed as being more prone to collaboration with the imperialist powers.

Ghana, Guinea, and Mali were the African states most often praised by Soviet writers. Their economic policies of closely restricting foreign investments and domestic capitalist enterprises were considered progressive and Soviet analysts also claimed that the economic programs of these states improved the conditions of the toiling masses.[214] Among the positive aspects cited were the independent monetary systems, old age pensions, and social security benefits, although the extent of these programs was greatly exaggerated by Soviet authors.[215]

---

[214] See Grishechkin, *op. cit.,* pp. 8–9; R. Avakov and R. Andreasian, "The Progressive Role of the State Sector," *Kommunist,* No. 13 (September, 1962) in *CDSP,* Vol. XIV, No. 41 (November 7, 1962), p. 10; and V. Tiagunenko, "Tendentsii obshchestvennogo razvitiia osvobodivshikhsia stran v sovremennuiu epokhu," *Mirovaia Ekonomika i Mezhdunarodnye Otnosheniia,* No. 3 (March, 1962), p. 31.

[215] *Tiagunenko,* Ibid., p. 31.

It was claimed in Soviet writings that the working people of Ghana (under Nkrumah) , Guinea, and Mali support their governments and that the broad people's masses play an active political role.[216] Although local capital was pictured as being weakly developed, it was believed that there was a sharp class struggle in these countries. Soviet authors praised the voluntary work programs and the supposedly communal system of land ownership and declared that Ghana, Guinea, and Mali have the pre-conditions for taking the non-capitalist path.[217]

Volume two of the third edition of the *Malaia Sovetskaia Entsiklopediia* went to press in October, 1958. It described the Convention People's Party of Ghana as a party of the national bourgeoisie but the Soviet view soon changed.[218] In his book *Afrika, 1956–1961,* Ivan Potekhin wrote in reference to Ghana: "The main guiding force in the country is the Convention People's Party, the party of a united national democratic front. Its program includes not only the demand for the destruction of imperialism and of all forms of oppression, but also for the elimination of capitalist exploitation and the building of a socialist society."[219] He asserted that the working class, which was still small, played an important political role and that the total number of wage workers at that time (1961) was 350,000.[220] This positive evaluation of the role of the Convention People's Party was initiated at least as early as 1960.[221] During the years 1958 and 1959, Sékou Touré's Parti Démocratique Guinéen was considered to be Africa's most radical

---

[216] See G. Usov, "Rabochii klass Afriki v bor'be protiv imperializma," *Mirovaia Ekonomika i Mezhdunarodnye Otnosheniia,* No. 6 (June, 1961) , p. 129 and Tiagunenko, *Ibid,* p. 24.

[217] See Tiagunenko, *Ibid.,* p. 29. For a discussion of the non-capitalist path of development, see the subchapter of this book entitled "The Non-Capitalist Path and the Evolution of African Socialism," pp. 181–200 and the subchapter entitled "Models for the Bypassing of Capitalism," pp. 200–208.

[218] *Malaia Sovetskaia Entsiklopediia,* third edition, Vol. II, p. 839.

[219] Potekhin, *Afrika, 1956–1961, op. cit.,* p. 52.

[220] *Ibid.,* pp. 52–53.

[221] See Potekhin, *Afrika smotrit v budushchee, op. cit.,* pp. 10 and 45.

party and stood alone, in the Soviet view, on the platform of progressivism.

Afrika: Entsiklopedicheskii Spravochnik, published in 1963, went one step further than Potekhin's 1961 book. It claimed that the Convention People's Party was based on the trade unions and other mass organizations.[222] Soviet writings stressed the weakness of the Ghanaian national bourgeoisie and cited this as one of the reasons why Ghana was capable of taking the non-capitalist path of development. This view was adopted at the same time that the Soviet analysts began to consider the Convention People's Party as progressive. In the early years of Khrushchev's rule, it was maintained that Nkrumah's administration "fostered the development of the national bourgeoisie."[223]

Facets of Ghanaian life favourably regarded by Soviet writers were the national monetary system, which was viewed as a necessary attribute of state sovereignty and a bastion of economic independence; the mutual assistance programs; common land-ownership; the state sector of the economy; the state bank; and the state's control over exports and transportation.[224]

Similar aspects of Guinean and Malian socialism were cited as progressive and Soviet writers asserted that these two nations also had the prerequisites for embarking on the non-capitalist path. Avakov and Andreasian claimed that the bourgeoisie in these states was minute, there was no feudal class, peasants lived in patriarchal-communal conditions, the parties in power were supported by the masses, and that these parties were led by the radical intelligentsia.[225] The past tense has been used in this paragraph because the Soviet analysis of

---

[222] *Afrika: Entsiklopedicheskii Spravochnik,* Vol. I (Moscow, 1963), p. 309.

[223] See A. Davidson, "The Gold Coast," *New Times,* No. 34 (August, 1956), p. 30.

[224] See Potekhin, *Afrika smotrit v budushchee, op. cit.,* pp. 10 and 45 and Potekhin, *Afrika, 1956–1961, op. cit.,* p. 53.

[225] Avakov and Andreasian, *op. cit.*

Guinean development changed toward the end of Khrushchev's rule.[226]

Soviet African specialists recognized certain progressive aspects of the Guinean and Malian political and economic programs but they left themselves an opening for a later change of opinion when they warned that the situation in these countries was still fluid and the future could not be predicted with certainty. V. Tiagunenko wrote in March, 1962:

> Most of the social and economic transformations carried out and contemplated in Guinea and Mali are not indeed capitalist measures. Objectively, this is a step toward the creation of conditions for the transition to the non-capitalist road of development. At the same time, one can not regard the social and economic situation in these countries as finally determined and settled. They are only at the very beginning of a long road. There is still before them a bitter and resolute struggle of the progressive forces against all reactionary and unstable elements for steady and unswerving advance on the road of non-capitalist development, the pre-conditions for which are present.[227]

In the September 28, 1958 referendum, Guinea voted not to join the French Community and it thereby became an independent nation. This act, made in defiance of Charles de Gaulle, endeared Guinea to Soviet writers and they portrayed Guinea as the most radical and progressive state in Africa. Volume two of the third edition of the *Malaia Sovetskaia Entsiklopediia*, which went to press in October, 1958, asserted that the Parti Démocratique Guinéen represented the peasantry, petty bourgeoisie, intelligentsia, native aristocracy, and part of the working class.[228] This analysis of the P.D.G. was in striking contrast to that of the Convention People's Party in Ghana, which was described as representing the national bourgeoisie.[229] Writing in January, 1959, A. Solonitskii de-

---

[226] See below, p. 109.

[227] Tiagunenko, "Tendentsii obshchestvennogo razvitiia osvobodivshikhsia stran v sovremennuiu epokhu," *op. cit.*, p. 32.

[228] *Malaia Sovetskaia Entsiklopediia*, third edition, vol. II, p. 882.

[229] See above, p. 104.

clared: "The achievement of political independence opens before the Guinean republic broad possibilities for the development of a healthy national economy."[230] He added that the Guinean people unanimously supported the P.D.G.

Soviet authors favorably discussed the policies of Sékou Touré's Guinean government during the following years. A *Pravda* article on April 7, 1960 asserted that Guinea was taking neither the capitalist nor the bourgeois path of development (it did not explain the difference between these seemingly similar paths) but was taking its own path which secures the best life for the Guinean people.[231] N. I. Gavrilov, in his book *Gvineiskaia Respublika,* averred that the P.D.G. united the "leading forces" of the Guinean people within its ranks.[232]

Another Soviet surveyor of the Guinean scene was Iu. Bochkarev. Writing in July, 1960, he claimed that the P.D.G. was a mass party and that its leaders had declared their opposition to the capitalist path of development. He also expressed pleasure in the fact that the Guinean government was combatting the practices of witch doctors. In regard to religion, Bochkarev stated: "The Democratic Party is aware of the need to dispel the religious myths with which the minds of the people are befuddled, and is taking steps in this direction."[233] He described the negative effects of Islam in Guinea but failed to mention any specific actions being taken against Islam by the Guinean government, possibly because no such actions existed in this predominantly Moslem country. Despite his generally positive report on Guinean life, he cautioned: "The situation there is indeed distinctive, and to be too hasty and try to fit

---

[230] A. Solonitskii, "Nezavisimaia Gvineiskaia Respublika," *Mirovaia Ekonomika i Mezhdunarodnye Otnosheniia,* No. 1 (January, 1959), pp. 100–101.

[231] "Gvineia na novom puti," *Pravda,* April 7, 1960, p. 3.

[232] N. I. Gavrilov, *Gvineiskaia Respublika* (Moscow, 1960), p. 117 footnote.

[233] Iu. Bochkarev, "The Guinean Experiment," *New Times,* No. 29 (July, 1960), p. 28.

it into any ready-made formula would be ill-judged."[234] In 1961, Sékou Touré received a Lenin Peace Prize. Nkrumah was not to receive one until 1962 and Keita until 1963. Guinea also sent a delegation to the Twenty-second Congress of the C.P.S.U. held in October, 1961. Guinea and the Soviet Union were enjoying a period of cordial relations.

A cooling in Soviet-Guinean relations occurred in November, 1961. In the so-called "teachers' plot," Sékou Touré charged that the Soviet Union was involved in an anti-government conspiracy planned by members of the teachers' union.[235] The Soviet ambassador, Daniel Solod, was expelled from Guinea. However, the Soviet Union decided to seek an improvement in relations with Guinea, rather than turn against her for her actions. Anastas Mikoyan was dispatched to Guinea in January, 1962 and his attitude was no less friendly than was the Soviet attitude prior to the "teachers' plot." In fact, Mikoyan asserted that Guinea was building a national democratic state.[236]   Therefore, Soviet analysts continued to cite Guinea as an example of progressivism and as moving toward the non-capitalist path of development.

In the October, 1963 issue of *Aziia i Afrika Segodnia*, I. Vasil'ev discussed Guinea. He called the Parti Démocratique Guinéen a "national progressive party" and claimed that all patriotic forces were united around the P.D.G., which stood on a platform of anti-colonialism and anti-imperialism.[237] Vasil'ev also averred: "In fact, at the head of Guinea from the very beginning to this day stand leaders who are not at all 'communist' or 'pro-communist.' President Sékou Touré, as well as the other leaders of the Guinean Republic, were, and remain, nationalist leaders."[238] This comment was not a barb

---

[234] *Ibid.*, p. 30.
[235] See "Guinea After Five Years," *Africa Report,* Vol. IX, No. 6 (June, 1964) , pp. 3–6.
[236] *Pravda,* January 12, 1962, p. 5.
[237] I. Vasil'ev, "Gvineia: proshloe i budushchee," *Aziia i Afrika Segodnia,* No. 10 (October, 1963) , p. 8.
[238] *Ibid.*, p. 9.

aimed at Touré since Vasil'ev went on to write that nationalism in an oppressed nation has a progressive, anti-imperialist
content.

During 1964, the Soviet view of Guinea changed. Although
neither Guinea as a country nor Sékou Touré was attacked
on basic issues, they were not mentioned as often in Soviet
articles dealing with Africa and were rarely singled out for
praise. Whereas Ghana, Guinea, and Mali had almost invariably been cited together as examples of African progressivism, Ghana and Mali alone now came to be cited. An
article by Iu. Ostrovitianov, which appeared in the June, 1964
issue of *Mirovaia Ekonomika i Mezhdunarodnye Otnosheniia,*
contained a long discussion of Ghana and Mali as examples
of development toward socialism but Guinea was not mentioned.[239] Also the 1964 edition of *Liudi i politika,* which went
to press in March, 1964, did not include a biographical sketch
of Touré, although it did have sketches of Nkrumah and
Keita.[240]

The most apparent reason for the new Soviet attitude seems
to have been Guinea's re-evaluation of its foreign policy com-
mitments. Guinea improved her relations with the Western
powers, especially France, and it also became disillusioned
with the quality of the aid sent by the Soviet Union. Therefore, Guinea showed less friendliness toward the socialist
countries and the Soviet African specialists responded by no
longer regarding Guinea as a leading progressive force in
Africa. This points out the close interrelationship between
Soviet theoretical writings and Soviet foreign policy. A country which has cordial relations with the Soviet Union is usually
considered progressive while this same country, when its relations with the U.S.S.R. cool to some extent, is no longer
viewed in this regard. However, such an interpretation does

---

[239] Iu. Ostrovitianov, "Sotsialisticheskie doktriny razvivaiushchikhsia
stran: formy i sotsial'noe soderzhanie," *Mirovaia Ekonomika i
Mezhdunarodnye Otnosheniia,* No. 6, 1964, pp. 82–91.
[240] *Liudi i politika, 1964* (Moscow, 1964).

contain an element of realism. The ideology is no longer out of touch with changing circumstances and although it is greatly eroded in a theoretical sense, it has become a more useful reflection of political exigencies. It has ceased to exist in a vacuum but, at the same time, in regard to the formulation of a foreign policy, it has become more of a servant than a master.

Mali was the third African country generally cited by Soviet political analysts as progressing toward non-capitalist development. When the Mali Federation disintegrated in August, 1960, and Mali (formerly the Soudan) and Senegal emerged as separate states, Soviet authors at once began to consider Mali progressive and Senegal reactionary. S. Wolk, writing in *New Times,* in September, 1960, declared that "the Soudanese bourgeoisie is very weak and the national-liberation movement is led by democratic elements closely linked with the people."[241] On the other hand, he claimed that in Senegal, the activity of the masses is suppressed and that Senghor's party represents the big bourgeoisie.[242]

It was affirmed in Soviet articles that the Union Soudanaise, the ruling party in Mali, was supported by the masses and that it was a "mass national-democratic party that speaks for the interests of the Mali people."[243] Soviet writers were also pleased by the fact that the Congress of the Union Soudanaise, held in September, 1960, called for a system of socialist planning.[244] Other Malian governmental programs cited as having positive results were the introduction of a national currency, state control of the basic sectors of the economy, nationalization of foreign concerns, government control of foreign trade, and the system of cooperative farming. It was pointed out that

---

[241] S. Wolk, "The Mali Coup," *New Times,* No. 36 (September, 1960), p. 18.
[242] See below, p. 112.
[243] V. Mikhailov, "Republic of Mali," *New Times,* No. 22 (May 30, 1962), p. 16.
[244] N. I. Gavrilov, "Respublika Mali—Molodoe nezavisimoe gosudarstvo Afriki," *Narody Azii i Afriki,* No. 4, 1961, p. 32.

collective work was practised in agriculture and that private land ownership was not well developed. Another important step, as viewed by Soviet analysts, was the law concerning land transactions. Potekhin wrote: "In order to facilitate the formation of cooperatives and to prevent the formation of a layer of rural bourgeoisie, the governments of Guinea and Mali have adopted laws which limit land transactions."[245]

In regard to Malian agriculture, Soviet writers hailed the establishment of cooperative and state farms and noted the creation of democratically elected village councils which settle problems related to land tenure. The chiefs were no longer in control of the land tenure system.[246] Iu. Dement'ev discussed the agricultural cooperatives in the July 1961 issue of *Mirovaia Ekonomika i Mezhdunarodnye Otnosheniia*. He stated:

At the end of 1960, the government adopted a law on cooperative agriculture in which the principle of voluntariness in the creation of cooperatives is emphasized and which indicates that the state is obliged in every way to aid their activities in material relations and to provide the necessary technical aid. According to law, the cooperative is a truly independent organization. Any kind of interference in its affairs by the administration, and furthermore, any decisions forced upon it, are not tolerated. The administration is only able to advise the cooperative. The general assembly of the cooperative may accept or not accept this advice.[247]

He also noted the absence of both feudalism and a class of kulaks and cited the existence of strong patriarchal-communal relations.[248]

The September 2, 1964 issue of *New Times* contained an interview with Madeira Keita, a member of the National Polit-

---

[245] Potekhin, *Afrika, 1956–1961, op. cit.*, p. 128.
[246] See A. B. Letnev, "Novoe v Maliiskoi derevne," *Sovetskaia Etnografiia*, No. 1 (January–February, 1964), pp. 81–82.
[247] Iu. Dement'ev, "Kooperirovanie v Maliiskoi derevne," *Mirovaia Ekonomika i Mezhdunarodnye Otnosheniia*, No. 7 (July, 1961), p. 110.
[248] *Ibid.*, p. 111.

ical Bureau of the Union Soudanaise.[249] Since this interview appeared in a Soviet journal, its content must have been looked upon favorably by Soviet political analysts. Keita expounded upon the Five Year Plan, the large state sector in industry, state control of foreign trade and transportation, the state bank, the national currency, the consumers' cooperatives, and the one party system. He also claimed that the traditional communes did not operate on truly socialist principles but they were being converted into socialist organizations.

* * *

President Léopold Senghor of Senegal and his Union Progressiste Sénégalaise were repeatedly viewed by Soviet African specialists as reactionary forces. After the dissolution of the Mali Federation in August, 1960, S. Wolk wrote: "Senghor and the party he leads, the Senegalese Progressive Union, speak for the big bourgeoisie, which is closely bound to French capital. Senghor himself comes from a Senegalese bourgeois family . . ."[250] Mikhail Kremnev described Senghor as a reactionary ideologist who represented the "bureaucratic top crust" and the book *Vstrecha s Afrikoi* claimed that "the humanistic 'socialism' of Senghor fits in with the nationalistic views of the reactionary wing of the Pan-African movement."[251] This latter source outlined the supposedly socialist ideas of Senghor and declared: "Such a discussion of socialism does not bring a refutation by the neo-colonialists. It serves to camouflage the development of capitalist foundations in a number of African countries with talk about the absence of classes in African society."[252]

It is interesting to note Ivan Potekhin's claim that Senegal has a small working class, consisting of only 100,300 hired

[249] Madeira Keita, "Madeira Keita on the New Mali," *New Times*, No. 35 (September 2, 1964), pp. 14–15.

[250] Wolk, *op. cit.*, p. 18.

[251] Mikhail Kremnev, "Africa in Search of New Paths," *World Marxist Review*, Vol. VI, No. 8 (August, 1963), p. 76 and Vadeev, *op. cit.*, p. 170.

[252] *Ibid.*, p. 170.

laborers (as of 1961) .[253] Viewed in context, the implication is that the absence of a large working class is a cause of Senegal's lack of political progressivism. However, an article by the Guinean leftist, J. Suret-Canale, which appeared in the February, 1961 issue of *International Affairs,* asserted that the Senegalese working class is the largest and most advanced in former French West Africa but it has been unable to "draw the peasant masses into the common struggle."[254] There is therefore disagreement on this point but Soviet journals agree that the working class does not support the Union Progressiste Sénégalaise. A Marxist-Leninist Senegalese party, the Parti Africain de l'Indépendance, is viewed by Soviet political experts as representing the Senegalese workers, peasants, and progressive intelligentsia.[255]

In addition to Léopold Senghor, another African leader often attacked in Soviet writings was Félix Houphouët-Boigny, President of the Ivory Coast. Houphouët-Boigny is generally regarded as a rather moderate African socialist but during the years immediately following World War II, he was a leading African leftist and headed the Rassemblement Démocratique Africain. He started to move away from his outwardly procommunist stance by 1950 and is now one of the most rightist African leaders. The communist view of Houphouët-Boigny is best summed up in this statement by Miroslaw Azembski, which appeared in the October 4, 1961 issue of *New Times:*

The President of the Ivory Coast Republic is Mr. Félix Houphouët-Boigny. Naturally he is an African by the colour of his skin, and, just as naturally, he is one of the richest planters in the country. Once upon a time he was all for progress and was one of the founders of the Democratic Union of Africa. Later, when he felt himself strong enough,

---

[253] Potekhin, *Afrika, 1956–1961, op. cit.,* p. 107.
[254] J. Suret–Canale, " 'The French Community' at the Hour of African Independence," *International Affairs,* No. 2 (February, 1961), p. 25.
[255] *Afrika: Entsiklopedicheskii Spravochnik,* Vol. II, *op. cit.,* p. 190.

he adopted Right-wing positions. Now he is a firm opponent of the Ghana-Guinea-Mali union.[256]

Until 1964, when Tanzania embarked on a more leftist course, Julius Nyerere was a moderate spokesman for African socialism. The Soviet analysts adopted a luke-warm attitude towards him and while not bitterly criticizing his views, they nevertheless opposed many of them. Iu. Tomilin charged that Nyerere's brand of socialism denied the existence of classes and side-stepped the question of eliminating private ownership in industry. However, he averred that Nyerere recognized the need to socialize land.[257] G. Usov criticized Nyerere for stimulating foreign investment.[258]

When describing the African variations on socialist doctrine, Soviet writers often included attacks on the Israeli and Yugoslav models of socialist development. As William Griffith has pointed out, quite a few Africans are attracted by the Yugoslav and Israeli examples of national socialist growth, partly because the Africans do not fear that these countries will try to dominate them, as the Soviet Union or China may.[259] In his authoritative book *Afrika smotrit v budushchee*, Ivan Potekhin recognized the fact that many African leaders, such as Senghor and Dia, have cited the significance of the Yugoslav and Israeli economic systems.[260] He claimed that Israeli workers are no better off than those in capitalist countries and are oppressed by the large monopolies. In regard to Yugoslavia, Potekhin asserted that the poor peasants are in a position

---

256 Miroslaw Azembski, "Report on the Ivory Coast," *New Times*, No. 40 (October 4, 1961), p. 28.
257 Iu. Tomilin, "East Africa Chooses the Way," *International affairs*, No. 1 (January, 1964), p. 45.
258 G. Usov, "Natsional'naia burzhuaziia i osvoboditel'noe dvizhenie v Vostochnoi Afrike," *Mirovaia Ekonomika i Mezhdunarodnye Otnosheniia*, No. 4 (April, 1962), p. 86.
259 See William Griffith, "Yugoslavia," in Zbigniew Brzezinski, ed., *Africa and the Communist World* (Stanford, 1963), pp. 116–141.
260 Potekhin, *Africa smotrit v budushchee, op. cit.*, p. 10.

similar to that of hired laborers. They are subject to the exploiting power of the well-to-do peasants.[261] N. Gavrilov
declared that the Israeli kibbutzim are really capitalistic.[262]
Another familiar Soviet theme was that, in regard to Africa,
Israel served as a Trojan horse of the imperialists.[263]

Most African socialist regimes in power have established
one-party systems but Soviet analysts rarely discussed this facet
of African socialism. The most probable reason is that these
one-party systems are not communist and many of them actually suppress the communist parties and movements within
their countries. Soviet authors usually looked favorably upon
the mass parties in power but were wary of approving them as
a general principle since they hoped for the establishment of
communist regimes in Africa. Among the infrequent pronouncements on the subject was one by I. Beliaev, who
praised the one-party rule of the Union Soudanaise in Mali
and asserted that it was supported by the people. He scoffed
at Western criticisms of one-party rule.[264]

Iu. Bochkarev lauded the Guinean one-party system and
claimed that the P.D.G. is supported by all the people. He
averred that Guinea's social and economic structure does not
have the proper foundations for the creation of a multi-party
system and then explained: "For, when there are, in substance,
no opposing classes in a country, one political party fully
suffices to express the interests of the broad masses."[265] Bochkarev was denying the existence of a class struggle in Guinea
and was therefore in disagreement with V. Tiagunenko who

---

[261] *Ibid.,* p. 15.
[262] N. Gavrilov, "Preobrazovanie Afrikanskoi derevni," *Aziia i
Afrika Segodnia,* No. 12 (December, 1962), p. 15.
[263] See *Ibid.,* p. 15; V. Nikolaiev, "Israel's Perilous Course," *International Affairs,* No. 10 (October, 1961), pp. 77–78; and V. Grigoriev,
"Israel: A Servant of Neo-Colonialism in Africa," *International Affairs,* No. 1 (January, 1961), pp. 124–125.
[264] Beliaev, *op. cit.,* p. 28.
[265] Iu. Bochkarev, "The Guinean Experiment," *New Times,* No. 24
(June, 1960), p. 26.

claimed that there was a sharp conflict of the classes in Guinea.[266] This demonstrates the Soviet manipulation of arguments to prove points since it is more likely that Bochkarev and Tiagunenko were fashioning cogent arguments than that they were sincerely in disagreement. Tiagunenko's article was aimed at emphasizing the political role of the masses in Guinea, Ghana, and Mali. The general Soviet position was that there is a class struggle through Africa and African socialists were often criticized for their belief that there is no class struggle in Africa.

Bochkarev's statement is interesting since it is in accordance with Marxist theory. Parties must represent classes and if there is one party which represents all of the people, there can not be antagonistic classes. Maybe this is another reason for the Soviet reluctance to discuss African one-party systems. Praising them would imply the existence of class harmony in the African countries.

V. Kudriavtsev declared that the one-party system is a reaction to bourgois democracy. The latter suffers from "parliamentary procrastination over issues which need urgent solution."[267] He claimed that the one-party system was sometimes used to consolidate dictatorships, as Youlou did in the Congo (Brazzaville) or as is now the case in Chad, where the south dominates the Moslem north. However, in countries which are taking the non-capitalist path, the party in power is supported by the advanced elements and is a national front.

Kudriavtsev called upon the advanced elements to support the one-party regimes and work within them in order to isolate the right-wing members in the leadership. He cautioned that these right-wing members might collaborate with the former colonial powers and he asserted that the advanced elements within these African parties should strive gradually

---

[266] See Tiagunenko, "Tendentsii obshchestvennogo razvitiia osvobodivshikhsia stran v sovremennuiu epokhu," op. cit., p. 24.
[267] V. Kudriavtsev, "Africa's Hopes and Anxieties," *International Affairs*, No. 11 (November, 1963), p. 44.

to gain control of them. The author added: "This is particularly the case in countries where there are no Communist parties but are individual Communists or sympathisers not united in a single party organisation."[268]

Kudriavtsev went on to cite the example set by the advanced elements in Mongolia.[269] He claimed that when the Mongolian People's Revolutionary Party was founded in 1921, there was as yet no working class. However, Mongolia took the non-capitalist path of development and the feudal-reactionary elements within the party were expelled in 1928. The working class was then in control.

Kudriavtsev concluded his discussion with this statement: "The question of a one-party or multi-party system is extremely complicated. Its solution depends on the concrete conditions existing in each African country, on the alignment of class forces within it, on the way the country develops, and on many other things. No set pattern or dogmatic, tidy propositions are possible."[270]

The Soviet view of African socialist ideology was therefore marked by an ambivalence. Soviet authors criticized many of the tenets of African socialism but since they did not want to malign the views of the African leaders whose friendship was being catered by the Soviet Union, they adopted a conciliatory position on many issues. These authors also professed a belief that African socialism could eventually evolve into scientific socialism. The Soviet Union was, to some extent, willing to compromise ideologically in return for continued joint action with the African states on certain international political issues. Soviet writers claimed that the socialist countries and the nations of Asia and Africa were united in their opposition to imperialism and E. Zhukov asserted that political and ideological differences between Ghana, Guinea, and the socialist countries did not prevent them from taking the

[268] *Ibid.*, p. 45.
[269] *Ibid.*, p. 45.
[270] *Ibid.*, p. 45.

same stand on major world problems.[271] He cited the issues of peace, disarmament, opposition to aggressive blocs, banning of nuclear weapons, and the abolition of military bases which are located on the territory of another country. Soviet political analysts therefore coordinated their ideological pronouncements with the flow of the Soviet Union's foreign policy. The dogmatic views of the Stalin era gave way to a more flexible, more realistic outlook during the Khrushchevian era.

---

[271] Zhukov. *op. cit.,* p. 19.

4 Socialism, the Class Struggle, and African Society: the Soviet Analysis

MOST AFRICAN SOCIALISTS CLAIM THAT THERE ARE NO CLASSES in Africa and that the traditional African societies which existed prior to the arrival of the colonialists were socialist. Both of these contentions were disputed by Soviet political experts, who averred that the African countries are now experiencing bitter class struggles and that class differentiation was beginning in Africa even before the colonial powers disrupted the course of African social evolution. These experts rejected the African socialist assertion that the African nations could return to the pre-colonialist socialist way of life since they took the position that such a way of life did not exist in the immediately pre-colonial period.

In regard to the contemporary period, Soviet Africanists minimized the extent of class hostility between the working class and the bourgeoisie and, instead, called for a united front, including these two classes, to oppose the imperialists. They declared that the foreign firms, not the native African bourgeoisie, were the chief exploiters of the African working class and also recognized that political independence could be achieved under national bourgeois leadership. Another of

119

their views was that nationalism in exploited nations had a democratic content.

Toward the end of the Khrushchevian era, Soviet political analysts began to emphasize the class struggle on an international level and wrote about a world revolutionary process. They subordinated the class struggles in individual countries to the one which they perceived in the international arena and thus stressed the unity of action between the socialist states and the new nations of Asia and Africa.

TRADITIONAL AFRICAN SOCIETY

One of the basic claims of the African socialists is that African society was socialist prior to the arrival of the colonialists. Soviet analysts disputed this contention and asserted that although many Africans lived in primitive-communal societies at that time, some of which were not touched by class conflict, class society was evolving and feudalism existed in some places.[272] Ivan Potekhin questioned the feasibility of the African socialist view that the African countries could return to the pre-colonialist socialist structure. He admitted that there were primitive-communal societies before the colonialists came to Africa but averred that these societies greatly differed from modern socialist societies and returning to them would not be advantageous. Potekhin wrote: "Many African peoples lived in primitive-communal society before the colonialists came, and knew neither exploitation nor the class division of society. If there was equality among these peoples, it was the equality of poverty; socialist society, on the other hand, is a society of abundance."[273]

Soviet researchers believed that feudalism was in the process of developing when the colonial period started and that there

---

[272] See A. S. Orlova, "O meste i roli traditsionnykh vlastei Afrikanskogo obshchestva v proshlom i nastoiashchem," *Sovetskaia Etnografiia*, No. 6, 1960, p. 104.
[273] Potekhin, *Africa: Ways of Development, op. cit.*, p. 63.

were feudal states in some parts of Africa in which nationalities (narodnosti) were already formed. At this time, nations
had not yet been formed.[274]

Soviet writers outlined a definite sequence of historical development which they claimed was pertinent to the African
continent, as well as to other parts of the world.[275] Under the
primitive-communal system, clans and tribes are the primary
social groupings. These clans and tribes have common languages and cultures, have no classes, and are based on ties of
kinship. When several tribes amalgamate, a nationality
(narodnost') is created. A nationality has a common language,
territory, and culture but not a common economy. It may have
a system of slavery but is usually primarily feudal. Communal
landholding is replaced by a system of feudal exploitation
and class differentiation proceeds rapidly.

As feudalism develops into capitalism, the nationality
changes into a nation (natsional'nost'). Private landholding
becomes prominent and a landless capitalist class forms in the
towns. Nations are composed of antagonistic classes and a
nation may contain people of many races. There is no relationship between race and nationhood. According to Ivan Potekhin, there were no nations in Africa until the end of the
nineteenth century.[276]

Soviet scholars still adhere to the famous definition of a

---

[274] See R. Avakov and G. Mirskii, "Class Structure in the Underdeveloped Countries," *Mirovaia Ekonomika i Mezhdunarodnye Otnosheniia*, No. 4, 1962. See Thornton, *The Third World in Soviet Perspective, op. cit.*, p. 278 and Ivan Potekhin, "Zadachi izucheniia etnicheskogo sostava Afriki v sviazi s raspadom kolonial'noi sistemy,"
Sovetskaia Etnografiia, No. 4, 1957, p. 103.

[275] For discussions of this topic, see Ivan Potekhin, "De quelques
questions méthodologiques pour l'étude de las formation des na-
tions en Afrique au Sud du Sahara," *Présence Africaine*, No. 17
(December, 1957–January, 1958), pp. 61–65; *Fundamentals of
Marxism–Leninism, op. cit.*, pp. 150–151; and Mary Holdsworth,
Soviet African Studies, 1918–1959: An Annotated Bibliography,
Part I, London: Royal Institute of International Affairs, Oxford
University Press, 1961, pp. 3–5.

[276] Potekhin, *Ibid.*

nation advanced by Stalin in his work, *Marxism and the National Question* (1913). Stalin asserted that a nation was a "historically evolved, stable community of language, territory, economic life, and psychological make-up manifested in a community of culture." It is curious to note that the 1960 edition of *Fundamentals of Marxism-Leninism* included this definition and attributed it to Stalin while the 1963 edition of the same work, although also citing the same definition, failed to mention its source.[277] This was obviously a result of the anti-Stalin campaign.

Ivan Potekhin discussed the development of African nations in an article appearing in *Présence Africaine* entitled, "De quelques questions méthodologiques pour l'étude de la formation des nations en Afrique, au Sud du Sahara."[278] His evaluation was in accord with Stalin's definition and he emphasized that a nation must have a common territory, language, culture, and economy. He specifically mentioned the Jews as proof of his point that there can't be a nation without a common territory.[279] He believed that the Jews do not constitute a nation.

Potekhin stressed that there were no nations before capitalism developed and that there were no African nations until the turn of this century because there was no capitalism in Africa. He wrote: "If one thus understands the word 'nation,' it must be evident that a nation is able to come into being only under capitalism and that nations are the product of capitalist development."[280] Potekhin claimed that nations were now in the process of formation and that this process was accompanied by a rise in national consciousness. Different African peoples are at different stages of development and the

---

[277] See *Fundamentals of Marxism–Leninism*, 1960 edition, p. 186 and 1963 edition, p. 151.
[278] Potekhin, "De quelques questions méthodologiques pour l'étude de la formation des nations en Afrique au Sud du Sahara," *op. cit.,* pp. 60–75.
[279] *Ibid.,* p. 61.
[280] *Ibid.,* p. 62.

boundaries between these stages are not precise. As a result, capitalist, feudal, and primitive-communal societies are all in existence on the African continent.

The Soviet analysis was marked by a recognition of three basic stages of African development: tribalism, nationality, and nation. The corresponding forms of economic relationships are communal, feudal, and capitalist. Therefore, as far as the Soviet critics were concerned, Africa is certainly not classless and most of it has not been since long before the arrival of the colonialists.

According to the pattern of development just presented, Africa was viewed in isolation from contacts with other continents but Soviet writers did recognize the impact of colonization on African societies. V. Ia. Katsman asserted that the colonialists helped develop feudal relations in some parts of Africa.[281] They strengthened the positions of the ruling classes as they collaborated with the leaders of the territories they conquered. Ivan Potekhin claimed that the colonialists exploited the Africans and prevented them from becoming proletarians because they realized the power of a possible unification of the class struggle of the proletariat with the national-liberation movement.[282] Most workers were migratory peasants and the colonialists held back the growth of the national bourgeoisie. They prevented the Africans from accumulating large reserves of capital. Potekhin stated: "Colonialism acted as an obstacle to the capitalist development of Africa and the emergence of the classes associated with capitalist society."[283] Avakov and Mirskii agreed with Potekhin's interpretation and declared: "The European bourgeoisie by no means went into overseas countries in order to implant there the prevailing capitalist production relationships. It

---

[281] V. Katsman and P. Kuprianov, "O meste i roli vozhdei v Afrikanskom obshchestve," *Sovetskaia Etnografiia*, No. 3, 1962, p. 149.
[282] Ivan Potekhin, "Some Aspects of the National Question in Africa," *World Marxist Review*, Vol. IV, No. 11 (November, 1961), p. 44.
[283] *Ibid.*, p. 44.

preserved the pre-capitalist and pre-feudal relationships every-where, utilizing them to enslave these countries, and it de-veloped capitalism only within definite limits."[284] Africa was unusual since the small degree of capitalism which did develop there was introduced from the outside and did not grow from within the domestic economic structure.[285]

Soviet African specialists concurred on the point that the slave trade had far-reaching effects on Africa's development. Potekhin wrote in 1962: "The specific characteristics of the historical development of the African peoples (the slave trade and so forth) engendered certain peculiar forms of transition from a preclass to a class society that are still not completely clear."[286] He was a little more precise in 1964 when he stated, in regard to the slave trade, that it "ruled out the possibility of the tribes merging into nationalities and nations and form-ing large centralised states."[287] Potekhin believed that Africa lagged behind other parts of the world because of colonial rule and the slave trade and that Africa's development was retarded for many centuries. He asserted that since gaining independence, the African countries have been able to de-velop during a period in which the world socialist system is advancing and the capitalist world is on the decline. These international factors should determine Africa's future course of growth.[288]

According to Soviet writers, the colonialists held back the formation of nations and were aided in this process by the missionaries.[289] They also prevented the tribes from merging

---

[284] Avakov and Mirskii, *op. cit.*, p. 278.

[285] See M. Braginskii, "Sotsial'nye sdvigi v tropicheskoi Afrike posle Vtoroi Mirovoi Voiny," *Sovetskaia Etnografiia*, No. 6, 1960, pp. 31–43.

[286] Ivan Potekhin, "Land Relationships in the Countries of Africa," *Narody Azii i Afriki*, No. 3, 1962. See Thornton, *The Third World in Soviet Perspective, op. cit.*, p. 239.

[287] Potekhin, "Legacy of Colonialism," *op. cit.*, p. 15.

[288] See Potekhin, *Afrika smotrit v budushchee, op. cit.*, p. 26.

[289] See Potekhin, "Some Aspects of the National Question in Africa," *op. cit.*, p. 42 and *Afrika: Entsiklopedicheskii Spravochnik*, Vol. I, *op. cit.*, p. 93.

into nationalities as they purportedly stressed the ethnic and linguistic differentiation in Africa and minimized the similarities among peoples. As seen by the Soviet analysts, African nations are at various levels of development and the main question is whether these evolving nations will be bourgeois or socialist.[290] This view strikingly contrasts with the Stalinist dictum that all nations are bourgeois and points out the Khrushchevian symbiosis of nationalism and socialism.[291]

Ivan Potekhin claimed that not only were the African nations still in the process of development, but that feudalism also is not completely evolved. He asserted:

> Feudal relations did not succeed in becoming fully developed in the countries of tropical Africa. Here there are no landlords, the land remains under communal ownership up to the present time, and each peasant cultivates only as much as he is able; the lack of land is felt only in certain regions. At the same time, numerous survivals of the pre-class socio-economic relations are preserved in these countries.[292]

Soviet scholars often linked African feudalism with tribalism. V. Ia Katsman averred that African feudalism is not the same as feudalism elsewhere because the peasants are not tied to the land and the organization of people into clans still exists.[293] He claimed that the tribes survive alongside the feudal states (remember that in the Soviet view, tribalism precedes feudalism) and that the chiefs have formed a feudal aristocracy as a result of the status given to them through the system of indirect colonial rule. However, Potekhin pointed out that "tribalism is not simply the intrigues of the imperialists."[294] He declared that there are elements of isolationism and patriotism in tribalism and that the cult of

---

[290] *Afrika: Entsiklopedicheskii Spravochnik, Ibid.,* p. 93.
[291] For a discussion of the Khrushchevian view of nationalism, see below, pp. 175–180.
[292] Potekhin, *Afrika, 1956–1961, op. cit.,* pp. 128–129.
[293] Katsman and Kuprianov, *op. cit.,* pp. 150–151.
[294] Potekhin, "Nekotorye problemy Afrikanistiki v svete reshenii XXII s''ezda KPSS," *op. cit.,* p. 14.

ancestors, a religious practice characteristic of pre-class society, is still preserved.

Soviet analysts saw a melange of class relationships in traditional African society and generally pictured tribalism as a negative force. They seemed to overemphasize the importance of classes and were quite far removed from a proper anthropological understanding of African tribal structures.

THE CLASS STRUGGLE IN AFRICA

Most African socialists have contended that the African countries are devoid of social classes and that the Marxian theory of class struggle is irrelevant to Africa. Soviet African specialists were in complete disagreement with this view as they claimed that all countries and continents are marked by class struggle and that this is an objective fact of historical development. K. Grishechkin averred that there are bourgeois and semi-feudal elements in Africa even though supposedly anti-communist propagandists deny the existence of a class struggle. Iu. Zhukov, also stressing the class struggle, maintained that agents of neocolonialism masquerade in Africa and speak about Arab, Islamic, and African socialisms.[295] Iu. Popov concurred and delivered a blistering attack on the African socialists who deny that there is a class struggle in Africa:

> These pro-imperialist circles, hiding behind talk about 'real African socialism,' are attempting to emasculate the class content of the proletarian struggle and to force the African working class to betray the principles of proletarian international as well as to drag into the African working-class movement the narrow nationalist slogan that 'all Africans are brothers.' However, this false bourgeois thesis will become less and less popular on the African continent. . . . The day is not far off when the all-conquering teachings

[295] Grishechkin, op. cit., p. 8 and Iu. Zhukov, "Vstrecha s Afrikoi," Pravda, May 19, 1964, p. 4.

of scientific socialism will triumph on the African continent.[296]

Another Soviet contributor to the issue of an African class struggle was R. Avakov. He pointed out that leaders in underdeveloped countries usually use the term "the people" rather than class categories. They preach class peace, citing the need for national unity, but they mislead the masses with this propaganda. Avakov then adopted a mild position vis-à-vis the Asian and African leaders and stated: "But one must bear in mind that appeals for class cooperation sound differently, for example, in Mali, where antagonisms are weak, and in India, where they are strong."[297] Avakov was therefore coming to terms with the views of the leaders in countries considered progressive by Soviet writers and was willing to overlook their claims that there is no class struggle in Africa.

In his famous address delivered in Sofia, Bulgaria in May, 1962, Nikita Khrushchev criticized those leaders of newly independent countries who rejected the applicability of the class struggle to their nations. He asserted: "Many of the leaders of the countries that have won their national independence are trying to pursue a kind of fence-sitting policy, which they call non-class, are trying to ignore the class structure of society and the class struggle, which are matters of fact in their countries."[298] Khrushchev noted that many underdeveloped countries reject capitalism and claim to be building socialism. They realize that socialism ensures rapid development but Khrushchev had a few questions concerning socialism in these countries: "But what kind of socialism do they have in mind? What do they mean by it? Which are the forces they would lean on in building socialism?"[299] He then supplied a partial answer to his own questions and warned:

---

[296] Popov, *op. cit.,* p. 11.
[297] "The U.S.S.R. and the Developing Countries," *op. cit.,* p. 17.
[298] Nikita Khrushchev, "Speech in Sofia," *Pravda,* May 20, 1962, pp. 1–3. See *CDSP,* Vol. XIV, No. 20 (June 13, 1962), p. 7.
[299] *Ibid.,* p. 7.

And those leaders who really have the best interests of the people, the working masses, at heart will sooner or later have to realize that only by leaning on the working class as the most consistent, most revolutionary class of society, in alliance with the peasantry and with the support of all progressive forces, can they bring about victory and the correct solution of fundamental social problems. They will either grasp this fact or they will be followed by others with a better understanding of life's demands.[300]

G. F. Kim echoed Khrushchev's position and declared: "The Communist and workers' parties in the countries of Asia and Africa persistently educate the working class and peasantry in the spirit of understanding the indisputable truth that the victories of socialism can only be achieved by means of class struggle."[301]

Why do the African socialist leaders deny the existence of a class struggle in their countries when divisions in society are obviously present, even if they are not in strict accordance with what Marxists consider to be classes? Two eminent noncommunist observers have provided answers to this question. Kenneth Grundy claimed that African leaders use the idea of classlessness to justify one-party rule and as a cover for their own positions of power. They set themselves up as the highest class and suppress their enemies while maintaining that there are not any classes. "In short, the denial of the presence of antagonistic social classes is a device utilised by ruling elites to bolster their regimes."[302]

Another analyst of this issue was David Morison. In his report to the conference at Uppsala, Sweden in November, 1963, he asserted:

---

[300] *Ibid.*, p. 7.

[301] G. F. Kim, "Soiuz rabochego klassa i krest'ianstva v natsional'noosvoboditel'nykh revoliutsiakh," *Narody Azii i Afrika,* No. 5, 1962, p. 10.

[302] Kenneth Grundy, "The 'Class Struggle' in Africa: An Examination of Conflicting Theories," *Journal of Modern African Studies,* Vol. II, No. 3 (November, 1964), p. 392.

The ideologies of present nationalist regimes in Africa deny the existence of classes and exclude the idea of class struggle. This is a convenient and natural standpoint for African elites who do not wish themselves to be identified as a class by opponents who might speak in the name of another class. But, however commendable is the idea of a classless society, in practice it is difficult to maintain. The ruling elite has a tendency to acquire the attributes of a class.[303]

Grundy and Morison have raised good points but another facet which must not be overlooked is the sincere desire of many African leaders to unify their nations. They try to minimize tribal and social divisions and promote unity in the task of nation building. They therefore emphasize that the people are a collective and that class divisions do not exist.

Soviet writers failed to use arguments similar to those set forth by Grundy and Morison, probably for fear of antagonizing the African leaders whose friendship was sought by the Soviet Union. Following the Marxist line, Soviet analysts believed that the leaders of any country represent the dominant class, and do not themselves constitute a class. Of course, Milovan Djilas claimed that the contrary was true in the Soviet Union.[304]

Ivan Potekhin maintained that African socialists overemphasize the socialist aspects of Africa's distant past and fail to take into account the class development which occurred during the past few centuries.[305] Potekhin admitted that African society was socialist long before the arrival of the colonialists but he differed with the views of most African socialists since he believed that class structure was evolving by the time

---

[303] David Morison, "Soviet Policy Towards Africa," in Sven Hamrell and Carl Gosta Widstrand, eds., The Soviet Bloc, China and Africa (Uppsala, Scandinavian Institute of African Studies, 1964), pp. 41–42.
[304] See Milovan Djilas, The New Class (New York, Praeger, 1957).
[305] Potekhin, "On 'African Socialism'," op. cit., p. 77.

the colonialists came to Africa. He also admitted that land in tropical Africa was not privately owned for many centuries but he pointed out that there have already been private land-holdings and property inequality for hundreds of years.

As far as Potekhin and other Soviet African specialists were concerned, the process of class formation in most African countries is not yet completed and class differentiation is not clear-cut.[306] There is not a class of feudal lords which opposes the working class and most areas do not have a class of large landowners.[307] The fluidity of the class relationships in the new nations of Asia and Africa was esoterically described by Iu. Ostrovitianov: "The social development of many young national states has little resemblance to the sharply sculptured forms of class struggle and is more like a graphic representation of the Brownian movement of particles in suspension, where the apparently chaotic nature of the phenomenon conceals its inner natural cause."[308] Avakov and Mirskii con-

> In contrast to the highly developed capitalist countries, the process of class formation is still not completed. The class structure of society is characterized by an unusually motley and mosaic-like pattern, by the presence of numerous classes and social groups. . . . Extreme heterogeneity, many social strata, and fluidity of class composition—these features are inherent in the classes in the underdeveloped countries.[309]

Ivan Potekhin cautioned that although the process of class formation has not been completed in Africa, one must not fall prey to the illusion that there is not a class struggle in Africa.[310] He went on to state:

---

[306] See Potekhin, "Nekotorye problemy Afrikanistiki v svete reshenii XXII s ' ' ezda KPSS," op. cit., pp. 9 and 12.
[307] Potekhin, "On 'African Socialism'," op. cit., p. 74.
[308] "The U.S.S.R. and the Developing Countries," op. cit., p. 2.
curred and offered a similar explanation:
[309] Avakov and Mirskii, op. cit., p. 279.
[310] Potekhin, "Nekotorye problemy Afrikanistiki v svete reshenii XXII s' 'ezda KPSS," op. cit., p. 10.

Exploiting elements and the section of the national intelligentsia which expresses their interests sedulously support these illusions, using them to cover up their selfish class interests. Finding themselves in authority as a result of the victory of the national revolution, they use this authority in the interests of personal enrichment and at the same time delay any social reforms designed to improve the life of the toiling masses of the people. When the latter come forward with their demands, the exploiting elements in power accuse them of treachery to the national interests.[311]

Potekhin then explained that the nationalism of an oppressed nation has two sides: one is the democratic content of this nationalism and the other is the ideology and interests of the exploiting leadership group which may be expressed in this nationalism. He also claimed, in regard to the absence of clear-cut class boundaries, that many Africans are half-peasant and half-proletarian. However, despite the variety of class relationships, Potekhin maintained that a petty bourgeois economy, with a corresponding petty bourgeois ideology, is dominant.[312]

Another aspect of the African class struggle which Potekhin recognized was the emergence of a new stratum of the native bourgeoisie.[313] He claimed that a group of high-salaried civil servants constitute a bureaucratic bourgeoisie and, in his view, this certainly was evidence that African society is not classless. Potekhin also discussed Ghanaian society in terms of classes. He asserted that there is a mixture of capitalist, feudal, feudal-patriarchal, and family-patriarchal elements and that in agriculture, capitalist and feudal relations are interwoven.[314] He stated: "The task of liquidating the remnants of feudalism

---

[311] *Ibid.*, p. 10.
[312] *Ibid.*, p. 12.
[313] See Potekhin, "On 'African Socialism,'" *op. cit.*, p. 78 and Potekhin, *Africa: Ways of Development, op. cit.*, p. 64.
[314] See Ivan Potekhin, "Ethnographic Observations in Ghana," *West Africa*, November 8, 1958, p. 1061 and Ivan Potekhin, "Etnograficheskie nabliudeniia v Gane," *Sovetskaia Etnografiia*, No. 3, 1958, p. 145.

is made difficult by the fact that the tribal chiefs are basically feudal princes. They are theocratic rulers who rely on the ancient religious beliefs of the people, on the still considerable survivals of the primitive-communal structure."[315] Potekhin stressed the weak position of the Ghanaian bourgeoisie and claimed that under colonial rule, large foreign monopolies controlled the economy and European and American goods were imported. This prevented the development of national capital.[316] Iu. Tomilin pointed out the concomitant idea that since the enterprises in Africa are usually owned by foreigners, the class struggle coincides with the anti-colonial struggle.[317]

In his book *Prezidentskie respubliki v Afrike*, published in 1963, V. P. Verin presented a class analysis of African societies and particularly castigated the leaders of the countries in the Afro-Malgash Union (U.A.M.) for their views that Africa is classless.[318] Verin made the unusual claim that the working class in tropical Africa was formed even before there was an African bourgeoisie. This certainly appears to be a non-Marxist assertion since, according to the Marxist dialectic, the bourgeoisie emerges as a class during the feudal period while the proletariat does not develop until the capitalist stage. However, Verin was not in conflict with Marxist thought since he emphasized the impact of colonialism on the class structure. He pointed out that the capitalists in tropical Africa were foreigners rather than Africans and that the African workers toiled in mines, on construction jobs, and on plantations which were under foreign control. Verin's singling out of the conservative leaders of the Afro-Malgash Union for their adherence to the idea that Africa is classless was in accordance with the views of other Soviet African specialists, who consistently considered these leaders to be the least progressive in Africa.

---

[315] Potekhin, "Etnograficheskie nabliudeniia v Gane," *Ibid.*, p. 146.
[316] Potekhin, "Etnographic Observations in Ghana," *op. cit.*, p. 1061.
[317] Tomilin, "East Africa Chooses the Way," *op. cit.*, p. 41.
[318] Verin, *op. cit.*, p. 106.

Soviet writers visually took the position that the dominant class in any society determines the character of that society. Avakov and Mirskii avowed: "In the final analysis, the choice of a path depends on which class becomes the leading force of society and then succeeds in attracting the masses; and what is the alignment of the class and political forces inside a country."[319] Although this is the official Marxist position, Soviet writers seemed to disregard it when confronted with actual situations which they had to analyze. This was because the Soviet political experts hoped for the spread of socialist ideas in Africa despite the weakness of the African proletariat. They even believed that the non-capitalist path could be initiated before the proletariat rises to a position of dominance.

Speaking in 1964 at the Moscow conference on underdeveloped areas, Georgii Mirskii modified the statement he had made two years earlier in conjunction with Avakov. Instead of maintaining the view that a state expresses the will of the dominant class, he asserted that "a state can express the combined point of view of several classes."[320] He went on to say that in most of the Asian and African states, the policies of the governments are largely determined by the "semi-bourgeoisie" or "quasi-bourgeoisie," which supports the idea that the state should play a leading role in the national economy.

In their 1962 analysis of the underdeveloped countries of Asia and Africa, Avakov and Mirskii divided these countries into six groups, determined by their class relationships and the nature of the class holding the reins of state power.[330] This was just one of many such categorizations provided by Soviet authors but it illustrates the point that Soviet writers thought of the African countries in terms of their class structure. Avakov and Mirskii included Nigeria with those countries in which capitalism is partly developed and in which

---

[319] Avakov and Mirskii, *op. cit.*, p. 277.
[320] "The U.S.S.R. and the Developing Countries," *op. cit.*, p. 14.
Note: Footnote numbers 321–329 have been eliminated.
[330] Avakov and Mirskii, *op. cit.*, pp. 293–295.

either the national bourgeoisie alone, or in conjunction with the feudal class, is in power. Guinea, Ghana, and Mali came under a different heading. They were described as having an evolving proletariat, practically no national bourgeoisie, and only rudimentary capitalist relations. The authors asserted: "The correlation of class and political forces in these countries has so evolved that an ever-increasing weight is being acquired by forces favoring the non-capitalist path of development."[331] The countries of French Africa, with the exceptions of Guinea and Mali, were placed with those states which the authors portrayed as being influenced by imperialism and in which the governments are patterned on those of imperialist nations. The proletariat in these countries was declared to be weak. Ethiopia fit into the category of countries with a developed feudal class, a small proletariat, little capitalist development, and almost no bourgeoisie. No sub-Saharan African states were included in the category of countries in which capitalism is well developed and the national bourgeoisie is in power, or in that in which the pro-imperialist bourgeoisie is in power, or forms a coalition with the feudal landowners.

Despite all of their articles and books concerning the class struggle in Africa, Soviet authors were careful not to criticize the ostensibly progressive leaders in Africa who are not proletarians, such as Nkrumah and Keita. Therefore, when it fit their purposes, they stressed the theme of anti-imperialism, rather than that of class struggle.

THE AFRICAN PROLETARIAT

Of course, Soviet analysts of the African scene emphasized the significant role which the proletariat must play during the transition to socialism. Potekhin explained that, in his view, the growth of proletarian class consciousness is of primary

---

[331] *Ibid.*, p. 294.

importance since the proletariat is "the only class whose interests are not connected with the preservation of private ownership of the means of production."[332] He also believed that the proletariat will grow more quickly than the national bourgeoisie because of limitations upon the capability of Africans to accumulate capital. Most enterprises are owned by foreigners or are under state control. The proletariat was seen as multiplying everywhere while the national bourgeoisie was considered to be very weakly developed.[333] A. M. Sivolobov strangely asserted that the African bourgeoisie is strongest in West Africa, especially in the ports along the Guinea Coast, and that the proletariat appeared rather early in these regions.[334] He didn't mention specific ports and therefore left his statement open to the implication that Accra may have a highly developed bourgeois class. This certainly was not Sivolobov's intention but it is curious that he did not let this glaring exception stand in the way of the framework he had drawn up, probably having ports such as Lagos and Abidjan in mind. Soviet writers of the late Khrushchevian era constantly claimed that the national bourgeoisie is quite impotent in Ghana.[335]

It is apparent that Soviet writers stressed the growing strength of the proletariat and the weakness of the national bourgeoisie so as to lend substance to their claims that Africa is ripe for the non-capitalist path of development. The existence of a well-developed national bourgeoisie would mean, in Soviet eyes, that capitalism is too great a factor to be bypassed.

Aspects of the evolving workers' movement in Africa which were cited by Soviet political specialists included an increase in the class consciousness of the workers, acceleration of strike activity, strengthening of trade unionism, improvement in the

---

[332] Potekhin, *Afrika smotrit v budushchee, op. cit.,* pp. 18–19.
[333] See Potekhin, "On 'African Socialism,'" *op. cit.,* p. 75 and Avakov and Mirskii, *op. cit.,* p. 285.
[334] Sivolobov, *op. cit.,* p. 10.
[335] See above, p. 105.

organization of proletarian forces, and the formation of new communist and workers' parties.[336] Growing influence in the independence movements on the part of the working class was also recognized and it was claimed that the workers played a large role in gaining independence for Ghana and Guinea.[337] Besides these positive facets of the workers' movement in Africa, it was also asserted that the standard of living of the African workers was the lowest in the world. Most African countries do not have a guaranteed minimum wage and usually pay is predicated upon the minimum necessities of the worker and does not take into account the fact that he generally has a family to support.[338]

D. I. Turchaninov maintained that as of 1962, there were twelve million African workers and that between two and three million of them were members of trade unions.[339] Since he also claimed that the population of Africa was 230 million people, the size of the working class was therefore quite small. The 1963 edition of *Fundamentals of Marxism-Leninism* concurred with Turchaninov on the statistic that there were twelve million African workers but set the number of trade union members at three million.[340]

One of the Soviet contentions was that the African working class is much more influential than its numbers would indicate. This is due to the fact that the African workers are concentrated around extremely large industrial enterprises and the transport industry and this leads to greater consciousness and organizational ability than if these workers

---

[336] See Sivolobov, *op. cit.*, p. 66 and V. Kiselev, "Rabochii klass i natsional'no-osvoboditel'nye revoliutsii," *Mirovaia Ekonomika i Mezhdunarodnye Otnosheniia*, No. 10 (October, 1963), p. 98.

[337] See Usov, *op. cit.*, p. 128.

[338] See Iu. Popov, "Rabochii klass Afriki," *Aziia i Afrika Segodnia*, No. 5 (May, 1963), p. 3 and Iu. Popov, "O nekotorykh chertakh rabochego dvizheniia v Afrike (Iuzhnee Sakhary)," *Narody Azii i Afriki*, No. 5, 1961, p. 47.

[339] D. I. Turchaninov, *Vseafrikanskaia Federatsiia Profsoiuzov* (Moscow, Izdatel'stvo VTsPS Profizdat, 1962), p. 5.

[340] *Fundamentals of Marxism-Leninism*, 1963 edition, *op. cit.*, p. 411.

were migrants who periodically returned to their villages.[341] However, Soviet writers did recognize the existence of a large migratory labor force.

Soviet spokesmen also stressed the point that the main enemy of the African working class is foreign imperialism, not the African national bourgeoisie. They explained that the entrepreneurial class in Africa is very weak and unable to accumulate capital and therefore owns very few enterprises. On the other hand, many large firms are in the hands of foreigners and it is in these firms that most of the African toilers work. These workers are exploited by their foreign employers, not by members of the national bourgeoisie. However, as G. Usov pointed out, some countries have local "feudal-bourgeois" elements which cooperate with the former colonialists subsequent to the achievement of independence and these elements are opposed by the workers.[342] Usov averred that the governments of Senegal and Nigeria were composed of people from this "feudal-bourgeois" group.

By emphasizing that the African workers see imperialism as their chief adversary, Soviet political analysts were really expressing their support for a four-class, rather than a three-class alliance. In communist parlance, a three-class alliance in an underdeveloped country features cooperation between the proletariat, peasantry, and petty bourgeoisie against the national bourgeoisie, which is portrayed as the prime enemy. A four-class alliance includes a bloc of the proletariat, peasantry, petty bourgeoisie, and national bourgeoisie opposed to imperialism. The difference between the two types of alliances lies basically in the fact that a three-class alliance fights domestic capitalism while a four-class alliance fights international imperialism. By advocating a four-class alliance, Soviet analysts were calling for cooperation between the proletariat and the national bourgeoisie.

Most African countries do not have communist or workers'

---

[341] See A. Zusmanovich, "Proletariat Afriki boretsia protiv imperializma," *Sovremennyi Vostok,* No. 5 (May, 1958), p. 30.
[342] Usov, *op. cit.,* p. 129.

parties. Soviet spokesmen explained this fact by pointing out that the African proletariat is still young and has not yet acquired an adequate degree of class consciousness. It also lacks organizational experience, a situation which has arisen partly as a result of the large number of migratory laborers.[343] Therefore, in the absence of communist and workers' parties, trade unions play an important role as organizations of the working class. *Fundamentals of Marxism-Leninism* asserted: "In Africa, where there are no working-class parties in most of the countries, an important part is played by the trade unions, which often assume the functions of political organizations."[344] Nikolai Gavrilov, writing in the February 7, 1962 issue of *New Times,* concurred and considered trade unions to be organs of the proletariat.[345] So did A. Sobolev, who claimed that trade unions can serve as a revolutionary vanguard.[346] However, D. I. Turchaninov, also writing in 1962, warned that the importance of trade unions as organs of the proletariat is limited. He declared that in those African countries which do not have revolutionary workers' parties, there is a dangerous tendency to bestow the tasks of these parties upon the trade unions. Such actions overestimate the role of the trade unions as broad mass organizations.[347] The Soviet view of this subject was therefore marked by caution: trade unions could serve progressive roles but they were not a complete substitute for workers' parties.

---

[343] See Potekhin, *Afrika, 1956–1961, op. cit.,* p. 137.
[344] *Fundamentals of Marxism-Leninism,* 1963 edition, *op. cit.,* p. 411.
[345] N. Gavrilov, "Splitters at Work in Africa," *New Times,* No. 6 (February 7, 1962), p. 18.
[346] A. Sobolev, *op. cit.,* p. 46.
[347] Turchaninov, *op. cit.,* p. 48. For a similar post-Khrushchevian view expressed by Africans, see Ibrahim Zakharia and Cuthbert Magigwana, "The Trade Unions and the Political Scene in Africa," *World Marxist Review,* Vol. VII, No. 12 (December, 1964), pp. 19–24. For an excellent analysis of the role of trade unions in Africa, see the June, 1965 issue of *Africa Report* entitled "Paradoxes of African Trade Unionism: Organizational Chaos and Political Potential."

Nikolai Gavrilov claimed in 1962 that there were 13–15 million wage and salary earners in Africa but that nearly 70% of them were farm workers, domestic servants, and free lancers. He averred that the industrial workers had the highest class consciousness but that they formed only the minority of the working force. He also noted that many of these industrial workers were employed only seasonally and returned home for the farming season.[348] Other Soviet writers produced much statistical information on the size of the working class in various African countries.[349] Their figures were generally similar but it is extremely difficult to make exact comparisons since they often used different bases for their analyses. Some dealt with the numerical size of the working class, some with the numerical size of the industrial workers only, while others used percentage figures. Even this latter method led to confusion since some percentage figures were relative to the whole population, some to the African population only (excluding white settlers), and some to just the male population. However, some important observations can be drawn. Those countries with the largest working classes were shown to be the Republic of South Africa, Angola, Northern Rhodesia (now known as Zambia), Southern Rhodesia (now known as Rhodesia), Nigeria, Tanganyika (now part of Tanzania), and Kenya. Guinea, Ghana, and Mali, usually cited by Soviet authors as the most progressive states in Africa, were conspicuously absent from most of the charts dealing with the size of the African working class and this points out a great inconsistency in the Soviet analysis of African affairs. When discussing the spread of socialism on the African continent, So-

---

[348] Gavrilov, "Splitters at Work in Africa," *op. cit.*, p. 17.
[349] See D. Vol'skii, "Profsoiuzy Afriki," *Sovremennyi Vostok*, No. 1 (January, 1959), p. 23; M. I. Braginskii, "O polozhenii rabochego klassa i profsoiuznom dvizhenii v kolonial'nykh stranakh Afriki," *Problemy Vostokovedeniia*, No. 5, 1959, p. 104; Popov, "O nekotorykh chertakh rabochego dvizheniia v Afrike (Iuzhnee Sakhary)," *op. cit.*, p. 47; Sivolobov, *op. cit.*, p. 4; and Usov, "Rabochii klass Afriki v bor'be protiv imperializma," *op. cit.*, p. 127.

viet observers stressed the historic role of the working class and considered the growth of this class to be one of the determining aspects of socialist development. However, they concomitantly claimed that Ghana, Guinea, and Mali, countries in which the working class is not particularly large, are the most progressive African states. The ideological tenet that socialism develops as the working class increases in strength was therefore sidestepped and it was recognized that socialism can begin to develop in countries which do not contain large working classes.

On the other side of the ledger, it should be pointed out that since Ghana, Guinea, and Mali are not especially populous, their working classes appear to be stronger when percentage figures are used, rather than when the numerical strength of their working classes is cited. According to G. Usov, the Ghanaian working class, as of 1960, comprised 8% of Ghana's population while the Guinean working class, as of 1959, made up 10% of Guinea's population. He failed to include statistics for Mali in his analysis.[350] When these percentage figures are used, Ghana and Guinea appear to have working classes which constitute fairly considerable sections of their populations but they still do not approach the figures of 20% for the Republic of South Africa and 19% for Angola. Actually, Iurii Popov claimed that Ghana's working class constituted 20% of Ghana's population, as of 1961, but all of his figures appear to be highly exaggerated when compared with other sources so that this statistic for Ghana can probably be dismissed as wishful thinking, rather than fact.[351]

The migratory labor force was usually viewed as an obstacle to the development of an organized working class. Nikolai Gavrilov pointed out that most migratory workers are not members of trade unions and went on to assert: "Without a doubt, the migrant workers are the most backward and least conscious part of the working class. In essence, they are half-

350 Usov, *Ibid.*, p. 127.
351 Popov, "O nekotorykh chertakh rabochego dvizheniia v Afrike (Iuzhnee Sakhary)," *op. cit.*, p. 47.

workers and half-peasants. Their consciousness is weighed down by patriarchal-feudal survivals."[352] M. I. Braginskii claimed that migration retards both the development of class consciousness and the formation of skilled cadres of workers.[353] Another Soviet writer praised Mali for trying to prevent the migration of the working force.[354]

Gavrilov averred that migratory labor becomes widespread only when capitalism is developing.[355] However, he foresaw a solution to the migratory problem and pointed to the example of the socialist countries: "The experience of the Soviet Union and of the people's democracies in Europe and Asia conclusively shows that the migration of the working force ends at the same time that a country begins to develop harmoniously its agriculture and industry."[356]

Despite their obvious hostility to migratory labor in Africa, Soviet analysts did not consider it in a completely negative way. Iu. Tomilin wrote in 1961:

The migration of man power and seasonal work are a serious drag on the consolidation of East Africa's working people into an organized working class. But migration has also a positive effect, for in travelling from place to place workers of various trades come into contact with each other, they learn more about the situation in other territories and exchange experience in fighting the exploiters. Finally, the migrating seasonal worker, closely bound up with life on the farm, brings to the peasants the revolutionary ideas of the towns.[357]

On this issue, as on many others, the Soviet position was marked by a certain ambivalence and by a chameleonic ability to blend in with changing circumstances.

---

[352] N. Gavrilov, "O migratsii rabochei sily v Zapadnoi Afrike," *Problemy Vostokovedeniia*, No. 3, 1959, p. 89.
[353] Braginskii, *op. cit.*, p. 107.
[354] Letnev, *op. cit.*, p. 85.
[355] Gavrilov, "O migratsii rabochei sily v Zapadnoi Afrike," *op. cit.*, p. 84.
[356] *Ibid.*, p. 90.
[357] Tomilin, "East Africa Will Be Free," *op. cit.*, p. 47.

The decisive role played by the working class in shaping the future of the African nations was a constant theme of the Soviet political specialists. Typical was this statement by Savel'ev and Sanovich: "The successes of the working class in the struggle for their economic and social rights, the firm union of the proletariat and peasantry are able to become the determining factor in the choice of the path on which the economically underdeveloped countries will proceed—the capitalist or non-capitalist."[358] However, despite the abundance of such pronouncements, Soviet writings of the Khrushchevian era always failed to advocate the creation of dictatorships of the proletariat in the African countries. The working class was singled out as being the most consistent fighter for socialism but an alliance between the workers and peasants was particularly stressed in Soviet articles and books. Soviet analysts recognized the importance of the African peasantry, who constitute the largest social grouping, and constantly used terms such as "the people" and "the masses." For the near future, they favored the creation of a national democratic state in which classes other than the working class would also play significant roles.[359] The period of proletarian dominance was relegated to the distant future and was not discussed in detail. A rather realistic interpretation of African affairs was therefore presented as the weakness of the African working class was taken into account and the African peasantry was recognized as a potent revolutionary force.

THE AFRICAN PEASANTRY

In the Soviet view, feudalism is not the most significant factor related to African agriculture. This was made clear at

---

[358] Iu. Savel'ev and I. Sanovich, "Polozhenie i bor'ba rabochego klassa Azii i Afriki," *Aziia i Afrika Segodnia,* No. 5 (May, 1962), p. 13.
[359] For a discussion of the national democratic state, see below, pp. 208–215.

a conference of communist experts on the underdeveloped countries, held in Prague in September, 1961 under the auspices of the *World Marxist Review*. These experts asserted that the struggle against feudalism in African agriculture is not the chief one. The main struggle must be directed against foreign monopolies and white settlers.[360] Ivan Potekhin wrote in his authoritative *Afrika smotrit v budushchee* that in most parts of Africa, there is not a feudal class which exploits the peasantry. He cited some regions of Nigeria and Uganda as exceptions.[361] He also averred that the land usually belongs to peasant communes, rather than to individual feudal landlords. However, Potekhin asserted that the tribal aristocracy often adopts feudal and semi-feudal methods of exploitation and uses the communal lands for its own benefit. Potekhin claimed that this is not real feudalism but is patriarchal feudalism.

Avakov and Mirskii agreed with Potekhin that feudalism is not prevalent in Africa. Following is their analysis of the agricultural situation in Africa:

> In most of the African countries, the peasantry lives under patriarchal-communal conditions, knowing neither feudal nor capitalist forms of land ownership. In the African countries, in contrast to many other underdeveloped countries, feudalists and rural bourgeoisie are, with rare exceptions, absent as classes. In the African countryside, the collectivist spirit is strong and private-property impulses are alien to an overwhelming part of the peasantry.[362]

On the other hand, some Soviet writers have pointed out the existence of feudalism and capitalism in certain parts of Africa. For example, V. Ia. Katsman described what he believed to be feudal and capitalist exploitation in Tanganyikan agriculture. He charged that the cooperatives in Tanganyika

---

[360] Iu. Bochkarev, "New Paths for New States," *New Times*, No. 41, (October 11, 1961), p. 14.
[361] Potekhin, *Afrika smotrit v budushchee, op. cit.*, p. 18.
[362] Avakov and Mirskii, *op. cit.*, pp. 284–285.

have a capitalist nature and do not practice the traditional system of tribal mutual aid.[363] Potekhin claimed that in many parts of Africa, the relationships between European landowners and African peasants "are very close to feudal relationships or even identical with them."[364] Potekhin also averred that tribal chiefs are feudal or semi-feudal rulers and are supported by the colonialists and he added: "Tribal separation, fanned by the colonialists and their subservient tribal chiefs, is the chief obstacle to a united national front in the colonies."[365] Iu. Tomilin concurred and asserted that most chiefs, who are puppets of the colonialists, are losing prestige among the people. However, he pointed out that some chiefs and tribal elders have joined the national-liberation movement and the prestige of these people is therefore buoyed.[366]

Another contributor to this discussion was A. M. Sivolobov. Greatly exaggerating the extent of class differentiation, he saw tribalism as a cover for both feudal and capitalist relations. He explained that the tribal leaders receive produce from other members of the tribe and this is really a form of feudal exploitation. In regard to capitalism among the African peasantry, Sivolobov wrote:

> The traditional concept of mutual aid rendered one another by members of the tribe in working their fields often serves as a cloak for capitalist exploitation also. A division into classes occurs within the tribes. Many peasants are ruined, forsake their lands, and go to seek work in the towns. Emigration, a characteristic feature of capitalism, has received wide development in modern Africa also.[367]

---

363 V. Ia. Katsman, "Rost imushchestvennoi differentsiatsii sredi Afrikanskogo krest'ianstva Tangan'iki posle Vtoroi Mirovoi Voiny," *Sovetskaia Etnografiia*, No. 1, 1961, pp. 83–93.
364 Potekhin, "Land Relationships in the Countries of Africa," *op. cit.*, p. 234.
365 Potekhin. "Africa Shakes Off Colonial Slavery," *op. cit.*, p. 88.
366 Iu. Tomilin, "East Africa Will Be Free," *International Affairs*, No. 5 (May, 1961), p. 47.
367 A. M. Sivolobov, *The National-Liberation Movement in Africa* (Moscow, Znanie Publishing House, 1961), See JPRS 10683, p. 7.

Thus feudal and capitalist elements were seen to be present in African agriculture but Soviet scholars believed that opposition to these "evil" influences should be subordinated to the struggle against foreign monopolies, a struggle in which the cooperation of all sectors of the African population is necessary.

The question of class differentiation among the African peasantry is highly complex. Soviet writers often shifted ground on this issue, depending upon the point which they wished to stress. In order to show the growth of revolutionary activity, they emphasized the antagonisms between classes but when they sought to portray the popularity and stability of the supposedly progressive regimes, such as those in Ghana, Guinea, and Mali, they minimized class contradictions. Thus, Nikolai Gavrilov was able to write in 1961 that class differentiation among the Malian peasantry had basically not yet begun.[368]

Ivan Potekhin, speaking in February, 1957 before a conference of the Institute of Ethnography of the Academy of Sciences of the U.S.S.R., declared: "We continue to talk about the African peasantry in general, although such a 'peasantry in general' has ceased to exist. The process of the decomposition of the peasantry is proceeding very rapidly. The African village is being torn by class contradictions."[369] Therefore, a statement made by Potekhin five years later seems quite contradictory: "Class differentiation of the peasantry in the great majority of African countries is still scarcely noticeable. The agricultural workers who have broken their connection with the land—the proletarians—are not numerous."[370] However, Potekhin again contradicted himself within this very same

---

[368] Gavrilov, "Respublika Mali—molodoe nezavisimoe gosudarstvo Afriki," op. cit., p. 33.

[369] See R. N. Ismagilova and L. D. Iablochkov, "Koordinatsionnoe soveshchanie sovetskikh Afrikanistov," Sovetskaia Etnografiia, No. 3, 1957, p. 185.

[370] Potekhin, "Land Relationships in the Countries of Africa," op. cit., p. 225.

article! He asserted: "It is scarcely possible to speak of the African peasantry as a homogeneous mass without class differentiations. Such a peasantry no longer exists in Africa."[371]

Soviet analysts perceived the existence of what they believed were capitalist relationships among the African peasantry. V. Ia. Katsman, when discussing Tanganyika, claimed that capitalist elements are rampant in the cooperative movement and that many wealthy people are establishing private property.[372] Potekhin declared that "in the African rural commune there is a stratum of planters and rich peasants who are farming on capitalist terms. It is these who control the bulk of commodity production."[373]

The Soviet attitude toward class differentiation among the African peasantry was marked by two major discrepancies. As has already been mentioned, the Soviet contentions that there are indeed class contradictions among the peasantry were at variance with their statements which sought to verify the absence of feudalism and capitalism from African agricultural relationships. Secondly, these same statements which avowed the absence of feudalism and capitalism were at odds with the general Soviet portrayal of African society as evolving through the stages of communalism, feudalism, and capitalism.[374] According to this analysis, present African society is in the process of nation-formation and social relationships are a melange of communalism, feudalism, and capitalism.

Soviet writers recognized the importance of the African peasantry. K. Ivanov asserted that the peasant is the "principle figure" in Africa and knows what it is like to be "a dispossessed proletarian."[375] V. Kiselev charged that the question of giving the land to those who work it is one of the most

---

[371] *Ibid.,* p. 242.

[372] Katsman, *op. cit.*

[373] Potekhin, "Land Relationships in the Countries of Africa," *op. cit.,* p. 242.

[374] For a discussion of this point, see above, pp. 121–123.

[375] K. Ivanov, "Present-Day Colonialism: Its Socio-Economic Aspect," part three, *International Affairs,* No. 10 (October, 1960), p. 20.

important facets of the revolutions in Asian and African countries but that the national bourgeoisie has everywhere failed to find a satisfactory solution to this problem.[376] It has not served the interests of the poor peasantry.

In the view of Potekhin, the peasants constitute the basic mass of the population in all African countries and A. M. Sivolobov described the peasantry as the "widest mass base for the national liberation movement in Africa."[377] Sivolobov claimed that the peasants suffered under both the colonialists and the feudal lords. Potekhin emphasized the significant role which the peasantry could potentially play in determining Africa's future course of development. He described the African peasantry as a "scattered, atomized mass of small commodity producers, illiterate, and extremely backward politically."[378] However, he averred that Africa's future is largely dependent upon who is able to unite the peasants and lead them, the working class or the bourgeoisie.

THE AFRICAN NATIONAL BOURGEOISIE

Soviet political writers usually pictured the African national bourgeoisie as having two facets, one being a tendency to compromise with imperialism and the other being a tendency to oppose imperialism and bring about progressive reforms.[379] The role of the national bourgeoisie at any given time was determined by an analysis of the relative attractions toward these two poles of political behavior. The national bourgeoisie was also believed to be divided into strata, Avakov and Mirskii wrote:

[376] Kiselev, *op. cit.*, p. 96.
[377] See Potekhin, "Nekotorye problemy Afrikanistiki v svete reshenii XXII s' 'ezda KPSS," *op. cit.*, p. 11 and Sivolobov, *op. cit.*, p. 6.
[378] Potekhin, *Ibid.*, p. 11.
[379] For example, see N. Savel'ev, "O roli burzhuazii v natsional'no-osvoboditel'nom dvizhenii," *Mirovaia Ekonomika i Mezhdunarodnye Otnosheniia*, No. 5 (May, 1962), pp. 97–102.

In the different countries, both the national and the pro-imperialist bourgeoisie consist of various strata. What strata are specifically included in each of these two groups of the bourgeoisie? . . . It should not be forgotten that these groups belong in one and the same exploiting class and that a process of interpenetration is proceeding between them. Therefore, the division itself is largely arbitrary.[380]

These authors then went on to identify the various strata as the industrial, trading, banking, usurer, and agricultural bourgeoisies. They explained that each stratum is divided into small, medium, and big bourgeoisie, with the banking bourgeoisie being an exception. This latter stratum contains only medium and big bankers. Avakov and Mirskii asserted that all of the strata previously mentioned are not necessarily present in each country.[381]

It should be pointed out that Avakov and Mirskii made a distinction between the national bourgeoisie and the pro-imperialist bourgeoisie. They belonged to a group of moderate writers who favorably regarded the regimes in power in most African countries and they therefore, in this instance, sought to give the term "national bourgeoisie" a rather positive flavor. By recognizing the pro-imperialist bourgeoisie as a separate entity, the authors implied that none of the national bourgeoisie are pro-imperialist. However, Mirskii often used a line of reasoning which was at odds with this distinction between the national and pro-imperialist bourgeoisies. In order to evaluate favorably many of the African political regimes, he argued that the leaders of many African countries were not members of the national bourgeoisie.[382] He frequently dis-

---

[380] Avakov and Mirskii, *op. cit.*, p. 289.

[381] *Ibid.*, p. 290.

[382] For example, see Mirskii, "Creative Marxism and Problems of the National-Liberation Movement," *op. cit.*, p. 12 and Uri Ra'anan, "Moscow and the 'Third World,'" *Problems of Communism*, Vol. XIV, No. 1 (January–February, 1965), p. 25. For an enlightening discussion of the statements made by Avakov, Mirskii, and other Soviet analysts of the African political scene, see the article by Ra'anan.

cussed groups which he labeled the "progressive intelligentsia" or "revolutionary democrats." Therefore, the term "national bourgeoisie" had a positive connotation in one context and a negative connotation in another.

Avakov and Mirskii claimed that the entire small and medium bourgeoisie are not necessarily part of the national bourgeoisie and that the entire big bourgeoisie is not necessarily pro-imperialist.[383] The Soviet view of the nature of the bourgeoisie in Africa was further confused by statements made by K. Ivanov and G. Usov. The former divided the bourgeoisie into three groups: foreign capitalists; compradores and collaborationist feudal and tribal rulers, and the national bourgeoisie.[384] Usov asserted that the petty bourgeoisie constitutes the majority of the national bourgeoisie.[385] He also averred that the right wing of the national bourgeoisie wants to take the capitalist path of development and that Jomo Kenyatta is a representative of the national bourgeoisie's left wing.

Soviet writers claimed that the African bourgeoisie is economically weak and has been unable to accumulate large amounts of capital.[386] This situation has arisen because the foreign firms dominated the economic life of the colonial areas and native capitalists were left little room for development. Ivan Potekhin asserted that the formation of the African national bourgeoisie is not complete.[387] African capitalists have not become a powerful force but Potekhin chided the African socialist leaders who deny the existence of a national bourgeoisie. He warned that this class has new opportunities for development in those African countries which have become independent.

---

[383] Avakov and Mirskii, op. cit., p. 291.

[384] Ivanov, "The National-Liberation Movement and Non-Capitalist Path of Development," part one, op. cit., p. 40.

[385] Usov, "Natsional'naia burzhuaziia i osvoboditel'noe dvizhenie v Vostochnoi Afrike," op. cit., p. 85.

[386] For example, see Ibid., p. 85.

[387] Potekhin, Afrika smotrit v budushchee, op. cit., p. 18.

K. Ivanov explained why Africans have been unable to accumulate large amounts of capital:

> The accumulation of national African capital is, therefore, very slow and takes place mainly in agriculture, the handicrafts, usury, trade and also in the small-scale and partly in the medium manufacturing industry. The Africans are barred from mining, the investment of capital in highly profitable branches of the economy, and export and import operations. All this makes the rising African bourgeoisie an opponent of the existing order of things.[388]

Ivanov's concluding remark sheds light on the fundamental Soviet view that the chief exploiter of the African worker is the foreign bourgeoisie, not the native national bourgeoisie.[389] The latter can act as a progressive force in opposing the remnants of colonialism and in joining an all-national anti-imperialist front.[390]

Many Soviet statements on the African national bourgeoisie emphasized the progressive tendencies of this class. E. M. Zhukov wrote: "The interests of imperialism and those of the national bourgeoisie are directly opposed."[391] K. Brutents asserted that, to some extent, the national bourgeoisie reflects the interests of the entire nation since it opposes both imperialism and feudalism.[392] Ivan Potekhin wrote early in 1956 that the colonial powers were attempting to use the national bourgeoisie as a middle-class force for stabilization but that, in fact, the national bourgeoisie is an anti-imperialist force.[393]

---

388 K. Ivanov, "Present-Day Colonialism: Its Socio-Economic Aspect," part two, *International Affairs*, No. 6 (June, 1960), p. 34.
389 For example, see Potekhin, *Africa: Ways of Development*, *op. cit.*, p. 52 and Potekhin, *Afrika smotrit v budushchee*, *op. cit.*, p. 20.
390 See Potekhin, *Afrika smotrit v budushchee*, *Ibid.*, p. 20.
391 E. M. Zhukov, "The Bankruptcy of the Imperialist System and International Relations," *International Affairs*, No. 3 (March, 1959), p. 67.
392 Karen Brutents, *Protiv ideologii sovremennogo kolonializma* (Moscow, Izdatel'stvo Sotsial'no-Ekonomicheskoi Literatury, 1961), p. 185.
393 Potekhin, "Politicheskoe polozhenie v stranakh Afriki," *op. cit.*

On the other side of the fence, the bad aspects of the national bourgeoisie were also pointed out. Khrushchev declared in his famous Sofia speech in 1962 that although the national bourgeoisie has not yet exhausted its progressive role, it has a dual nature and leans more toward reaction as contradictions develop between the workers and the propertied classes.[394] Avakov and Mirskii wrote: "The national bourgeoisie which holds the power or influences government policy, manifests in every case a natural striving toward economic independence. The national capitalists dream of reaching the level of the financial magnates in the developed capitalist countries and of occupying a position of equality in the family of the international financial oligarchy."[395]

In another article, Mirskii asserted: "It would be an oversimplification to assume that the national bourgeoisie will surely become the ruling class in all or the majority of African countries."[396] He cited the powerful influence of the world socialist system and the increasing prospects for the noncapitalist path of development. This was a logical outgrowth of his general thesis that many African leaders are not members of the national bourgeoisie.

OTHER AFRICAN SOCIAL GROUPS

Soviet authors often discussed the African intelligentsia as if it constituted its own class. Avakov and Mirskii called it a "category of people" who support the ideology of nationalism. The majority of the intelligentsia express the interests of the national bourgeoisie but some members may "switch to positions of protecting the interests of the workers and join the nucleus of Marxist parties."[397] The intelligentsia was therefore viewed as a potentially progressive force.

---

[394] Khrushchev, "Speech in Sofia," *op. cit.*
[395] Avakov and Mirskii, *op. cit.*, p. 299.
[396] Mirskii, "Creative Marxism and Problems of the National-Liberation Movement," *op. cit.*, p. 13.
[397] Avakov and Mirskii, *op. cit.*, pp. 291–292.

L. A. Gordon and L. A. Fridman analyzed the intelligentsia and considered this group to be extremely important in the transition of the underdeveloped countries to socialism. They even asserted that the intelligentsia can play the guiding role in this transition:

> The semi-proletarian position of the basic mass of the intelligentsia is of great significance. As the experience of a number of countries of Asia and Africa shows, these groups are under certain conditions, capable not only of participating, but even of playing the guiding role in the transition to socialist transformation. The powerful upsurge of the world revolutionary process, the hegemony of the international proletariat in the social progress of humanity on the whole guarantees in several former colonies and semi-colonies, the success of the anti-capitalist measures, even in a situation in which the proletariat and its party have not yet become the leader of the all-people's struggle.[398]

The authors' assertion that the basic mass of the intelligentsia is in a semi-proletarian position is indeed highly questionable and it would probably be more accurate to state that they bear a great resemblance to the national bourgeoisie.

Besides the great significance which they attached to the intelligentsia, Gordon and Fridman also mentioned the novel idea that the proletariat need not be the leader of the masses when measures are taken which lead toward the non-capitalist path of development. The hegemony of the proletariat in individual countries is not necessary since it was purported that the proletariat enjoys a position of hegemony on an international scale.[399]

Once the African countries become independent, native administrators replace the colonial officials and a bureaucracy begins to develop. Soviet observers looked with disfavor upon this spread of bureaucratization and praised Ghana, Guinea,

---

[398] L. A. Gordon and L. A. Fridman, "Nekotorye osobennosti sotsial'noi struktury razvivaiushchikhsia stran," *Narody Azii i Afriki,* No. 6, 1964, p. 18.
[399] For a discussion of this idea, see below, pp. 170–174.

and Mali for their efforts to brake this tendency. They feared that government and party officials would become elitist and L. Aleksandrovskaia asserted that the bureaucratic elite must inevitably become bourgeois.[400] Georgii Mirskii claimed that the bureaucrats and landowners are allied with the imperialist monopolies.[401] He also averred that in the majority of the tropical African countries, the bureaucratic elite is in power.

Soviet African specialists stressed the point that Africa is capable of taking the non-capitalist path of development. Some countries, such as Ghana, Guinea, Mali, Algeria, and the United Arab Republic, were shown to have particularly good prospects for taking this path and Soviet theorists were therefore faced with a doctrinal problem. According to communist theory, the national bourgeoisie builds capitalism. From this it follows that Soviet writers could not possibly label certain African governments as "national bourgeois" while at the same time claiming that these governments in question are capable of leading their countries along a non-capitalist path. However, to what class do the leaders of these countries belong if not to the national bourgeoisie? Soviet theorists solved this problem by creating new categories to fit the leftist and purportedly progressive African leaders. One of these, which referred only to sub-Saharan political figures, was that of "Negro democrats." K. Ivanov used this term in October, 1960 and stated that "Negro democrats" are neither bourgeois nor feudal. They understand colonial exploitation and some of them have even belonged to Marxist study groups. Ivanov opposed calling these people "nationalists" or "compradores" since this would be a dogmatic approach. He averred that "Negro democrats" are intellectual African liberation leaders who do not have working-class views.[402]

---

[400] "The U.S.S.R. and the Developing Countries," *op. cit.* p. 20.
[401] Mirskii, "Creative Marxism and Problems of the National-Liberation Movement," *op. cit.,* p. 12.
[402] Ivanov, "Present-Day Colonialism: Its Socio-Economic Aspect," part three, *op. cit.,* p. 20.

Another recently created category is that of "revolutionary democrats." V. Tiagunenko wrote that this group includes the petty bourgeois intelligentsia, students, and the revolutionary officers' corps.[403] As has already been mentioned, Mirskii used this term in an article which appeared in the March–April, 1963 issue of *Mirovaia Ekonomika i Mezhdunarodnye Otnosheniia.*[404] He was soon roundly criticized by L. Stepanov and R. Avakov, the latter being Mirskii's former collaborator.[405] They accused him of over-simplification when analyzing the nationalistic and anti-democratic factors present in the United Arab Republic. Their general line of attack was that Mirskii was too favorably oriented toward many African regimes and that he failed to recognize some negative aspects which are associated with "revolutionary democracy."

Stepanov and Avakov wrote that although the national bourgeoisie has two facets, the situation is even more complicated in those African countries in which the local bourgeoisie has not taken shape as a class and in which the proletariat has not yet formed. In these countries, power is held by small, urban and rural producer-proprietors and included in the power structure are the broad masses of the peasantry, the intelligentsia, army circles, and bureaucrats. The authors stated that these intermediate social groups have the most diverse ideological and political tendencies and constitute a "revolutionary democracy" only in some situations. "Revolutionary democrats" can play a progressive role in many liberated countries and Stepanov and Avakov actually maintained that the Russian Trudoviks were an example of "revolutionary democrats!"

---

[403] V. Tiagunenko, "Na glavnuiu revoliutsionnuiu magistral," *Krasnaia Zvezda,* November 11, 1964, p. 3.
[404] See above, p. 149.
[405] For the attack by Avakov and Stepanov, see Avakov and Stepanov, *op. cit.,* pp. 51–53. For the highly authoritative article on which Avakov and Mirskii collaborated, see Avakov and Mirskii, *op. cit.* For a discussion of all these writers, see the article by Ra'anan, *op. cit.*

In their assault on the ideas of Mirskii, the authors maintained: "Viewing the place of revolutionary democracy in the contemporary national-liberation movement, one must never forget about its petty-bourgeois nature, its being weighted down by bourgeois illusions and political inconsistency."[406] However, they did not fail to recognize the positive side of "revolutionary democracy" and claimed that it brings the masses into political activity. Thus the concept of "revolutionary democracy" filled a theoretical void for the Soviet ideologists and although the term was usually used to describe regimes looked upon favorably by the Soviet Union, negative facets of "revolutionary democracy" were also identified. The insistence of Stepanov and Avakov that "revolutionary democracy" is not completely rosy, as Mirskii seems to have believed, was probably intended as a safety valve device. In case leaders identified as "revolutionary democrats" would swerve from the path Moscow considers progressive, the Soviet political analysts would have a theoretical base from which to explain this action.

It appears to have been no accident that the terms "Negro democrat" and "revolutionary democrat" were introduced at the same time that Soviet writers were emphasizing the ability of African countries to bypass the capitalist stage of development. They served as necessary ideological complements to this new concept of African historical development.

When Soviet scholars looked at the class struggle in Africa, they sought to determine the proclivity of each class to socialism. Ivan Potekhin carefully analyzed this question and concluded: "The working class, the peasantry, the intelligentsia and the large town petty bourgeoisie (artisans, small traders, etc.), almost the entire population, have no reason to be in favour of the capitalist way of development. Socialism is the only way to happiness for them."[407] He then identified the elements which oppose socialism: feudal, semi-feudal, and

---

[406] Avakov and Stepanov, *op. cit.,* p. 53.
[407] Potekhin, "On 'African Socialism'," *op. cit.,* p. 75.

those members of the national bourgeoisie who are associated with foreign enterprises. All of these groups are unpatriotic.

Potekhin favorably evaluated the role of the African intelligentsia. He claimed that although the preponderant majority of the workers and peasants do not understand the ideas of socialism, the patriotic intelligentsia helps them acquire an understanding of these socialist concepts. He therefore seemed to place the intelligentsia in the position of being the vanguard which can raise the masses to a higher level of political consciousness. According to Lenin's *What is to Be Done?*, this role should be played by a revolutionary workers' party. Potekhin declared: "There exists in Africa an intelligentsia which has mastered the scientific principles of socialism and is ready to devote all its strength and knowledge for the good of its people."[408] As Herbert Dinerstein has correctly pointed out, the members of the African intelligentsia do not own much land and would not be hurt by socialism.[409]

ROLES OF THE CLASSES IN THE NATIONAL-LIBERATION MOVEMENT

According to Soviet writers, the national-liberation movements in the African countries are aimed at gaining independence from the imperialists and also at ending the exploitation practiced by local feudalists.[410] Many segments of the population join the struggle, including the national bourgeoisie, and the national-liberation movements therefore have an all-people character. Ivan Potekhin claimed that all social strata take part, except for some tribal leaders and members of the feudal aristocracy. He declared that each

---

[408] *Ibid.*, p. 75.
[409] Herbert Dinerstein, "Soviet Doctrines on Developing Countries: Some Divergent Views," in Kurt London, ed., *New Nations in a Divided World* (New York and London, Praeger, 1963), p. 88.
[410] See Orlova, *op. cit.*, p. 104.

social group brings its own goals, demands, and prejudices into this movement.[411]

The national-liberation movement was extremely important to Soviet authors since it was believed that independence can only be gained as a result of an upsurge of the forces of liberation. E. Dolgopolov wrote: "The colonialists have never in the whole course of history voluntarily granted independence to the colonial peoples, and they never will do so; they are compelled to grant it only when the national-liberation movement has become so strong that they are unable to deal with it."[412] Since the national-liberation movement has such vital tasks, of extreme importance is the question of who has hegemony over it.

Until the Khrushchevian era, it was maintained by Soviet scholars that the proletariat must strive to gain hegemony over the national-liberation movement and that independence could only be achieved under proletarian leadership. In their authoritative book *Narody Afriki,* published in 1954, Ol'derogge and Potekhin declared: "In African colonies, the working class is the only force capable of gathering around itself all anti-imperialist forces, of leading them in the struggle for national independence and for the radical reconstruction of the entire economic and political life."[413] However, Soviet political analysts of the Khrushchevian era recognized the fact that the national bourgeoisie could lead the national-liberation movements and gain independence for their countries. Ivan Potekhin, writing in his historical *Afrika, 1956–1961,* asserted:

In consequence of the relative backwardness of the African countries, the weakness and small size of the working classes, because of the absence of communist parties and inadequate

---

[411] Ivan Potekhin, "Kharakternye cherty raspada kolonial'noi sistemy imperializma v Afrike," *Problemy Vostokovedeniia,* No. 1, 1960, p. 20.
[412] E. Dolgopolov, "National-Liberation Wars in the Present Epoch," *International Affairs,* No. 2 (February, 1962), p. 17.
[413] Ol'derogge and Potekhin, *op. cit.,* p. 659.

political experience among the workers, the leadership in the national-liberation movement of the peoples of Africa and in its organizations belonged to the national bourgeoisie and also to the petty-bourgeois democratic intelligentsia. But the working class, its trade unions and its communist parties actively participated in the struggle, playing in it a major, sometimes decisive role.[414]

E. Zhukov made a similar realization in an article written for *Pravda* in August, 1960:

It is known that at the head of the majority of new national states of Asia and Africa stand bourgeois political leaders who usually take a position under the nationalist flag. However, this cannot belittle the progressive historical importance of the breakthrough that has taken place on the imperialist front. The working class is the most consistent enemy of imperialism. Nevertheless, Lenin considered it natural that at the beginning of any national movement, the bourgeoisie plays the role of its hegemonic force (leader) and urged that in the struggle for the self-determination of nations, support be given to the most revolutionary elements of the bourgeois-democratic national-liberation movements.[415]

Although Soviet writers recognized the leadership of the national bourgeoisie, they did not expect the African working class to remain acquiescent. V. Tiagunenko asserted: "In the majority of liberated countries, the proletariat did not have hegemony over the national liberation revolution." However, he went on to state: "In those countries in which a revolutionary situation has unfolded or is rapidly unfolding, the working class must naturally be prepared to make use of it and take power into its hands."[416]

Despite the contention that the national bourgeoisie can lead the anti-imperialist, anti-colonial struggle, Soviet critics emphasized the importance of an alliance of the workers and

---

[414] Potekhin, *Afrika, 1956–1961, op. cit.,* pp. 26–27.
[415] Zhukov, "Significant Factor of Our Times," *op. cit.,* p. 18.
[416] Tiagunenko, *op. cit.,* p. 3.

peasants, which should form the core of a national front. G. F. Kim asserted that the working class is capable of becoming the decisive political force in the national-liberation movement but that this is possible only if the workers form an alliance with the peasants.[417] V. Pavlov described such an alliance as the core of the national front. Only the workers and peasants support all the policies of this front.[418]

Soviet writers recognized national bourgeois leadership of the anti-imperialist front but claimed that only the working class, in alliance with the peasantry, is able to consummate the anti-imperialist, anti-feudal, democratic revolution. The working class can lead the people along the non-capitalist path, develop industry, raise the standard of living of the people, and carry out far-reaching agrarian reforms.[419]

Soviet surveyors of the African scene advocated the creation of anti-imperialist national fronts in the African countries, in accordance with the tactic of a four-class alliance.[420] They stressed a flexible approach to the problems of the anti-imperialist movement and E. M. Zhukov declared: "Above all, Lenin pointed out that the struggle against imperialism, like any other progressive historical process, could take the most varied and sometimes contradictory forms. The proletarian party would be guilty of a grave error if it expected only fully consistent, straight line, 'pure' anti-imperialist actions."[421] The author went on to state: "Anti-imperialist activity might be led by parties and groups very far removed

---

[417] G. Kim, "O gosudarstve natsional'noi demokratii," *Aziia i Afrika Segodnia*, No. 10 (October, 1962), p. 3.

[418] V. Pavlov, "Soiuz rabochego klassa i krest'ianstva i sotsial'nye preobrazovaniia na Vostoke," *Aziia i Afrika Segodnia*, No. 10 (October, 1961), p. 13.

[419] See V. Li, "O nekapitalisticheskom puti razvitiia," *Aziia i Afrika Segodnia*, No. 11 (November, 1961), p. 12.

[420] For example, see Usov, "Natsional'naia burzhuaziia i osvoboditel'noe dvizhenie v Vostochnoi Afrike," *op. cit.*, p. 87.

[421] E. M. Zhukov, "The October Revolution and the Rise of the National-Liberation Movement," *International Affairs*, No. 9 (September, 1957), p. 40.

not only from the working class but even from the working population in general."[422]

Iu. Bochkarev averred that the nucleus of the national front is the alliance of workers and peasants. The former are the most progressive forces while the latter are the most numerous. In accordance with the flexible Soviet approach to this question, Bochkarev wrote: "The experience of the collaboration of Communists and other patriotic forces shows that it is fruitful for the national interests."[423]

The 1961 *Program of the C.P.S.U.* stated that the "national front embraces the working class, the peasantry, the national bourgeoisie and the democratic intelligentsia."[424] The *Draft Program*, after mentioning that the alliance between the working class and peasantry is the core of the national front, went on to assert: "The national front also embraces the urban petty bourgeoisie and the democratic intelligentsia."[425] There was therefore a difference in wording between the *Draft Program* and the final text, with the latter including the national bourgeoisie in the national front while the former included the urban petty bourgeoisie but not the national bourgeoisie. The final draft seemingly conveyed a more liberal interpretation.

Fundamentals of Marxism-Leninism described the working class as the "forefront" of the national-liberation movement. It is the most consistent anti-imperialist force. The peasantry "forms the broadest mass basis of the national-liberation movement." It is unable to become the leading force because of its backwardness and high level of illiteracy. Since the peasantry constitutes the majority of the population in the underdeveloped countries, the working class must ally with it in

---

[422] *Ibid.,* p. 41.
[423] Bochkarev, "Communists are Doughtiest Fighters for National Independence," *op. cit.,* p. 20.
[424] *Program of the Communist Party of the Soviet Union, op. cit.,* p. 45.
[425] *Draft Program of the Communist Party of the Soviet Union* (Moscow, Foreign Language Publishing House, 1961), p. 37.

order to become the leader of the national-liberation movement.[426]

Soviet scholars recognized the significant role played by the national bourgeoisie in the independence movements and G. Usov wrote: "The history of the national-liberation movement shows that, under definite conditions and at a definite stage of this movement, the national bourgeoisie is capable of anti-imperialist and anti-feudal actions."[427] Ivan Potekhin even foresaw cooperation between the working class and the national bourgeoisie after the achievement of independence: "In the struggle for independence, the national bourgeoisie and the working class formed a common front, and since the tasks of the anti-imperialist revolution have not yet been fully accomplished, the basis still exists for joint action in the future."[428] Despite the moderate statements made about the national bourgeoisie by Soviet authors, communist analysts did not fail to emphasize the role to be played by the communists in the underdeveloped countries. The Eighty-one Party Statement of 1960, to which the C.P.S.U. adhered, stated: "The aims of the Communists accord with the supreme interests of the nation. The reactionaries' effort to break up the national front under the slogan of 'anti-communism' and isolate the Communists, the foremost contingent of the liberation movement, weakens the national movement."[429] Since this document was somewhat of a compromise between the Soviet and Chinese positions, its line was a little to the left of most Soviet articles on the subject.

One of the faults which Soviet political specialists found with the national bourgeoisie, in addition to its purported tendency to compromise with the imperialists, was this class's inability to solve the agrarian problem. G. Kim explained that

---

[426] *Fundamentals of Marxism-Leninism,* 1963 edition, *op. cit.,* p. 397 (1960 edition, pp. 497–498).

[427] Usov, Natsional'naia burzhuaziia i osvoboditel'noe dvizhenie v Vostochnoi Afrike," *op. cit.,* p. 82.

[428] Potekhin, "On 'African Socialism,' " *op. cit.,* p. 75.

[429] Jacobs, *op. cit.,* p. 34.

in the initial states of the national-liberation movement, the peasantry usually follows the leadership of the national bourgeoisie since the latter promises to implement a radical solution to the agrarian problem. However, the national bourgeoisie does not live up to its promises and the peasantry strives to continue with the all-democratic revolution, until it is consummated.[430]

During the Khrushchevian era, Soviet writers revised the traditional doctrine of the two-stage revolution. According to orthodox Marxist-Leninist thought, revolutions in underdeveloped areas first pass through a bourgeois-democratic phase and then through a socialist phase. However, these two phases became more intermingled in Soviet thinking during the years of Khrushchev's rule, such as in the concept of national democracy.[431] In accordance with the more favorable attitude adopted toward the national bourgeoisie, Soviet observers discerned many aspects of the bourgeois-democratic revolution which were considered progressive and claimed that the national-liberation movements in the colonial areas are going even further, in a positive direction, than did previous bourgeois-democratic revolutions. V. Tiagunenko asserted:

> Making some kind of analogy, it is possible to say that the revolution in colonial and dependent countries goes beyond the framework of classical bourgeois-democratic revolutions. Under the pressure of the people's masses, the socio-economic transformation inescapably turns against capitalism. The national bourgeoisie, even if it is in power, is not among the forces obstructing this objective process.[432]

Tiagunenko also indicated that a flexible approach is needed in order to understand developments in underdeveloped areas: "The practice of the revolutionary struggle daily brings about the creation of new forms and methods of solving the basic socio-economic problems."[433] E. M. Zhu-

---

[430] Kim, "Soiuz rabochego klassa i krest'ianstva v natsional'no-osvoboditel'nykh revoliutsiakh," *op. cit.*, p. 7.
[431] See below, p. 215.
[432] Tiagunenko, *op. cit.*, p. 2.
[433] *Ibid.*, p. 2.

kov also pointed out the need for flexibility since the most important aspect of the national-liberation movements is their anti-imperialist character. Zhukov wrote: "But one thing— the main thing—cannot be doubted: at any stage, *and in any form,* the national-liberation struggle of the peoples of the East is of a profoundly progressive and revolutionary character, in that it weakens imperialism and undermines the world capitalist system based on the exploitation of the workers and popular oppression."[434]

K. Ivanov claimed that current national-liberation movements and revolutions of oppressed peoples should not be considered bourgeois-democratic.[435] Georgii Mirskii expressed a similar point of view at the 1964 Moscow conference on underdeveloped areas as he declared: "The national liberation and democratic revolution is not necessarily to be regarded as a bourgeois one; it must and often does go far further than the bourgeoisie desire."[436] Another statement supporting this viewpoint appeared in the 1963 edition of *Fundamentals of Marxism-Leninism.* It sought to revise the Soviet analysis of two-stage revolutions:

> Firstly, the struggle for the accomplishment of the democratic and socialist tasks does not necessarily take the form of two separate independent revolutions, but in general merely constitutes two phases of a single revolutionary process. Secondly, in the course of it the elements of the democratic and socialist revolutions are interwoven, as a result of which the fulfillment of a number of tasks of the socialist revolution is possible in the initial, democratic, stage.[437]

This bible of Khrushchevian thought also adopted a liberal attitude toward the development of proletarian revolutions.

---

[434] Zhukov, "The Bankruptcy of the Imperialist Colonial System and International Relations," *op. cit.,* p. 66. The italics are my own.
[435] Ivanov, "The National-Liberation Movement and Non-Capitalist Path of Development," *op. cit.,* p. 39.
[436] "The U.S.S.R. and the Developing Countries," *op. cit.,* p. 13.
[437] *Fundamentals of Marxism-Leninism,* 1963 edition, *op. cit.,* p. 487.

Possibilities for such revolutions were recognized in many circumstances as it was stated that they could arise from bourgeois-democratic revolutions, from national-liberation movements, and from anti-fascist or anti-imperialist struggles of liberation.[438]

In addition to this new analysis of the two-stage revolution, Soviet scholars began to think of the two stages in even another way. Approaching the usual African socialist position on this issue, Soviet writers frequently conceived of the two stages as being the achievement of political independence and the reorganization of the economy along socialist principles. A statement by Ivan Potekhin revealed this new interpretation: "Over a large area of the continent, the first stage of the national revolution has been completed: political power has been transferred from the European imperialist Powers to local national forces."[439]

It is interesting to compare this view of Potekhin with that of Kwame Nkrumah. Writing in *I Speak of Freedom,* Nkrumah maintained: "Before I address myself to the new task before us, let me once again emphasize that without the first revolution—the political revolution—we should never have been in a position to plan the future. The history of these past ten years has shown indubitably that political power is the inescapable prerequisite to economic and social power."[440] Nkrumah then went on to claim that Ghana was on the threshold of the second revolution, the economic and social one.[441]

Soviet authors constantly discussed national-liberation but did not really stress the nationalistic facet of this movement. They thought more in terms of nationalism as a force aimed at eliminating colonialism, rather than as a post-independence manifestation of chauvinism. Communists are generally averse to excessive nationalism and extol internationalism.

---

[438] *Ibid.,* p. 173 (1960 edition, p. 213).
[439] Potekhin, "The African Peoples Forge Unity," *op. cit.,* p. 84.
[440] Nkrumah, *I Speak of Freedom, op. cit.,* p. 162.
[441] *Ibid.,* p. 163.

They feel that professions of national unity actually gloss over the existence of bitter class struggles.

In regard to liberation, these authors emphasized the freeing of the masses from colonial rule. They believed that once this was achieved, the economy could begin to develop along socialist principles and the class struggle would become intensified. During the struggle for independence, most classes united in opposition to the imperialists.

It has been shown that the Soviet political analysts of the Khrushchevian era generally adopted a moderate position in regard to the independence movements in the African countries. They recognized the important role played by the national bourgeoisie and appreciated the weakness of the African proletariat. However, there was one brief period when Soviet writers followed a more leftist line and exaggerated the actions of the proletariat, while minimizing those of the national bourgeoisie. This occurred during 1959 and early 1960 and was not limited to the analysis of Africa. This method of interpretation was applied to all underdeveloped areas and India, in particular, was treated in this manner.[442] The Soviet leaders probably realized that they had become too optimistic in regard to the revolutionary potential of the national bourgeoisie and to the possibilities for the new nations of Asia and Africa to become socialist (communist). It is conceivable that Sino-Soviet ideological differences may have had some bearing upon the new Soviet stand. The Soviet leadership therefore backtracked to a more leftist position and, at the same time, sought a systematic analysis of just what was the nature of the various complex facets of African and Asian

[442] For a discussion of Soviet writings on India during the years 1959 and 1960, see the author's master's thesis, "The Strategy and Tactics of the Communist Party of India During the Formation and Implementation of the 'United Front' in India, 1934–1939," Columbia University, 1964. The Soviet sources cited all deal historically with the "United Front" period, rather than with contemporary Indian politics, but the more leftist interpretation is nevertheless obvious when the books discussed are compared with Soviet sources from 1955–1958 and 1961–1964.

politics. There were very few analytical articles dealing with this subject during 1959 and early 1960 but the hiatus in reporting was ended by E. M. Zhukov's authoritative *Pravda* article of August 26, 1960 and by Potekhin's panoramic *Afrika smotrit v budushchee*.[443] There was also a greater attempt to foster the development of communist parties in Africa during the 1959–1960 period and the journal *The African Communist* was founded in 1959.[444]

Another possible explanation for the leftist phase in Soviet analysis is that this turn leftward was a response to developments in Cuba. It must be remembered that Fidel Castro gained control over Cuba on January 1, 1959 and that the leftist attitude adopted in Soviet articles began shortly thereafter. This certainly does not prove any causality but Soviet observers may have seen Castro's revolution as an alternative to socialist (proletarian) revolution throughout the underdeveloped world. Castro was a charismatic nationalist leader who advocated radical social and economic reform but who nevertheless denied that he was a communist. He had great international appeal and may therefore have been seen as a rival to communism. These considerations may have led Soviet analysts to look askance at revolutions led by non-proletarian figures.

Castro gradually moved leftward and in the summer of 1960, there was a sharp deterioration in relations between Cuba and the United States. In October, 1960, the United States began to embargo most items meant for delivery to Cuba. It was during this period that Soviet scholars developed the concept of national democracy, apparently having the Cuban model in mind.[445] The concept was first announced following the Moscow Conference of communist parties, held in November-December, 1960, but had been presaged in an

---

[443] For references to Zhukov's article, see above, pp. 98, 118 and 158 and below, p. 208. Potekhin's book is cited throughout this book.
[444] See below, p. 199.
[445] See below, pp. 212–213.

article by Zhukov which appeared in *Pravda* on August 26.[446] The end of the Soviet leftist period also came at this time and it is conceivable that as Soviet analysts came to see Cuba as a progressive example for other underdeveloped nations, they simultaneously altered their view of the national bourgeoisie. The Cuban experience had shown that national bourgeois leaders could indeed participate in the carrying out of radical reforms and set the stage for socialism. It should be pointed out that Castro did not actually call his revolution "socialist" until April, 1961 and did not declare himself a "Marxist-Leninist" until December 1, 1961.

As has been mentioned, the Soviet leftist phase emphasized the role played by the proletariat. A. A. Guber even claimed that the working class had gained hegemony in the national-liberation movements and his statement is typical of Soviet pronouncements of that period:

> The working class of the enslaved countries has participated with increasing vigour in the national-liberation struggle and has won hegemony in this movement. It has regarded the gaining of national independence merely as a stage, a necessary requisite for social change and the subsequent growing over of the national colonial revolution into a Socialist revolution. The national bourgeoisie saw in national independence the attainment of its ultimate aim, namely, the establishment of its undivided rule in a sovereign state.[447]

The questions of class struggle and national-liberation are extremely relevant to the Soviet assessment of socialism in Africa. From the Soviet point of view, the prospects for socialism in any country are determined by an analysis of its class relationships and the position of each class vis-à-vis the seat of state power. In addition, as will be shown below, Soviet authors linked the Soviet Union and other socialist coun-

---

[446] See below, p. 208.
[447] A. A. Guber, "Distinctive Features of the National-Liberation Movement in the Eastern Colonial and Dependent Countries," *International Affairs*, No. 3 (March, 1959), p. 72.

tries with the class struggles in the underdeveloped states, claiming the existence of a world revolutionary process.

NATIONALISM AND INTERNATIONALISM

K. Ivanov stated that the three main progressive forces of our time are the world socialist system, the international workers' movement, and the national-liberation movement.[448] Soviet writers attempted to link these three phenomena in order to show a close relationship between the Soviet Union and the countries of Asia and Africa and they stressed the theme of joint action against international imperialism. Ivan Potekhin wrote that the world features a fight of imperialism against an alliance of the three forces just mentioned while a *Kommunist* editorial of January, 1962 declared: "The national-liberation movement can develop successfully only in direct relation with other integral components of the world revolutionary process."[449] The other components cited were the socialist camp fighting imperialism, the proletariat in the capitalist countries fighting monopolies, and the fights for peace and disarmament.

Soviet writers stressed imperialism rather than capitalism and thus coupled the U.S.S.R. with the underdeveloped countries. Mirskii and Stepanov asserted: "The bitter struggle in the Afro-Asian countries is taking place alongside the competition of the two world systems—socialism and imperialism."[450] An unsigned article in *Sovremennyi Vostok* claimed that the forces of socialism and those of the national-liberation move-

---

[448] Ivanov, "The National-Liberation Movement and Non-Capitalist Development," part one, *op. cit.*, p. 43.
[449] Potekhin, *Africa: Ways of Development, op. cit.*, p. 72 and "The National-Liberation Movement is an Integral Part of the World Revolutionary Process," *Kommunist*, No. 2 (January, 1962), pp. 15–20. See *CDSP*, Vol. XIV, No. 6 (March 7, 1962), p. 5.
[450] Mirskii and Stepanov, *op. cit.*, p. 103.

ments were joined in a common front against imperialism.[451] It was maintained elsewhere that the international struggle between socialism and imperialism is the most important factor affecting the outcome of the national-liberation movements.[452] The interrelationship between the underdeveloped nations and the socialist countries was also touched upon by E. M. Zhukov in his significant *Pravda* article of August 26, 1960:

> The states of Asia, Africa and Latin America are defending their independence and sovereign rights under the banners of anti-colonialism and anti-imperialism. It is quite natural, therefore, that in the most fundamental problems of an international nature, in questions of war and peace, the positions of the non-socialist states of the East and those of the socialist states coincide and cannot but coincide.[453]

Despite their inclusion of national-liberation movements in the world revolutionary process, Soviet analysts actually thought more about how the nations of Asia and Africa could help them in their struggle against imperialism, rather than about how the Soviet Union could help the underdeveloped nations in their struggle against the colonial powers. This was made clear in the Soviet polemics with the Chinese as it was maintained that the chief contradiction of our era is between socialism and imperialism, not between the oppressed nations and imperialism, as the Chinese had suggested.[454] The Soviets feared the Chinese attempt to rally the Asian and African states behind her on a racial and anti-colonialist basis and

---

[451] "Vsepobezhdaiushchie idei kommunizma," *Sovremennyi Vostok,* No. 11 (November, 1958), p. 6.

[452] G. F. Kim, "Sorevnovanie dvukh sistem i ekonomicheski slabo razvitye strany Vostoka," *Sovremennyi Vostok,* No. 11 (November, 1959), p. 13.

[453] Zhukov, "Significant Factor of Our Times," *op. cit.,* p. 18.

[454] See Georgii Mirskii, "The Proletariat and National Liberation," *New Times,* No. 18 (May 1, 1964), p. 7 and V. Kudriavtsev, "Africa in One Formation," *Izvestiia,* October 10, 1963, p. 2 (see *CDSP,* Vol. XV, No. 41 (November 6, 1963), p. 20).

stressed the unity of the socialist states with those of Asia and Africa so that the Soviet Union would not be excluded from the mainstream of Afro-Asian revolutionary activity. V. Kudriavtsev attacked the Chinese position and wrote: "Politicians must have nationalist blinkers on their eyes if they do not see the great results of unifying the mighty stream of a single anti-imperialist movement, of realizing Lenin's idea of the leadership of the working class as a condition for victory in the anti-imperialist struggle."[455] Kudriavtsev was therefore advocating a single anti-imperialist movement which included the socialist states as well as the nations of Asia and Africa. He then went on to state: "Every attempt to divorce the national-liberation movement of the African peoples from the world revolutionary process and from its deciding center can only lead to the weakening of this movement, to a strengthening of imperialist positions in the African countries."[456]

By late 1962, Soviet scholars came to maintain that the class struggle must be viewed on an international, rather than on a national, scale. However, a few other Soviet arguments led up to this concept. In April, 1960, G. Skorov claimed that the working class plays the leading role in the world anti-imperialist struggle. The victorious proletariat has an international task of liberating peoples from colonialism and strengthening their political and economic independence.[457] By referring to the victorious proletariat, Skorov seemed to have the Soviet Union in mind.

In April, 1962, K. Ivanov further placed the development in Asian and African countries into an international framework. First, he analyzed colonialism and mentioned a world division of labor:

> In effect, present-day colonialism is not confined to relations between the metropolitan countries and the colonies; it is

---

[455] Kudriavtsev, *ibid.*, p. 21.
[456] *Ibid.*, p. 21.
[457] G. Skorov, "Torzhestvo Leninizma i narody Vostoka," *Mirovaia Ekonomika i Mezhdunarodnye Otnosheniia*, No. 4 (April, 1960), p. 26.

a whole system of international relations established in the world by imperialism which it wants to uphold, retain, and consolidate regardless of everything, at least in the part of the world where it still has influence. Hence, to understand the essence of colonialism, it must be viewed from the general standpoint of the general laws governing imperialism and the world division of labour which has taken shape on its basis, and also of the relevant international political and economic relations.[458]

Ivanov then discussed national-liberation movements and placed them in an international framework also:

Another result is that the struggle for national liberation is increasingly becoming an international struggle, a struggle against capitalism and imperialism (the trusts remain the foundation of capitalism and colonialism) ; that the national-liberation movement extends beyond the local or even continental framework, and actually becomes a world-wide struggle, including the world-wide struggle for peace and general and complete disarmament, undermining the foundations of imperialism.[459]

The positions held by Skorov and Ivanov laid the groundwork for G. F. Kim's introduction of a novel concept which is of extreme relevance to the question of the African class struggle. Writing similar articles in *Narody Azii i Afriki* and *Aziia i Afrika Segodnia,* Kim introduced the idea that the class struggle in the underdeveloped countries cannot be viewed just in terms of the classes present in those countries. He asserted:

A union of states, personifying the rule of the toilers with the working class at their head, and of the peoples of young sovereign states, which have arisen on the wreckage of colonial empires, realizes on an international scale the Leninist idea of a union of the working class with the many million semi-proletarian and non-proletarian masses. The problem of the union of the working class and peasantry, tran-

---

[458] Ivanov, "Present-Day Colonialism and International Relations," *op. cit.,* p. 40.
[459] *Ibid.,* p. 43.

scending the national framework, has become, in such a manner, an international factor.[460]

The author then went on to state: "The union of the socialist countries and of the countries which have attained independence through the course of the national-liberation revolutions, has already become the decisive factor of international life."[461]

Kim's doctrine maintained that the underdeveloped countries, in which the peasants constituted the majority of the population and the working class was quite weak and disorganized, could evolve in the same manner as countries led by the working class. This was possible since the socialist countries, in which the working class purportedly is in power, can act as the leader of an international alliance of workers and peasants. Therefore, the underdeveloped countries could conceivably construct socialism, despite the fact that their own working classes were far removed from the seat of state power. Concomitant with this idea was the oft-expressed Soviet contention that the underdeveloped countries could skip the capitalist stage of development and proceed directly to socialism.[462] It was claimed that this was made possible by the fact that the proletariat had already seized power in some countries, such as the Soviet Union, and that the proletariats of these advanced countries could help the underdeveloped ones on the road to socialism.

Kim actually foreshadowed his new analysis of the international class struggle in an article appearing in *Sovremennyi Vostok* in November, 1959. Without going as far as he later did in his 1962 articles, Kim implied that one must look further than the role of the proletariat in individual countries. The moral support given to the national-liberation

---

[460] Kim, "Soiuz rabochego klassa i krest'ianstva v natsional'no-osvoboditel'nykh revoliutsiakh," *op. cit.,* p. 5 and Kim, "O gosudarstve natsional'noi demokratii," *op. cit.,* p. 5.

[461] Kim, "Soiuz rabochego klassa i krest'ianstva v natsional'no-osvoboditel'nykh revoliutsiakh," *Ibid.,* p. 5.

[462] For a discussion of bypassing capitalism, see below, pp. 200–208.

movements by the socialist nations must be taken into account when determining the revolutionary nature of these movements.

> It was formerly supposed . . . that proletarian leadership of the national-liberation movement as a decisive factor of the success of the revolution will become possible only as a result of the rising up, of the strengthening of the positions and development of the political maturity of the proletariat within each country taken individually. At the present time, it is impossible to be limited to this only. The enormous role of the proletariat in the national-liberation movement under present conditions is expressed even in the moral support of the national-liberation movement by the world socialist system.[463]

Kim's views were later expanded upon by K. Ivanov. Writing in the September, 1964 issue of *International Affairs,* he claimed that Lenin analyzed the national-colonial question in terms of world economic relationships, rather than in terms of the developments in individual countries.[464] He also maintained that when considering the economic base of society, one must look at international economic relationships, not at those in individual nations:

> To a Marxist it is clear that the causes impelling the national-liberation movements in the U.A.R., Algeria, Burma, Ghana and other countries and turning them against capitalism and imperialism are rooted in modern material production rather than the superstructure—the sphere of ideology, form of government of politics in general. They are rooted in economic life on a world scale, not in the framework of individual nations.[465]

Thus Soviet scholars advanced many arguments in order to show the close interrelationship between the socialist states

---

[463] Kim, "Sorevnovanie dvukh sistem i ekonomicheski slabo razvitye strany Vostoka," *op. cit.,* p. 13.
[464] Ivanov, "The National-Liberation Movement and Non-Capitalist Path of Development," part one, *op. cit.,* p. 35.
[465] *Ibid.,* p. 35.

and the emerging nations of Asia and Africa. The class struggles and national-liberation movements in these nations were shown to have been significantly affected by their purported ties with the victorious Soviet proletariat and it was even claimed that without the existence and power of the socialist camp, the national-liberation movements would never have been successful.

Ivan Potekhin asserted that the victories of national revolutions in Africa were due to three factors: the people's movements in the colonies, the influence and strength of the world socialist system, and the struggle of the proletariat in the capitalist countries.[466] Soviet authors seemed to emphasize the second of these factors and Iurii Bochkarev wrote: "The mounting strength of the socialist commonwealth and the support its members give the peoples of Asia, Africa and Latin America is today the decisive international factor in the success of national-liberation revolutions."[467]

Another familiar Soviet theme was that the October Revolution initiated the downfall of imperialism and opened up prospects for colonial revolutions.[468] An attempt was made to identify pre-revolutionary Russia as a colonial country and thereby associate it with the nations of Asia and Africa. Karen Brutents asserted: "The first socialist revolution was victorious in a backward country which was dependent on the imperialist brigands of the West. At the same time, pre-revolutionary Russia itself was the hearth of colonial oppression.[469] Other contentions frequently made by Soviet writers were that the

---

[466] Potekhin, "Nekotorye problemy Afrikanistiki v svete reshenii XXII s' 'ezda KPSS," *op. cit.*, p. 8.
[467] Iu. Bochkarev, "The Soviet Union and the National-Liberation Movement," *New Times,* No. 26 (July 3, 1963), p. 6.
[468] See Potekhin, "Politicheskoe polozhenie v strankh Afriki," *op. cit.*, p. 23; Bochkarev, "Communists are Doughtiest Fighters for National Independence," *op. cit.*, p. 13; and "Replies of N. S. Khrushchev to Questions of Editors of Ghanaian Times, Alger Républicain, Le Peuple and Botataung," *op. cit.*, p. 11.
[469] Brutents, *Protiv ideologii sovremennogo kolonializma, op. cit.*, p. 9.

socialist states defend the newly-independent nations from the imperialists and give them "brotherly" aid.[470]

* * *

The Soviet analysis of African nationalism is particularly important since nationalism is one of the major components of African socialism and may be viewed as a viable alternative to the development of communism in the African nations. Soviet critics were careful to differentiate between the nationalism present in the underdeveloped countries of Asia and Africa and that in the countries of the socialist camp. The former is directed against the imperialist powers and was therefore seen as progressive in certain instances, but the latter is a threat to Moscow's grip over the European members of the socialist camp and was therefore deemed reactionary. Of course, Soviet writers did not discuss nationalism in quite these terms but as one can easily read into their statements, the considerations just mentioned were obviously in their minds.

During the Khrushchevian era, nationalism was the dominant force on the African continent as one nation after another received its independence from the colonial powers. The Soviet leaders seem to have decided that the Soviet Union's main task in Africa was not to stress the road to communism but was to emphasize the anti-imperialist nature of the African nationalist movements. The immediate aim was not to gain the African countries as adherents to the socialist camp but to deny control over these nations to the imperialist powers. It must be realized that the African nations had formerly been considered reserves of the imperialist camp. The denouement of this relationship, which is the way the Soviet analysts pictured the process of decolonization, was therefore seen as a significant step forward by Soviet observers. Consequently, Soviet writers were careful not to antagonize the African nationalist leaders and treated the subject of nationalism in a

---

[470] See Kudriavtsev, "Fighting Africa's Daily Round," *op. cit.,* and Potekhin, "Nekotorye problemy Afrikanistiki v svete reshenii XXII s' 'ezda KPSS," *op. cit.,* p. 13.

rather favorable manner. Of course, as Richard Pipes has pointed out, this was not the Soviet Union's first flirtation with the force of nationalism in the underdeveloped nations. The friendships established with Ataturk and Chiang Kai-shek were well remembered.[471]

Before 1955, Soviet sources described nationalism as a negative force which serves the interests of the bourgeoisie and the imperialists. Volume twenty-nine of the second edition of the *Bol'shaia Sovetskaia Entsiklopediia*, which went to press in November, 1954, defined nationalism as a "reactionary bourgeois ideology and policy which defends the interests of the bourgeoisie of a given nation under the cover of the fraudulent flag of 'all-national' interests . . ."[472] It went on to claim that "bourgeois nationalism is a weapon of imperialist reaction." The encyclopedia maintained that the struggle against bourgeois nationalism is one of the most important preconditions for the success of the national-liberation movements.[473] It also asserted that the liquidation of social and national oppression can take place only under the leadership of the communist and workers' parties.[474]

Volume six of the third edition of the *Malaia Sovetskaia Entsiklopediia*, which went to press in September, 1959, adopted a more favorable position in regard to nationalism. It stated that nationalism is sometimes progressive, such as in the colonial countries where it is directed against feudal and colonial oppression.[475]

The rather leftist Soviet interpretations of events in Asia and Africa during the year 1959 emphasized the role played by the proletariat but did not correspondingly derogate the

---

[471] Richard Pipes, "Nationalism and Nationality," in Leonard Schapiro, ed., *The U.S.S.R. and the Future* (New York and London, Praeger, 1962), p. 72.
[472] *Bol'shaia Sovetskaia Entsiklopediia*, second edition, Vol. XXIX, p. 287.
[473] *Ibid.*, p. 288.
[474] *Ibid.*, p. 299.
[475] *Malaia Sovetskaia Entsiklopediia*, third edition, Vol. VI, p. 483.

force of nationalism. As this statement by S. I. Tiul'panov indicates, nationalism was not necessarily considered to be bourgeois and the proletariat was deemed to be a supporter of nationalism:

> The nationalist ideology of the colonial working class is not in any way supplementary, secondary to its internationalist policy. Proletarian internationalism as a determining trait of the ideology of the proletariat in no way diminishes the fact that in a given concrete historical situation, the proletariat of colonial countries above all emphasizes its role as the bearer of the nationalist idea, as the leading force in the national-liberation struggle.[476]

When Soviet analysts began their new assessment of developments in the underdeveloped countries in the latter half of 1960, they were less enthusiastic about nationalism and, while still praising its strong points, they did not fail to point out its detrimental facets. The 1961 *Program of the C.P.S.U.* first discussed the positive side of nationalism in the countries of Asia and Africa:

> In many countries, the liberation movement of the peoples that have awakened proceeds under the flag of nationalism. Marxists-Leninists draw a distinction between the nationalism of the oppressed nations and that of the oppressor nations. The nationalism of an oppressed nation contains a general democratic element directed against oppression, and Communists support it because they consider it historically justified at a given stage.[477]

However, it then asserted that the "anti-popular circles" in these countries emphasize the reactionary aspects of nationalism and obstruct social progress. They adhere to theories of socialism of the national type and have a petty-bourgeois con-

---

[476] S. I. Tiul'panov, "Nekotorye teoreticheskie voprosy raspada kolonial'noi sistemy imperializma," *Vestnik Leningradskogo Universiteta* (Seriia Ekonomiki, Filosofii i Prava), No. 11, 1959, p. 11.
[477] *Program of the Communist Party of the Soviet Union, op. cit.,* p. 45.

ception of socialism. These circles purportedly hinder the national liberation movements and mislead the people.[478]

These statements on nationalism referred only to "oppressed nations" and the countries of the socialist camp were not included in this category. The nationalism evident in these countries was analyzed quite differently:

> Nationalism is the chief political and ideological weapon used by international reaction and the remnants of the domestic reactionary forces against the unity of the socialist countries. Nationalist sentiments and national narrowmindness do not disappear automatically with the establishment of the socialist system. Nationalist prejudice and survivals of former national strife are a province in which resistance to social progress may be most protracted and stubborn, bitter and insidious.[479]

Thus nationalism which opposes the interests of the imperialists was viewed favorably and that which opposes the interests of the Soviet Union was looked upon as anathema.

Karen Brutents' book, *Protiv ideologii sovremennogo kolonializma,* was published in 1961 and the author was quite explicit in pointing out the negative facets of nationalism in Asia and Africa. He charged that nationalism is the policy of the bourgeoisie and that its advocates try to make believe that the interests of the whole nation are served. The bourgeoisie uses nationalism as a weapon to push the class struggle of the workers into the background.[480] Brutents also maintained that nationalism preaches class cooperation and thus works to the advantage of the bourgeoisie.[481]

The author then made a statement which went rather far in castigating nationalism. In fact, it was probably the harshest condemnation of nationalism made by Soviet writers during the Khrushchevian period. Brutents asserted:

---

[478] *Ibid.,* pp. 51–52.
[479] *Ibid.,* p. 24.
[480] Brutents, *Protiv ideologii sovremennogo kolonializma, op. cit.,* p. 45.
[481] *Ibid.,* p. 199.

The masses are beginning to be convinced that at this stage, nationalism is less and less able to come forward as a form of anti-imperialist national consciousness and is becoming more and more limited. In search of a philosophy which would consistently express their anti-imperialist strivings, they are turning ever more frequently to the socialist ideology, the genuine bearers of which are the Communist Parties.[482]

Despite his attacks on nationalism, Brutents did not fail to mention that nationalism has a positive side. He averred that it can be a progressive force since it is anti-imperialist, anti-feudal, and is based on economic and political sovereignty.[483]

The 1963 edition of *Fundamentals of Marxism-Leninism* contained a balanced account of nationalism and did not paint a picture as rosy as that presented in the 1960 edition. Many entries in the two editions were identical but the earlier version did not discuss as many negative facets of nationalism. Both editions adopted a flexible approach to the subject and stated: "Marxist-Leninism approaches nationalism, as it does all social phenomena, from a concrete historical point of view, i.e., from the point of view of the interests of social progress. Lenin repeatedly warned against abstract formulations of the question of nationalism. . . ."[484] The positive and negative aspects of nationalism were then outlined, with the earlier edition toning down references to the latter.[485] Both editions maintained that nationalism can help the masses acquire a sense of dignity but warned against "racial or national exclusiveness."[486]

The 1960 edition of *Fundamentals of Marxism-Leninism* contained a section on nationalism which did not appear in the 1963 edition. It asserted: "Gradually many countries, peoples and whole continents became victims of colonialism. The

---

[482] *Ibid.,* p. 201.
[483] *Ibid.,* p. 198.
[484] *Fundamentals of Marxism-Leninism,* 1963 edition, *op. cit.,* p. 401 (1960 edition, p. 492).
[485] Compare p. 402 of the 1963 edition with p. 493 of the 1960 edition.
[486] *Ibid.,* 1963 edition, p. 402 (1960 edition, p. 493).

national question was now not one of the rights and fate of individual national minorities, but of the majority of mankind, the majority which the imperialists had enslaved by force or cunning and made subjects of their colonial empires.[487] It seems possible that this section was deleted from the later edition because it sounded too much like the line taken by the Chinese, who were attempting to align the nations of Asia and Africa on the basis of their common colonial histories.

Thus the Soviet analysis of nationalism during the period from late 1960 to the end of Khrushchev's rule was marked by an equivocal attitude. It was considered progressive since it was opposed to imperialism but was at the same time viewed as a brake upon the development of scientific socialism because it suppressed the class struggle. However, an editorial appearing in the May, 1964 issue of *Kommunist* took a position which favorably reflected upon nationalism. It maintained that nationalism, if it is truly based upon patriotism, "must inevitably develop on the side of socialism."[488] Therefore, nationalism was viewed as a progressive force and the Soviet leaders continued to woo the African nationalist leaders.

[487] *Ibid.*, 1960 edition, p. 488.
[488] "Soiuz sil sotsializma i natsional'no-osvoboditel'nogo dvizheniia," *Kommunist* editorial, No. 8 (May, 1964), p. 9. Underlining is my own.

5 The Soviet View of Africa's Future Transition to Scientific Socialism

SOVIET SCHOLARS CRITICIZED AFRICAN SOCIALISM ON MANY grounds and affirmed that the future happiness of the African peoples lies in their acceptance of scientific socialism. However, these Soviet experts seemed to be quite confused as to the paths which should be taken by the Africans to attain a truly socialist society. They discussed a non-capitalist path of development, national democratic states, and the bypassing of capitalism in accordance with the Mongolian and Central Asian models and often made contradictory statements regarding the relationships between the alternatives just cited. They were also inconsistent when attempting to differentiate between the non-capitalist path and socialism. These analysts asserted that the African socialist leaders could become adherents of the working-class ideology of scientific socialism but they also examined the role of the African communist parties, which provided an alternative to the radicalization of the nationalist parties.

THE NON-CAPITALIST PATH AND THE EVOLUTION OF AFRICAN SOCIALISM

On November 12, 1882, Friedrich Engels addressed a letter to Karl Kautsky in which he discussed revolutions in those

181

colonial countries where there was a native problem (as distinguished from colonies like Canada and Australia). He asserted:

> Once Europe is organized, and North America, that will furnish such colossal power and such an example that the semi-civilized countries will follow in their wake of their own accord. Economic needs alone will be responsible for this. But as to what social and political phases these countries will then have to pass through before they likewise arrive at socialist organization, we today can only advance rather idle hypotheses, I think. One thing alone is certain: The victorious proletariat can force no blessings of any kind upon any foreign nation without undermining its own victory by so doing.[489]

This letter raised many points which are of great relevance to current Soviet views on the course of African revolutions. First of all, Engels claimed that the advanced countries would have their socialist revolutions before the underdeveloped countries. This was a basic Marxist tenet until the time of the Russian Revolution but has since been revised. When Russia experienced its socialist revolution, it was a backward agrarian country and events since 1917 have shown that the advanced European countries have failed to comply with the prophesy made by Engels. However, prospects for socialist revolutions in the underdeveloped countries have greatly increased during the last ten years. Instead of considering revolutions in these nations just the ripples caused by revolutionary waves in the advanced industrial nations, Soviet observers came to view the revolutions in Asia and Africa, along with the successful revolutions in the socialist bloc countries and the workers' movements in the industrialized countries, as an integral part of a world revolutionary process.

Secondly, Engels mentioned that the advanced countries could serve as examples for the "semi-civilized countries."

---

[489] Letter from Engels to Kautsky, London, November 12, 1882 in Lewis Feuer, ed., *Marx and Engels: Basic Writings on Politics and Philosophy* (Garden City, Doubleday, 1959), p. 452.

Soviet writers of the Khrushchevian era constantly stressed this theme, citing the U.S.S.R. as the example to be followed. They claimed that the Soviet Union had overcome economic backwardness in a short period of time and had become one of the most technologically advanced states in the world. They pointed out that the Soviet people enjoy a high standard of living.

Thirdly, Engels did not outline the course to be followed by revolutions in the underdeveloped countries. He maintained that an attempt to determine the political and social consequences of these revolutions would be idle hypothesizing. Marx and Lenin also failed to present rigid blueprints for the paths to be followed by these countries and Soviet theorists therefore had a free hand to develop their own concepts to fit the patterns of growth manifested throughout Asia and Africa.

Finally, Engels asserted that conditions for socialist revolutions must develop within each country and the victorious proletariat of one country cannot export its revolution. This view was maintained by Soviet writers, although they still pointed to the Soviet model of development.[490]

According to Soviet scholars, the nations of Africa must proceed to either capitalism or socialism. There is no third path.[491] It was often affirmed that the African nations have a choice between these two paths and this seems to deny historical inevitability.[492] Africa was viewed as being capable of taking either path and Ivan Potekhin wrote: "The capitalist road is not closed to the African peoples and countries, of course. All the prerequisites for the development of capitalism are at hand:"[493]

---

[490] For example, see the speech by Mikoyan, "Gana privetstvuet Sovetskogo gostia," *Pravda*, January 13, 1962, p. 3 and Potekhin, *Africa: Ways of Development, op. cit.*, p. 46.

[491] See "Soiuz sil sotsializma i natsional'no-osvoboditel'nogo dvizheniia," *op. cit.*, p. 9.

[492] For example, see Iudin, *op. cit.*, p. 9.

[493] Potekhin, *Africa: Ways of Development, op. cit.*, p. 45.

Although avowing that revolutions cannot be exported, Soviet authors mentioned that the world socialist system "leaves its imprint on the ideology and political program of the bourgeois nationalists."[494] In a similar vein, Potekhin asserted that without the presence of the world socialist system, nations would have no opportunity to construct socialism without having first passed through the capitalist stage of development. He claimed that the socialist states aid the underdeveloped countries, protect them from the imperialists, and serve as models for development.[495] Another theme was that the advantages of socialism over capitalism will become more evident as the economies of the Soviet Union and other socialist countries become stronger.[496] The U.S.S.R. was therefore seen as an important factor in the African nations' choice of roads of development.

In the eyes of Soviet analysts, capitalism is discredited in Africa because it was the system practiced by Africa's colonial rulers.[497] It was also maintained that the African nations do not want to take the long capitalist path traversed by the Western powers. They hope to overcome economic backwardness rapidly. Avakov and Andreasian wrote: "History has left them no time to move along the capitalist path. To catch up with the 20th century within the lifetime of one generation, that is their vital need."[498] Potekhin stated that an important question for Africa is which is the shortest possible way to raise the material and cultural levels of the people and at the same time eliminate the remnants of colonialism.[499] *Fundamentals of Marxism-Leninism* also touched upon this topic.

---

[494] Brutents, *Protiv ideologii sovremennogo kolonializma, op. cit.,* p. 186.

[495] Potekhin, *Africa: Ways of Development, op. cit.,* p. 46.

[496] See A. Gatsoiev, F. Politkin, and P. Khmylov, "Two System Competition and the Young States," *International Affairs,* No. 9, 1964, p. 82.

[497] See Tiagunenko, "Tendentsii obshchestvennogo razvitiia osvobodivshikhsia stran v sovremennuiu epokhu," *op. cit.,* p. 22 and Potekhin, *Afrika smotrit v budushchee, op. cit.,* p. 3.

[498] Avakov and Andreasian, *op. cit.,* p. 9.

[499] Potekhin, *Afrika smotrit v budushchee, op. cit.,* p. 3.

It claimed that the newly-independent states cannot repeat the capitalist pattern set by the European nations because they will not be able to exploit colonies and use them as sources of raw material and as outlets for their goods. It went on to state that the people in the underdeveloped nations are opposed to the classical capitalist course since they realize the suffering of the working people and the accumulation of capital which it engenders.[500]

Soviet writers believed that the Africans are becoming greatly attracted to socialism, of one variety or another. They cited the fact that most African governments claim to be based on socialist principles and averred that the number of Africans adhering to Marxism-Leninism is constantly increasing. "Socialism has become more popular than any other idea in Africa today."[501] Nikita Khrushchev iterated a similar view during an interview in 1963. Referring to the underdeveloped nations, he declared: "Personally, I am deeply convinced that the peoples, some sooner, others later, will choose socialism."[502]

A comprehensive explanation of why the underdeveloped nations should accept socialism was presented by K. Ivanov. He wrote:

> Socialism, as a social order, simultaneously gives the peoples a practical example of how to extricate themselves from the quagmire of backwardness and poverty and to reach the heights of modern civilization during the life span of a single generation. Furthermore, it gives all backward nations and peoples the possibility of eliminating the inherited inequality and ensures the prerequisites for a more or less simultaneous transition of all countries—backward and advanced—to Communism 'within a single historical epoch.' This is no fantasy but a true prospect, in full accord with

---

[500] *Fundamentals of Marxism-Leninism*, 1963 edition, *op. cit.*, p. 418.
[501] Potekhin, "Pan-Africanism and the Struggle of the Two Ideologies," *op. cit.*, p. 48.
[502] "Replies of N. S. Khrushchev to Questions of Editors of Ghanaian Times, Alger Républicain, Le Peuple and Botataung," *op. cit.*, p. 12.

the present level of the productive forces and the experience in economic construction in the developed Socialist countries.[503]

Ivanov was not only claiming that the underdeveloped nations could take the path leading to socialism, but was also maintaining that they could achieve communism during the same "historical epoch" as the Soviet Union and other countries of the socialist camp.

According to Soviet writers, the ideology of scientific socialism is being disseminated in Africa by the African communist parties and by the communist parties of the colonial countries.[504] In addition, certain representatives of the national intelligentsia and some leading political parties and social organizations were considered to be adherents of scientific socialism and they help spread this ideology. Many of these people received Marxist training in the colonial countries.[505]

Soviet observers also asserted that the masses lean toward socialism and influence the bourgeoisie in this direction. During its initial years in power, the bourgeoisie is rather weak and is forced to pay attention to the views of the masses.[506] Another theme was that socialism does not appear spontaneously.[507] People must work hard in order to achieve it. This view seems to imply voluntarism rather than determinism in the course of historical development but none other than Nikita Khrushchev was one of its adherents.

Another view maintained by Soviet spokesmen was that people of non-proletarian origin favor the development of so-

---

[503] Ivanov, "The National-Liberation Movement and Non-Capitalist Path of Development," part one, *op. cit.,* p. 42.
[504] See Potekhin, "Nekotorye problemy Afrikanistiki v svete reshenii XXII s' 'ezda KPSS," *op. cit.,* p. 15.
[505] See Potekhin, "Kharakternye cherty raspada kolonial'noi sistemy imperializma v Afrike," *op. cit.,* p. 20.
[506] Brutents, *Protiv ideologii sovremennogo kolonializma, op. cit.,* p. 187.
[507] See E. M. Zhukov, "Velikaia Oktiabr'skaia Revoliutsiia i natsional'no-osvoboditel'naia bor'ba narodov," *Pravda,* November 5, 1964, p. 3.

cialism in their countries.[508] This seems to contradict the orthodox Marxist tenet that class determines consciousness but Soviet writers of the Khrushchevian era did just that, by implication rather than by actual statement. They frequently used the theme that the ideology of people can change and that non-proletarians are able to undergo an ideological evolution and eventually become adherents of scientific socialism. This line of reasoning began to appear in 1962 (it should be remembered that Fidel Castro declared himself a Marxist-Leninist on December 1, 1961) and Cuban developments may have prompted the Soviet theorists to take this new position. Of course, communists have used similar arguments many times in the past, with Mao Tse-tung being a prime exponent of such views.

As Georgii Mirskii saw the underdeveloped countries of Asia and Africa, the intelligentsia and army often have the leading roles. They create revolutionary or national democracies which express the interests of specific classes but are not necessarily bourgeois. Mirskii averred: "But the society in which they operate is of a transitional nature and the ideology of these people can undergo an evolution. Since they sometimes possess real power, they are in a position to change course sharply. The course taken depends on the political views of the leaders and on how closely they are linked with the masses and how much they express their interests."[509] Krasin and Li asserted that in many countries which do not have communist organizations, there are influential revolutionary groups within the mass democratic parties. These groups lean toward Marxism-Leninism and are active within the Union Soudanaise of Mali, the Parti Démocratique Guinéen, Convention People's Party of Ghana, and other African parties.[510]

---

[508] "The U.S.S.R. and the Developing Countries," *op. cit.*, p. 24.
[509] Mirskii, "Creative Marxism and Problems of the National-Liberation Movement," *op. cit.*, p. 13.
[510] Iu. Krasin and V. Li, "O zakonomernostiakh nekapitalisticheskogo razvitiia osvobodivshikhsia stran," *Voprosy Filosofii*, No. 8, 1964, p. 36.

A. Sobolev, writing in the *World Marxist Review,* gave this advice: "If a revolutionary democrat or a member of the national bourgeoisie is willing to take one step forward, it is the duty of the Marxists to help him take two."[511] He then maintained: "There is, then, the possibility that many revolutionary democrats will come over to the positions of scientific socialism, to the positions of the working class."[512] Iurii Bochkarev also believed that nationalist leaders could eventually become scientific socialists. In discussing communists, he wrote:

> They take a fraternal and attentive attitude to those nationalist leaders who are sincerely striving to lead their countries out onto the road of socialism but who, in virtue of various objective and subjective reasons, have not yet come to scientific socialism. The Communists believe that life itself, the logic of the struggle, a study of the experience of socialist countries will lead these people to scientific socialism.[513]

There are two reasons which suggest that Fidel Castro's declaration of his adherence to Marxism-Leninism may have precipitated the Soviet belief that leaders of underdeveloped nations may come over to Marxist-Leninist positions. First of all, the question of timing must be considered. The first comprehensive Soviet article on this subject, as related to the general Soviet outlook on Asia and Africa, appeared in the March, 1962 issue of *Mirovaia Ekonomika i Mezhdunarodnye Otnosheniia* and was written by V. Tiagunenko. Castro's declaration was on December 1, 1961. Secondly, Tiagunenko specifically cited the Cuban revolution in his analysis and claimed that it could serve as an example for other nations:

> With the joining together of specific conditions, the transition of the most farsighted representatives of the nonproletarian elements to the position of the working class

---

[511] Sobolev, *op. cit.,* pp. 41–42.
[512] *Ibid.,* p. 42.
[513] Bochkarev, "Communists are Doughtiest Fighters for National Independence," *op. cit.,* p. 26.

has become a real possibility. The experience of the development of the Cuban revolution has shown that representatives of the radical petty bourgeoisie, during the course of the development of an authentic people's revolution, are able to come to the position of the working class and socialism and become members of the ranks of active fighters for the socialist reconstruction of society. But, of course, there are possibilities and occasions for treason to the interests of the toilers, for a temporary retreat, for a departure from the further development of the revolution. However, the ultimate tendency is the transition to socialism by all peoples.[514]

Although advocating the Cuban path, Tiagunenko was careful to leave room for future backtracking from his position. He accordingly mentioned that there could be lapses in revolutionary advancement.

Soviet writers frequently cited the possibility of the African nations taking the non-capitalist path of development and Ivan Potekhin, while averring that the majority of African states have the prerequisites for taking the capitalist path, simultaneously maintained that these states also have the objective preconditions for taking the non-capitalist path.[515] Other Soviet analysts, such as Rybakov, asserted that all countries in tropical Africa, including the most backward, are capable of traversing it while Mirskii declared: "In present-day conditions any country irrespective of its development level can set foot on the road to socialism."[516] Nikita Khrushchev joined the stream of statements on this subject. In his Report on the 1961 Party Program, he asserted: "The seething

---

[514] Tiagunenko, "Tendentsii obshchestvennogo razvitiia osvobodivshikhsia stran v sovremennuiu epokhu," op. cit., p. 33.
[515] Potekhin, "Nekotorye problemy Afrikanistiki v svete reshenii XXII s' 'ezda KPSS," op. cit., p. 11. Also see Brutents, Protiv ideologii sovremennogo kolonializma, op. cit., p. 335. For discussions of the non-capitalist path see E. M. Zhukov, "Significant Factor of Our Times," op. cit., p. 18 and Potekhin, Ibid., p. 11.
[516] "The U.S.S.R. and the Developing Countries," op. cit., p. 10 and Mirskii, "The Proletariat and National Liberation," op. cit., p. 8.

underdeveloped countries of Asia, Africa and Latin America, pursuing to the end the national-liberation, anti-imperialist revolution, will be able to carry out the transition to socialism. In the present era, practically any country, irrespective of the level of its development, can take the path leading to socialism."[517]

In the Soviet view, the non-capitalist path is applicable not only to pre-capitalist countries but also to those which already have the rudiments of capitalist relations.[518] A. Sobolev even contended that countries with well-developed capitalist systems can take the non-capitalist path! However, he explained that "sufficient material and class preparation" must occur in these countries before they can build socialism.[519] Sobolev went on to write: "This transition, however, will not take place spontaneously, solely as the result of objective processes. The primary role in non-capitalist development is played by the subjective factor, i.e., by the activity of the revolutionary classes, by their correct policy."[520] According to the author, the non-capitalist path carries out the same social and material roles as capitalism but does it with greater rapidity and less pain.[521]

Soviet writers maintained that the non-capitalist path corresponds to the interests of the majority of people living in the recently liberated countries.[522] It was concomitantly claimed that *only* the non-capitalist path can satisfy the desires of the masses.[523] Those social groups which are purportedly pleased with this path are the working class, peasantry, petty bour-

---

[517] Khrushchev's Report on the Party Program, *Pravda*, October 19, 1961, p. 8.
[518] See V. Tiagunenko, "Aktual'nye voprosy nekapitalisticheskogo puti razvitiia," *Mirovaia Ekonomika i Mezhdunarodnye Otnosheniia*, No. 10, 1964, p. 14.
[519] Sobolev, *op. cit.*, p. 42.
[520] *Ibid.*, p. 42.
[521] *Ibid.*, p. 43.
[522] See Verin, *op. cit.*, p. 4.
[523] See Brutents, *Protiv ideologii sovremennogo kolonializma, op. cit.*, p. 332.

geoisie, and progressive intellingentsia.[524] Another theme was that the non-capitalist path would be impossible without the existence of the world socialist system.[525]

What are the prerequisites for taking the non-capitalist path? Soviet authors cited many: the bourgeoisie which promates capitalism must be weak or absent and the middle bourgeoisie must also not be numerous; the capitalist enterprises must belong to foreign firms rather than to native capitalists; the petty bourgeoisie must be similar to the working class and must not support capitalism; communal land tenure under which land cannot be bought or sold is desirable; a strong state sector of the economy is also advantageous; the working class should have a high degree of consciousness and organizational ability; and, of course, the powerful world socialist system, which enabled colonial areas to become independent, must play a significant role.[526]

Feudalism was not seen as an obstacle to the non-capitalist path and it was also affirmed that as industry develops in the new states, the proletariat will grow more rapidly than the bourgeoisie.[527] S. I. Bruk and N. N. Cheboksarov succinctly summed up the capabilities of a nation to take the non-capitalist path with the statement that where the national bourgeoisie is economically and politically strong, it is the chief force in the process of national consolidation but where it is weak or absent, conditions exist for the non-capitalist path.[528]

Alexander Dallin has correctly pointed out the paradoxical position taken by Soviet ideologists on the issue of the non-capitalist path. According to traditional Marxist theory and

---

[524] See Kim, "O gosudarstve natsional'noi demokratii," *op. cit.,* p. 2.
[525] See "The U.S.S.R. and the Developing Countries," *op. cit.,* p. 16 and Grishechkin, *op. cit.,* p. 7.
[526] See Grishechkin, *Ibid.,* p. 7 and Potekhin, *Afrika, 1956–1961, op. cit.,* pp. 143–144.
[527] Grishechkin, *Ibid.,* p. 7 and Potekhin, *Afrika, 1956–1961, op. cit.,* pp. 143–144.
[528] S. I. Bruk and N. N. Cheboksarov, "Sovremennyi etap natsional'nogo razvitiia narodov Azii i Afriki," *Sovetskaia Etnografiia,* No. 4, 1961, p. 78.

as advanced by contemporary Soviet analysts, the succession of historical stages is feudalism, capitalism, socialism, and communism. However, the advocates of the non-capitalist path asserted that the capitalist stage can be bypassed even though the base for socialist development has not yet been developed. Dallin wrote in regard to this concept: "The impotence of the national bourgeoisie and the existence of the village 'commune' in Africa were strong arguments for those who maintained that a non-capitalist path was open to all African states, however underdeveloped. Thus, in a peculiar application of what has been called the dialectics of backwardness, unreadiness for capitalism became equated with readiness for socialism."[529]

Soviet scholars realized that many countries were not yet capable of taking the socialist path and the non-capitalist path was therefore devised as an advance toward socialism which was not capitalistic. Usually, capitalism is the direct predecessor of socialism. S. Ogurtsov affirmed that the question of constructing socialism in the former colonial countries had to be subordinated to the possibilities of non-capitalist development, at least for the present. However, he was quick to point out that prospects for the immediate creation of socialist societies are becoming more favorable.[530]

G. Starushenko, writing in the September, 1962 issue of *Kommunist*, also discussed the non-capitalist path as an alternative to the immediate construction of socialism. He stated that many countries are not yet capable of the latter task and that the non-capitalist path is a step forward in their social development:

> The conditions for immediately carrying out revolutionary socialist transformations and for embarking on the socialist path have today not matured in all the countries. Not all countries have a sufficiently organized working class, a peasantry ready to accept the leadership of the working

[529] Alexander Dallin, "The Soviet Union: Political Activity," in Brzezinski, *op. cit.*, p. 19 footnote.
[530] Ogurtsov, *op. cit.*, p. 10.

class, and a Marxist-Leninist Party. Does this mean that in these countries social development must slow down or even come to a halt? Of course not. Revolutionary Marxists, having studied the special features and tendencies in the life of the young states, have established that they can have a progressive development along a non-capitalist path that will eventually lead to socialism.[531]

Soviet observers of the African scene contended that the non-capitalist path can be taken even in those countries in which the proletariat has not clearly developed as a class.[532] R. Avakov, speaking at the 1964 Moscow conference on under-developed areas, recognized the absence in tropical Africa of a well-formed proletariat and queried: "Is it necessary to postpone the struggle for transition to the non-capitalist path until the appearance of a proletariat and its maturing as a class? Cannot the peasants, led by the progressive intelligentsia and revolutionary democrats, reach this goal?"[533] African countries cited by Soviet writers as having embarked on the non-capitalist path are Ghana, Guinea, and Mali, while Algeria and the United Arab Republic were also considered to have taken steps in this direction.[534] In addition, this path was believed to be immediately relevant to the East African countries, particularly Kenya.[535]

Georgii Mirskii asserted that since the proletariat is weak and not very influential in many countries, the revolutionary democrats can lead these countries along the non-capitalist path.[536] These revolutionary democratic leaders usually come

---

[531] Starushenko, op. cit., p. 9.
[532] Grishechkin, op. cit., p. 9.
[533] "The U.S.S.R. and the Developing Countries," op. cit., p. 17.
[534] See L. Aleksandrovskaia, "Kooperativenoe dvizhenie," Aziia i Afrika Segodnia, No. 10 (October, 1963), pp. 16–17; "Soiuz sil sotsializma i natsional'no-osvoboditel'nogo dvizheniia," op. cit., p. 7; Tiagunenko, "Na gravnuiu revoliutsionnuiu magistral," op. cit., p. 3; and "Okonchatel'noe krushenie kolonializma neizbezhno," Pravda editorial, January 5, 1965, p. 1.
[535] Tomilin, "East Africa Chooses the Way," op. cit., p. 42.
[536] Georgii Mirskii, "O nekapitalisticheskom puti razvitiia byvshikh kolonii," Pravda, January 31, 1965, p. 5.

from the middle class or peasantry but they are influenced by the example of the socialist countries and can advance from capitalist to socialist ideology.[537] Mirskii emphasized that the leading role played by the revolutionary democrats in initiating the non-capitalist path of development for their countries in no way negates the role of vanguard in the building of socialism played by the proletariat. "The working class will exert an increasing, and in the end dominating, influence on the policy and ideology of the revolutionary democrats. It will thereby be fulfilling its historic mission."[538]

Nikita Khrushchev also recognized that the revolutionary democrats can lead their nations on the non-capitalist path. During the course of an interview on December 22, 1963, he welcomed the declarations of revolutionary democrats that they desired to build socialism and maintained that these people seek the non-capitalist path of development.[539] The national democratic state was seen as a suitable form for this transition but Khrushchev claimed that other forms of development are also possible.

Soviet analysts were quite pleased with the prospects for the non-capitalist path in Africa but K. Grishechkin pointed out some impediments to the adoption of this course of development.[540] He claimed that members of the native intelligentsia educated in capitalist countries have accepted bourgeois ideology and many of them live luxuriously and are divorced from the people. Another factor to be considered is the backwardness of the working class, while yet another is the incorrect view of socialism held by many African leaders.

In a section entitled "The Historical Necessity of the Transition From Capitalism to Socialism," the 1961 *Program of the Communist Party of the Soviet Union* discussed the

---

[537] Mirskii, "The Proletariat and National Liberation," *op. cit.*, p. 9.
[538] *Ibid.*, p. 9.
[539] "Replies of N. S. Khrushchev to Questions of Editors of Ghanaian Times, Alger Républicain, Le Peuple and Botataung," *op. cit.*, p. 13.
[540] Grishechkin, *op. cit.*, p. 8.

role of the working class and that of the communist party as its vanguard, during the transition from capitalism to socialism. Apparently the transition to socialism, bypassing capitalism, is of quite a different nature, as the section of the *Program* entitled "The National-Liberation Movement" makes clear.[541] As explained above, Soviet scholars believed that non-proletarian elements could lead their countries along the non-capitalist path and that this path could be taken despite the weakness of the working class. However, in regard to the transition from capitalism to socialism, the analysis was quite different as the role of the working class was emphasized. The *Program* explicitly stated: "The dictatorship of the proletariat and the leadership of the Marxist-Leninist party are indispensable conditions for the triumph of the socialist revolution and the building of socialism."[542] It later went on to declare:

> Soviet experience has fully borne out the Marxist-Leninist theory that the Communist Party plays a decisive role in the formation and development of socialist society. Only a party that steadfastly pursues a class, proletarian policy, and is equipped with progressive revolutionary theory, only a party solidly united and closely linked with the masses, can organize the people and lead them to the victory of socialism.[543]

What has led Soviet theorists to formulate such divergent analyses of the different transitions to socialism? The answer must lie in the fact that capitalist countries have large proletariats, and are therefore capable of fostering powerful communist parties, while the underdeveloped countries of Africa, setting out on the non-capitalist path of development, have weak proletariats and therefore present unfavorable conditions for the growth of influential communist parties. Realizing the existence of this situation, but at the same time hoping

---

[541] See *Program of the Communist Party of the Soviet Union, op. cit.,* pp. 42–48.
[542] *Ibid.,* p. 11.
[543] *Ibid.,* p. 19.

for the advent of socialism in Africa, Soviet observers had to devise blueprints for the development of socialism in Africa under non-proletarian leadership. This was a rather realistic approach since waiting for the crystallization of the proletariat as a class and the setting up of a dictatorship by this class could take many decades. It was also perceptive since numerous African leaders desire socialism, though it is not of the "scientific" variety, and this fact seriously weakens the old Stalinist arguments that only the working class can truly advocate and work toward the socialization of society.

Soviet writers seemed to be enmeshed in a terminological jumble of concepts related to various transitions to socialism. They discussed the non-capitalist path, the bypassing of capitalism on the Mongolian and Central Asian models, the national democratic state, and the building of socialism (as in Cuba). The lines of reasoning were often confusing and different policies were intermingled with the result that the sequence of the phases leading up to socialism was frequently blurred and statements by analysts were sometimes contradictory.

Such a problem of clarity was evident in regard to the question of a non-capitalist path. This form of development was usually interpreted as a preliminary to the construction of socialism and Georgii Mirskii asserted: "The reforms now being carried out in these countries are non-capitalist measures. This is still not socialism, but it is the primary stage of the transition to socialist construction."[544] The analysis proffered by Mikhail Kremnev, though a little more cautious, was in a similar vein: "The choice of the non-capitalist way does not necessarily mean choosing the socialist way. Nevertheless, socio-economic changes of a non-capitalist order pave the way to socialism, especially in countries where capitalist relations are not yet deeply rooted."[545] However, disagreement among

---

[544] "The U.S.S.R. and the Developing Countries," *op. cit.*, p. 16.
[545] Kremnev, *op. cit.*, p. 75.

Soviet writers was evident as N. G. Pospelova contended that the non-capitalist path is the socialist path.[546]

Since Soviet theorists condemned African socialism but still hoped for the institution of scientific socialism in Africa, they advocated either the bypassing of the capitalist stage of development or the formation of national democratic states. They often became lost in their own ideological morass as an article by G. F. Kim amply illustrates.[547] Kim claimed that when the working class gains hegemony over the national-liberation movement, the national democratic state gives way to the next stage of development, the non-capitalist. The latter is the path of constructing socialism. Kim seemed to be stating that the non-capitalist path follows the institution of a national democratic state, which is rather ridiculous since Soviet writers cited countries which have taken the non-capitalist path but did not cite any countries as having passed through the national democratic stage (unless Cuba is to be considered under this category). Kim's confusion appears to have stemmed from his view that the non-capitalist path and the building of socialism are one and the same thing but this runs counter to the general Soviet position on this issue, unless Pospelova's assertion is given some weight.

Soviet writers stressed the purported ideological evolution of the African leaders toward scientific socialism and hoped that the African nationalist parties would eventually become parties of the Marxist-Leninist type. However, the formation of communist parties in the African countries was not ignored since these parties provided an alternative to the radicalization of the nationalist parties. In the traditional communist

---

[546] N. G. Pospelova, "Ekonomicheskie, klassovye i politicheskie osnovy gosudarstva natsional'noi demokratii i ego funktsii," *Vestnik Leningradskogo Universiteta* (Seriia Ekonomiki, Filosofii i Prava), No. 23, 1962, p. 135. There also appeared to be disagreement over whether "non-capitalist development" is the same as "building socialism." See the article by Ra'anan, *op. cit.*

[547] Kim, "O gosudarstve natsional'noi demokratii," *op. cit.*, p. 5.

style, African communists were to attempt to increase their influence within the nationalist parties but, at the same time, preserve their own organizational base and develop it as a rival source of strength. This was particularly true in the moderate African states and less evident in the leftist states, such as Ghana, Guinea, and Mali, in which communist parties were not active. Although many African communist parties are weak and have a rather nebulous existence, there seem to be such parties in Somalia, Madagascar (Malagasy Republic), Zambia, Zanzibar, Basutoland, Algeria, Morocco, Tunisia, Sudan, Nigeria, Republic of South Africa, United Arab Republic and Libya.[548] A communist party has recently been created in Senegal and it appears to be aligned with Communist China in its internecine struggle with the Soviet Union.[549] Mention should also be made of the illegal Parti Africain de l'Indépendance in Senegal, which is in fact a Marxist-Leninist party adhering to the Moscow line.

Many African regimes persecuted the communists in their nations since they saw them as agents working against the existing order. Such actions did not greatly influence Soviet state relations with these countries because the Soviet Union sought cordial ties with most African leaders but this statement by Georgii Mirskii shows the Soviet concern about such persecution of communists: "In certain liberated countries, some suggest that socialism can be built without socialists, and moreover, by eliminating and even persecuting those who are most interested in socialist development. It is impossible to combine socialism with anti-Communism. The goals of the

---

[548] See William Zartman, "Communism in Africa," in Jeanne Kirkpatrick, ed., *The Strategy of Deception: A Study in World-Wide Communist Tactics* (New York, Farrar, Straus, 1963), pp. 165–192; Walter Kolarz, "The Impact of Communism in West Africa," *International Affairs* (London), Vol. XXXVIII, No. 2 (April, 1962), pp. 156–169; Dan Kurzman, *Subversion of the Innocents* (New York, Random House, 1963); and U.S. Department of State, Bureau of Research and Intelligence, *World Strength of Communist Party Organizations* (Washington, 1964).
[549] See *Africa Report*, Vol. X, No. 7 (July, 1965), p. 28.

Communists are inseparable from the interests of the people's masses."[550]

The Soviet Union simultaneously carried out two seemingly contradictory tasks. The first was an attempt to establish bonds of friendship with the African leaders for the purposes of influencing the course of development taken in the African countries and of securing the African nations as allies on many issues of Cold War politics. The second was an effort to increase communist strength in the African nations and to steer the African nationalist parties toward the adoption of Marxism-Leninism. This latter task often brought the communists into rivalry with nationalist leaders. Although communist parties were organized in some countries, the idea of overthrowing African governments seems to have been subordinated to the effort to increase influence within the existing state structures. Soviet writers did not stress the revolutionary potential of the African communist parties and instead cited the possibility of the African nationalist parties becoming Marxist-Leninist parties. Discussing the programs of African parties which express the interests of the masses, Mikhail Kremnev wrote: "These programs, of course, do not rest on a Marxist foundation. But one can envisage the possibility of the influence of the growing working class increasing in these parties and turning them into mass parties of the Marxist-Leninist type."[551]

A leftist phase in the Soviet analysis of events in Africa began in 1959 and was accompanied by a Soviet attempt to foster the creation of new communist parties in Africa and to strengthen those communist parties which were already in operation.[552] *The African Communist,* a generally pro-Moscow journal published in London, was significantly founded in the fall of 1959 and was intended to be the organ of the

[550] Mirskii, "Creative Marxism and Problems of the National-Liberation Movement," *op. cit.,* p. 18.
[551] Kremnev, *op. cit.,* p. 76.
[552] Richard Lowenthal has cited this fact in "The Sino-Soviet Split and its Repercussions in Africa," in Hamrell, *op. cit.,* p. 137.

Communist Party of South Africa, although its scope actually encompassed events throughout Africa. Richard Lowenthal correctly pointed out that the articles in this journal are accepted as authoritative by the communist press outside of Africa and he also pictured *The African Communist* as an instrument of the Soviet drive to help organize the communists on the African continent:

> Since the first appearance of the journal The African Communist—officially published from London on behalf of the South African Communist Party, and in fact edited as a policy-making organ and a 'collective organizer' for the whole of Tropical Africa—there has been a systematic, Soviet-directed campaign to push the development of Communist parties in Africa.[553]

Thus communist parties in Africa are still quite weak but are increasing in number and strength. Their development is being backed by Moscow despite the facts that the Soviet Union values its friendship with many African governments and Soviet political observers proffer the view that the African socialist leaders may indeed become Marxist-Leninists. As William Griffith has explained, communist support in the underdeveloped nations usually comes from the newly-educated elites who are unable to find a positive role for their talents and who feel alienated from the people in their homelands because of their higher level of education and their contacts with outside cultural and material standards.[554] Support also comes from the landless peasantry and the embryonic working class.

MODELS FOR THE BYPASSING OF CAPITALISM

Soviet theorists discussed the non-capitalist path of development and frequently pointed to the examples set by Mon-

---

553 *Ibid.*, p. 137. Also see Richard Lowenthal, "China," in Brzezinski, *op. cit.*, p. 188.
554 William Griffith, "Communist Polycentrism and the Underdeveloped Areas," in London, *op. cit.*, p. 275.

golia and by some of the peoples of the Soviet Union. Capitalism did not take root in the underdeveloped countries, as had been expected by the ideologists of the Stalinist period, and Soviet scholars saw the possibility of proceeding directly to socialism by skipping the capitalist stage. In June, 1962, a special conference was held on this very subject.[555] This concept of historical evolution was considered to be particularly relevant to sub-Saharan Africa and G. F. Kim explained that in this region, a "national working class" has not yet been formed or is still in the process of crystallization.[556]

Ivan Potekhin led the Soviet political analysts in contending that the bypassing of capitalism in no way runs counter to the views of Karl Marx. He claimed that it is not essential for all peoples to pass through every historical stage and then went on to justify his view in terms of the thinking of Marx and Engels:

> Marx and Engels maintained that there is a definite sequence of socio-economic formations, and that is is impossible for feudal society to succeed capitalism. But nowhere and never did they write that all peoples must inevitably pass through all the stages of historical development. The works of Marx and Engels do not present a detailed and fully elaborated theory of the non-capitalist development of backward nations to socialism without passing through capitalism. Such a possibility did not yet exist in their lifetime and so there was no practical reason for such a theory.[557]

Actually, Potekhin's justification was based upon what Marx and Engels did not state, rather than upon what they did. However Potekhin asserted elsewhere that Marx and Engels recognized the possibility of peoples bypassing certain

---

[555] See Z. Osmanova, "Vsesoiuznaia nauchnaia sessiia 'Zakononernosti Perekhoda Ranee Otstalykh Narodov k Sotsializmu i Kommunizmu, Minuia Stadiiu Kapitalizma'," *Narody Azii i Afriki,* No. 1, 1963, pp. 237–240.
[556] See Kim, "Soiuz rabochego klassa i krest'ianstva v nationsal'noosvoboditel'nykh revoliutsiakh," *op. cit.,* p. 5.
[557] Potekhin, *Africa: Ways of Development, op. cit.,* p. 39.

historical stages. They did not go into much detail since conditions for such a path did not exist during their lifetime and the theory of bypassing stages was left for Lenin to develop.[558]

Another view held by Soviet writers was that countries which have already started to progress along the capitalist path need not pass through all aspects of the capitalist stage.[559] The non-capitalist path is open even to those nations which have rudimentary capitalist relations. This concept appears to contradict completely one of the basic tenets of Karl Marx: "No social order ever disappears before all the productive forces for which there is room in it have been developed. . . ."[560] Potekhin attempted to interpret this statement by Marx in a way which was in accordance with his own views but he only produced a futile and pointless exercise in terminological dexterity.[561]

While maintaining that capitalism can be bypassed, Soviet theorists simultaneously claimed that the socialist stage may not be avoided! This argument was certainly at variance with Soviet pronouncements on the non-capitalist path and was usually used in open or veiled attacks upon the Chinese, who hoped to accelerate their progress toward communism through the "Great Leap Forward." In his *Afrika smotrit v budushchee*, Potekhin affirmed that according to scientific socialism, socialism inescapably comes right after capitalism, which was another way of stating that socialism cannot be bypassed.[562] At the Twenty-first Congress of the C.P.S.U., Nikita Khrushchev was quite explicit on this point: "First, the transition

---

[558] Potekhin, "On 'African Socialism'," *op. cit.,* p. 72. For a discussion of Lenin's contribution to the subject of bypassing capitalism, see Gene Overstreet, "Soviet and Indian Communist Policy in India, 1935–1952," doctoral dissertation, Columbia University, 1959, pp. 31–32.
[559] See Mirskii and Tiagunenko, *op. cit.,* p. 31.
[560] *A Contribution to the Critique of Political Economy,* in Feuer, *op. cit.,* p. 44.
[561] Potekhin, *Africa: Ways of Development, op. cit.,* p. 37.
[562] Potekhin, *Afrika smotrit v budushchee, op. cit.,* p. 13.

from the socialist stage of development to the higher phase is a logical historical process that one cannot arbitrarily violate or bypass. The Marxist-Leninist parties consider the building of communist society to be their ultimate goal. But society cannot leap from capitalism to communism, skipping the socialist stage of development."[563]

Soviet authors therefore twisted their theories to fit in with the courses of development they desired to see. Capitalism, which is a system alien to Marxist-Leninists, may be bypassed but socialism, considered to be a progressive stage, may not. Reconciling these two views would have been quite a chore so it was not attempted.

The Soviet emphasis upon skipping capitalism began at least as early as the beginning of 1956. D. Tumur-Ochir, writing in *Voprosii Folosofii,* asserted: "The experience of the development of the peoples of the U.S.S.R. and M.N.R. uniquely shows the peoples of the colonial and dependent countries the true path to the liquidation of imperialistic and feudal oppression, to the overcoming of their age-old backwardness and to the construction of socialism, bypassing capitalism."[564] However, the 1960 edition of *Fundamentals of Marxism-Leninism* did not contain a section included in the 1963 edition entitled, "Immediate Prospects of Historical Development of the Countries Liberated From Colonial Oppression." This section discussed the bypassing of capitalism and the role of state capitalism in the underdeveloped areas.

As seen by Soviet writers, the bypassing of capitalism is linked with the victory of the proletariat in the advanced countries, such as the U.S.S.R., and with the aid given to the underdeveloped countries by this victorious proletariat.[565]

[563] N. S. Khrushchev, "Speech to Twenty-first Congress," *Pravda,* January 28, 1959, (see *CDSP,* Vol. XI, No. 5, March 11, 1959, p. 13).
[564] D. Tumur-Ochir, "O nekapitalisticheskom puti razvitiia otstalykh stran k sotsializmu," *Voprosy Filosofii,* No. 1, 1956, p. 62. M.N.R. is the Mongolian People's Republic.
[565] See Tiagunenko, "Aktual'nye voprosy nekapitalisticheskogo puti razvitiia," *Mirovaia Ekonomika i Mezhdunarodnye Otnosheniia,* No. 10, 1964, p. 13.

The nations of Asia and Africa can proceed toward socialism even though they do not have a developed working class because, according to the internationalization of the class conflict, the proletariat of the socialist countries can act as an international vanguard. It was frequently affirmed that Mongolia advanced toward socialism without being led by its weak working class because it allied with the victorious proletariat of the U.S.S.R.[566]

Soviet authors contended that various peoples of the Soviet Union proceeded to socialism without having first passed through the capitalist stage and they took pride in their assertion that different areas of the U.S.S.R., despite their contrasting levels of development, were able to arrive at socialism virtually simultaneously.[567] They also pointed out that all nationalities did not bypass capitalism by the same means.[568] Furthermore, it was contended that some peoples advanced to socialism immediately from their primitive-communal structure.[569]

The experience of the Kazakh Republic was often cited by Soviet analysts as an example of the bypassing of capitalism. M. S. Dzhunusov wrote an entire book on the subject and he stated that the path taken in the Kazakh Republic could serve as a guide for the peoples of Asia and Africa.[570] He also maintained:

Affirming the program of struggle for the transition of countries with underdeveloped economic relations to socialism without passing through the whole cycle of capitalist development, the communist parties of these countries take into consideration, above all, the instructive experience of

[566] See Sobolev, op. cit., p. 46. Also see above, pp. 171–174.
[567] See K. Ivanov, "The National-Liberation Movement and Non-Capitalist Path of Development," part two, International Affairs, No. 12, 1964, p. 15.
[568] Ibid., p. 12.
[569] Potekhin, Afrika smotrit v budushchee, op. cit., pp. 25–26.
[570] M. S. Dzhunusov, O zakonomernostiakh perekhoda narodov ranee otstalykh stran k sotsializmu (Alma-Ata, Izdatel'stvo Akademii Nauk Kazakhskoi SSR, 1961), p. 225.

the peoples of the Soviet East, who were the first in the history of the world to have taken the non-capitalist path of development to socialism.[571]

The peoples of the northern regions of the Soviet Union were also pointed to as having proceeded to socialism from their primitive level of development. V. Uvachan explained that prior to 1917, the Northern minorities had a social structure intermediary between class society and primitive tribalism. The tribal system was in the process of disintegration and the tribe was losing its function as the basic social grouping.[572] Uvachan later hailed the exemplary role of the Northern peoples:

> The change-over to socialism, bypassing capitalism, is a great historical feat, one that was made possible by the October Revolution which abolished colonial oppression and proclaimed the principles of equality and fraternity of all peoples. . . . There are still many primitive peoples in the world. The experience gained in the Soviet Union in liquidating the economic and cultural backwardness of the Northern minorities may thus be of interest.[573]

Soviet writers singled out the non-capitalist path taken by Mongolia as the prime example of the dictum that backward countries can proceed to socialism with the help of the victorious proletariat of the advanced countries.[574] Also contributing substantially to the analysis of this historic process was Yumjagiyn Tsedenbal, Premier of the Mongolian People's Republic and First Secretary of the People's Revolutionary Party. In reference to his country's building of socialism, he stated:

---

[571] *Ibid.,* p. 5.
[572] V. Uvachan, *Peoples of the Soviet North* (Moscow, Foreign Languages Publishing House, 1958), p. 18.
[573] *Ibid.,* p. 125.
[574] See B. Shirendyb, "Uspekhi stroitel'stva sotsializma v Mongol'skoi Narodnoi Respublike," *Sovetskoe Vostokovedenie,* No. 5, 1958, p. 52 and N. Shimmel, "From Feudalism to Socialism," *New Times,* No. 28 (July 12, 1961), pp. 9–10.

The contact between the working people of Russia and Mongolia, which steadily became wider and stronger after the October Revolution, was of decisive help in this respect. This was, in fact, a class alliance between the victorious working class of Russia and the Mongolian arats (peasants), which ensured the victory of our revolution, and thanks to which we were able to step out successfully along the road to socialism without going through the capitalist stage.[575]

Tsedenbal maintained that Mongolia was primarily a backward country in which stock-breeding was the basic livelihood and in which the working class had not yet formed. The People's Revolutionary Party was exclusively a peasant organization fighting for national liberation but it came into close contact with the international communist movement and assimilated the teachings of Marxism-Leninism. The M.P.R.P. (Mongolian People's Revolutionary Party) therefore became armed with a working class ideology but Lenin advised it not immediately to become a communist party because certain economic, cultural, and national tasks had to be accomplished prior to taking this step. The M.P.R.P. came to represent the interests of the working people. In the words of Tsedenbal: "Our experience has shown that a political party of the working people guided by Marxist-Leninist teachings, can, in certain conditions, successfully lead the struggle in an underdeveloped country where the working class has not yet emerged or where, if it has, it is numerically small."[576] There appears to be a contradiction since how can there be a political party of the working people if a working class does not exist? However, in fairness to Tsedenbal, he seems to be maintaining that there may be some working people organized as a political party despite the fact that these people do not constitute a large or cohesive class force.

According to Tsedenbal, Mongolia became a "people's republic" in 1924 and, at that time, the Third Congress of the

---

[575] Y. Tsedenbal, "From Feudalism to Socialism," *World Marxist Review*, Vol. IV, No. 3 (March, 1961), p. 12.
[576] *Ibid.*, p. 13.

People's Revolutionary Party "decided to build a socialist society without going through capitalism, that is, to by-pass a whole historical epoch in its social development."[577] The party created an anti-imperialist national front but preserved its complete operational independence.[578]

The Mongolian experience discussed by Tsedenbal was not simply historical reminiscing but was intended as an instructional guide for the peoples of Asia and Africa, a point which was made quite clear by the author. He mentioned that some Asian and African nations had already taken steps along the non-capitalist path and then asserted: "After throwing off the yoke of foreign oppression, these countries face the task of getting rid of the same social contradictions as did Mongolia after the victory of the revolution—the contradictions between the national interests and international imperialism; between the peasants and the feudal elements, etc."[579] Tsedenbal maintained that these countries must concentrate on the struggle against imperialism and create national fronts based upon an alliance of the workers and peasants.

Tsedenbal's advice to the progressive forces in the Asian and African nations contained three fundamental tactical points: form a national anti-imperialist front, maintain organizational independence and freedom of action, and do not establish communist parties too soon. Since these views appeared in *New Times* and *World Marxist Review* and since Tsedenbal was closely aligned with the Khrushchevian leadership of the Soviet Union, it may be assumed that his comments were looked upon favorably by Soviet political analysts and that these analysts concurred in his recommendations.

It should be noted that in addition to citing certain peoples of the Soviet Union and the experience of the Mongolian people in bypassing capitalism, Soviet writers also mentioned

---

[577] Y. Tsedenbal, "Mongolia's Path," *New Times*, No. 47 (November 25, 1964), p. 9.
[578] Tsedenbal, "From Feudalism to Socialism," *op. cit.*, p. 13.
[579] *Ibid.*, p. 17.

that some peoples in China, North Korea, and North Vietnam traversed the non-capitalist path of development.[580]

THE NATIONAL DEMOCRATIC STATE AS A TRANSITION TO SOCIALISM

The concept of a national democratic state was launched at the conference of eighty-one communist parties held in Moscow in November–December, 1960 but was foreshadowed in Zhukov's significant *Pravda* article of August 26, 1960. Zhukov asserted that the cooperation of the workers, peasants, intelligentsia, and certain sections of the bourgeoisie will be possible for a prolonged period and then used the identical line of reasoning later to be used in the *81 Party Statement*:

> The struggle for the solving of all-national democratic tasks, the implementation of land reform, the creation and strengthening of national industry, the liquidation of all kinds of remnants and residues of feudalism, the unrestricted annulment of all fettering agreements which at one time were forced upon the countries by the colonialists, and a foreign policy of peace and nonparticipation in military blocs created by the imperialist powers—this is the positive platform which can and in fact does unite the broadest strata of the population in the former colonial and semi-colonial countries.[581]

Not only did Zhukov's pronouncement precede the inception of the doctrine of national democracy by at least three months, it also included the phrase "all-national democratic tasks."

Ivan Potekhin's book, *Formirovanie natsional'noi obshchnosti iuzhnoafrikanskikh bantu,* was published in 1955

---

[580] See S. N. Rostovskii, "Leninskoe uchenie o nekapitalisticheskom puti razvitiia," *Problemy Vostokovedeniia*, No. 2, 1960, p. 27 and M. G. Kirichenko, "O nezavisimom gosudarstve natsional'noi demokratii," *Kommunist*, No. 11 (November, 1961), p. 108.

[581] Zhukov, "Significant Factor of Our Times," *op. cit.*, pp. 3–4.

and at least three Western specialists on Soviet attitudes toward Africa have claimed that Potekhin introduced the concept of national democracy in this work.[582] These writers appear to have made a mistake in interpretation for there is evidence that Potekhin did not conceive of national democracy at this early date.

The statement cited by other authors, and which has led to confusion on the issue of national democracy, is the following:

> The general historical situation is now such that people's democracy (narodnaia demokratiia), which guarantees the leading role of the proletariat and opens to the country the path to socialism, is becoming the political form of the liberation of peoples under the yoke of imperialism. And this means that with the liquidation of the colonial regime in such countries, there will be formed not a bourgeois, but a socialist nation. The rate of formation of the socialist nation will be determined by the rate of transition of the democratic revolution into a socialist one.[583]

Potekhin was discussing people's democracy (narodnaia demokratiia), such as those in Eastern Europe, not national democracy (natsional'naia demokratiia) but the translations of this statement made by Holdsworth and Lewis maintained that "narodnaia demokratiia" was actually national democracy. An analysis of Potekhin's views contained within this statement also reveal that he could not possibly be thinking of national democracy. He claimed that "narodnaia demokratiia" "guarantees the leading role of the proletariat" and that a socialist nation will be created following "the liquidation of the colonial regime." Both of these tenets are incon-

---

[582] Mary Holdsworth, *Soviet African Studies, 1918–1959; An Annotated Bibliography*, Vol. II, *op. cit.*, p. 57; Lewis, *op. cit.*, p. 377; and William Shinn, Jr., "The National Democratic State: A Communist Program for Less-Developed Areas," *World Politics*, Vol. XV, No. 3 (April, 1963), p. 384 footnote.

[583] Ivan Potekhin, *Formirovanie natsional'noi obschchnosti iuzhno-afrikanskikh bantu* (Moscow, 1955), pp. 12–13.

sistent with the concept of national democracy, as expressed in 1960, but are certainly pertinent to the path of people's democracy.

The 81 Party Statement, issued in December, 1960, introduced the concept of national democracy. It contended that an alliance of the working class and peasantry is the basis of a broad national front and then defined national democracies as those nations which uphold their political and economic independence, fight imperialism and military blocs, do not permit military bases on their territory, fight imperialist capital, reject dictatorship and despotic forms of government, and give their people democratic rights, such as the right to establish political parties.[584] This new concept was designed to meet changing circumstances in the underdeveloped countries and Nikita Khrushchev, speaking on January 6, 1961, made this point clear: "The Communists are revolutionaries and it would be bad if they failed to see the new opportunities that are arising and did not find new methods and forms that lead most surely to the achievement of the established goal."[585]

The concept of national democracy has been consistently supported by Soviet theorists while Chinese writers have been rather cool toward it. In fact, Pavlov and Red'ko claimed that the Chinese reject this concept.[586] Therefore, it seems improbable that the idea of national democracy was devised as a compromise between the Soviet and Chinese positions on developments in the underdeveloped nations and it is much more likely that the concept was introduced by Soviet ideologists as a reaction to new events in Asia and Africa. Richard Lowenthal has advanced this latter view:

But it is contended here that the concept of 'national democracy' was devised primarily not as a reaction to the

---

[584] Jacobs, *op. cit.,* p. 32.
[585] N. S. Khrushchev, "Za novye pobedy mirovogo kommunisticheskogo dvizheniia," *Kommunist,* No. 1 (January, 1961), p. 27.
[586] V. I. Pavlov and I. B. Red'ko, "Leninskii soiuz mirovogo sotsializma s natsional'no-osvoboditel'nym dvizheniem," *Narody Azii i Afriki,* No. 5, 1963, p. 21.

Sino-Soviet dispute, but in response to the real problems facing Soviet and communist strategy in the ex-colonial nations, and that some new strategic formula of this kind would have had to be invented by the Soviet leaders at the present stage, even if no dispute with Peking existed, because the classical communist two-stage theory of the revolution in colonial and ex-colonial countries had proved obviously inadequate to the situation in the growing number of former colonies emerging into independence; . . .[587]

A national democratic state represents the broad masses of the population and is a coalition of patriotic forces. It is a united front of the working class, peasantry, democratic intelligentsia, and the anti-imperialist strata of the national bourgeoisie. The national bourgeoisie is just one of the groups involved in creating this state and does not assume a role of leadership. Countries on the road to national democracy are neither bourgeois nor socialist but are of a transitional type and may be called democratic nations.[588]

A national democratic state carries out the prerequisites for the transition to socialism and is not itself a socialist state. Soviet writers claimed that national democracy leads to the non-capitalist path but how this form of transition differs from the non-capitalist path which does not evolve out of national democracy was not made clear. As was frequently pointed out in Soviet articles and books, the countries of sub-Saharan Africa were considered to be capable of taking the non-capitalist path.[589] If this was so, what was the purpose of a national democratic state? It was to serve as the prime model for underdeveloped countries but it did not exclude the possibility that some nations will take the non-capitalist path outlined earlier, although not too clearly, in Soviet writings. Soviet analysts were trying to outline different transi-

---

[587] Richard Lowenthal, "On National Democracy: Its Function in Communist Policy," *Survey*, No. 47 (April, 1963), p. 120.
[588] Bruk and Cheboksarov, *op. cit.*, p. 77. Also see Starushenko, *op. cit.*, p. 15; Li, *op. cit.*, p. 12; and Kim, "O gosudarstve natsional'noi demokratii," *op. cit.*, pp. 2–3.
[589] See above, pp. 189–190.

tions to socialism without formulating a prescribed rigid pattern.

The concept of a national democratic state was put forth just prior to Cuba's affirmation that its revolution was of a socialist nature and developments in Cuba may have influenced Soviet theorists in the formulation of this concept. B. Ponomarev, writing in the May, 1961 issue of *Kommunist,* asserted: "The idea of the national-democratic state advanced by the Communist and Workers' Parties is not the fruit of ivory-tower meditations; life itself has given rise to it."[590] Without specifically stating that the concept was based upon the Cuban experience, Ponomarev strongly implied that this was the case. He declared: "Major revolutionary transformations have taken place in Cuba in two years. . . . The Cuban people have accomplished the tasks of the agrarian and anti-imperialist, democratic and national-liberation stage of the revolution and are going further."[591] He then cited Ghana, Guinea, Mali, and Indonesia for their struggle against imperialism.

Soviet writers usually did not label Cuba a national democratic state but references to Cuba in articles dealing with the national democratic state were abundant. For example, Pavlov and Red'ko maintained that the Cuban revolution has shown that only a revolutionary democratic dictatorship led by the working class can bring the national-liberation revolution to completion. They asserted that in Cuba, the conservative bourgeois elements were removed from the government and replaced by representatives of the proletariat, radical petty bourgeoisie, and poor peasantry.[592] V. Korionov also pointed to the Cuban revolution as an example for other countries. He wrote:

---

[590] B. Ponomarev, "Concerning the National Democratic State," *Kommunist,* No. 8 (May, 1961). See *CDSP,* Vol. XIII, No. 22 (June 28, 1961), p. 5.

[591] *Ibid.,* p. 3.

[592] V. I. Pavlov and I. B. Red'ko, "Gosudarstvo natsional'noi demokratii i perekhod k nekapitalisticheskomu razvitiiu," *Narody Azii i Afriki,* No. 1, 1961, pp. 38–39.

The example of Cuba teaches that if the Cuban people were able to realize the anti-imperialist, anti-feudal revolution and successfully defend it from all attacks by the American imperialists, then any other people is in a position to do it. The possibility in Latin America of a transition from the anti-imperialist revolution to the revolution resolving socialist tasks, formerly was only theoretical. Revolutionary Cuba showed that this possibility could be translated into action. The successful development of the Cuban revolution is new eloquent evidence of the deep qualitative changes occuring in our time in the huge world of economically underdeveloped countries.[593]

William Shinn has described Cuba's reluctance to accept the label of national democracy and this is probably the reason why Cuba was not cited as a national democratic state in most Soviet writings.[594] However, there is one specific reference to Cuba in this regard, made by G. F. Kim in the October, 1962 issue of *Aziia i Afrika Segodnia*: "The experiences of the Cuban revolution show that here, the national democratic stage was a short one. After the withdrawal from the government of the conservative bourgeois elements and the strengthening in it of revolutionary Maxist forces, the revolution transcended the limits of national democracy to become a socialist revolution."[595]

S. Ogurtsov analyzed the national democratic state and seemed to imply that this type of state should be created as a stalling tactic until such time as the working class is able to take over the leadership of the nation:

But since there is no proletariat in certain countries of Asia and Africa, or it has not yet become strong and does not have its own political organization capable of leading the masses, the representatives of other revolutionary-democratic circles can assume the mission of leaders for the limited time needed for the proletariat to mature. In

[593] V. Korionov, "Velichaishaia sila sovremennosti," *Kommunist,* No. 14 (September, 1961), p. 44.
[594] Shinn, *op. cit.*, p. 383.
[595] Kim, "O gosudarstve natsional'noi demokratii," *op. cit.*, p. 5.

present-day conditions in many of the underdeveloped countries, the task of the working class consists not in securing a guiding role for itself, for which it is not yet ready, but in winning allies, in rallying the entire people around itself. Only after this can it become the predominant force and complete the historical process of development of society under its guidance.[596]

The author also warned that the national democratic state does not always lead to a non-capitalist path of development.

Soviet spokesmen believed that the concept of a national democratic state is applicable to the sub-Saharan nations of Africa and Anastas Mikoyan asserted that the Guinean people are "building their national democratic state."[597] However, they were quick to point out that the national democratic stage is not inevitable. Pavlov and Red'ko maintained that when the national bourgeoisie refuses to join the progressive forces and instead compromises with imperialism and feudalism, the working class and its party (the authors did not specify that it must be a communist party) can remove the bourgeoisie from power and establish a people's democracy. It was also considered possible that a national democracy may evolve into a people's democracy through peaceful means.[598] In addition, forms of transition to the non-capitalist path, other than national democracy, were deemed to be conceivable by Soviet writers: "It is not impossible, indeed it is very probable, that the revolutionary creativity of the masses will put forward other state forms, other methods of solving the tasks of the transition period. But it is not possible to forecast them in advance."[599] This flexible approach is also evident in an article by A. Sobolev, who emphasized the importance

---

[596] Ogurtsov, op. cit., p. 11.
[597] Mikoyan speech, Pravda, January 12, 1962, p. 5. For discussions of the applicability of national democracy to Africa, see Grishechkin, op. cit., p. 7 and Verin, op. cit, p. 140.
[598] Pavlov and Red'ko, "Gosudarstvo natsional'noi demokratii i perekhod k nekapitalisticheskomu razvitiiu," op. cit., pp. 39–40.
[599] Tiagunenko, "Na glavnuiu revoliutsionnuiu magistral," op. cit., p. 3.

of national peculiarities: "National democracy will be translated into the language of each country and will emerge on the historical scene in a distinctive national garb."[600]

The idea of national democracy modified the concept of the two-stage revolution as the bourgeois-democratic and socialist phases became closely connected and rather indistinguishable. It also recognized the importance of nationalism in the underdeveloped areas of the world and the weakness of communism, and of the working class, in these regions. Since the current African leadership was considered to be an integral part of the proposed national democratic states, it would not have cause to be alienated by the introduction of this concept.

THE ROLE OF STATE CAPITALISM

Soviet analysts believed that state capitalism in the underdeveloped nations of Asia and Africa may play a progressive role but also warned that it could be used by ruling elites for their own interests. Everything depends upon the specific situation: "In the final analysis, the nature of the state sector depends on the correlation of class forces in the given country and is determined by the nature of the regime and the attitude of the ruling circles toward the paths of historical development, as well as by the foreign policy orientation of the governments."[601] This statement by Avakov and Andreasian sums up the Soviet position on this issue and is particularly revealing in that it considers the foreign policy orientation of a government to be a factor in the determination of that government's program of state capitalism. The authors explained that those countries which seek economic independence, and therefore receive the help of the socialist camp, have state sectors which are anti-imperialist. The state

---

[600] Sobolev, *op. cit.,* p. 43.
[601] Avakov and Andreasian, *op. cit.,* p. 9.

sector was deemed most progressive in countries like Ghana, Guinea, and Mali, where class and political forces favored a non-capitalist path of development.

The 1963 edition of *Fundamentals of Marxism-Leninism* maintained that state capitalism in the underdeveloped nations is very different from state-monopoly capitalism in the advanced Western countries. The former system is opposed to monopolies while the latter permits the monopolies to control the state machinery. "All this warrants the conclusion that at the present stage in the liberated non-socialist countries state capitalism plays a progressive role."[602] However, this guidebook was careful to point out that state capitalism does not always serve the anti-imperialist cause and that it sometimes allows the bourgeoisie to gain control over the state sector.

Soviet writers generally praised the measures taken by the underdeveloped nations in strengthening the state sector of their economies and contended that a strong state sector is one of the conditions necessary for the formation and development of a national democratic state.[603] After gaining political independence, the struggle for economic independence is of prime importance and the state sector aids by opposing the machinations of foreign monopolies. However, these writers did not fail to mention some negative features of state capitalism. Potekhin claimed that under this system, property actually belongs to a class of capitalists, not to the people as a whole, while Mirskii and Tiagunenko asserted that the standard of living of the toiling classes has not risen since the achievement of political independence.[604] Mirskii declared elsewhere:

---

[602] *Fundamentals of Marxism-Leninism*, 1963 edition, *op. cit.*, p. 419. Also see Anastas Mikoyan, "Speech to the Eighth Congress of the Communist Party of China," *op. cit.*, p. 9 and V. Li, "Dva litsa odnogo klassa," *Aziia i Afrika Segodnia*, No. 3 (March, 1962), p. 7.
[603] I. Tiul'panov, "The Problem of State Capitalism in Underdeveloped Countries," *Vestnik Leningradskogo Universiteta* (Seriia Ekonimiki, Filisofii i Prava), Vol. XVI, No. 1 (March, 1961). See JPRS 8370, August, 1961, p. 3.
[604] Potekhin, *Afrika smotrit v budushchee*, *op. cit.*, p. 16 and Mirskii and Tiagunenko, *op. cit.*, p. 28.

The intelligentsia and bureaucracy, though they may support 'socialism,' insist on preserving ownership by the employer. Why are socialist ideas popular among them, when these ideas are foreign to their class? For example, the 'groundnut bourgeoisie' of Senegal call themselves socialists; yet the new bourgeoisie has no conflict of interests with imperialism, but profits by co-operation with it. The fact is that it is interested in developing the state sector because the state sector in turn is what sustains it economically.[605]

In a similar vein was this statement by V. Pavlov:

The logical development of the public sector will be the most evident and convincing proof for the petty bourgeoisie, the semi-proletarian masses, and above all for the peasantry, of the fact that no capitalism—not even the most democratic, not even the 'semi-socialist,' etc.—can overcome its exploiting nature and free the workers from poverty and social inequality, and that the manufacturing capacity created in the public sector can be put at the disposal of the fundamental interests of the working masses only in conditions of socialism.[606]

Soviet analysts contended that state capitalism can accelerate economic development and strengthen a nation's defense against the imperialists. They also maintained, or at least hoped, that state capitalism could lead to an imitation of the Soviet system: "The development of the state-owned sector of the economy enables the sovereign states of the East to take advantage to a certain extent of the experience of economic planning which the Soviet Union and the other Socialist countries readily share with friends."[607] As David Morison has pointed out, Soviet leaders seemed to feel that the presence of state-controlled economies in many African countries may increase the chances of Soviet influence in these areas.[608]

---

[605] "The U.S.S.R. and the Developing Countries," *op. cit.,* pp. 14–15.
[606] Pavlov, "Soiuz rabochego klassa i krest'ianstva i sotsial'nye preobrazovaniia na Vostoke," *op. cit.,* p. 13.
[607] Zhukov, "The Bankruptcy of the Imperialist Colonial System and International Relations," *op. cit.,* p. 67.
[608] Morison, *op. cit.,* p. 33.

Under colonialism, the state sector was considered to be a tool of the monopolies and was used to retard the national-liberation movement. However, its role changed with the granting of independence.[609] Large enterprises were built with state funds, or with private capital under state control, and they resist foreign control while benefiting the whole nation.[610] State capitalism helps overcome economic backwardness and often leads to the nationalization of foreign firms.

State capitalism was deemed to be a step toward socialism but was not itself socialistic. It creates predispositions for the transition from capitalism to socialism but in order for state capitalism to be converted into socialism, state power must be transferred from the exploiters to the exploited.[611] O. Ul'rikh claimed that the state sector in Ghana, Guinea, and Mali was not only anti-imperialist, but anti-capitalist as well.[612] In fact, Avakov and Andreasian stressed the point that the class struggle continues during the development of the state sector:

> The growth and consolidation of the state sector takes place in a bitter class struggle. This struggle unfolds between the opponents of the consolidation of the role of the state in the economy—the feudal lords and the big bourgeoisie—on one hand, and advocates of the development of the state sector—the working class, the peasantry, the progressive intelligentsia and the major part of the national bourgeoisie—on the other hand.[613]

The struggle for a state sector of the economy unites the working class and the peasantry and, according to Ponomarev,

---

[609] See G. Usov, "Gosudarstvennyi sektor v ekonomike stran Vostochnoi Afriki," *Mirovaia Ekonomika i Mezhdunarodnye Otnosheniia*, No. 2, 1963, p. 52.

[610] See Potekhin, *Afrika smotrit v budushchee, op. cit.*, p. 43 and "Replies of N. S. Khrushchev to Questions of Editors of Ghanaian Times, Alger Républicain, Le Peuple and Botataung," *op. cit.*, p. 12.

[611] Potekhin, *Ibid.*, p. 16.

[612] O. Ul'rikh, "Osnova industrializatsii," *Aziia i Afrika Segodnia*, No. 10 (October, 1963) , p. 14.

[613] Avakov and Andreasian, *op. cit.*, p. 9.

state capitalism can "give the progressive forces an opportunity to occupy ever more important positions in production and to increase their political influence."[614]

State capitalism was considered to be economically progressive since it benefits the people and politically progressive since it opposes imperialism. However, Soviet writers warned that it is indeed ambivalent and could turn into state monopoly capitalism. Another negative feature of state capitalism is that it is financed by increasing the taxes paid by the workers and by attracting foreign capital.[615] Despite their emphasis on state capitalism in the underdeveloped nations, Soviet observers recognized that the public and private sectors of the economies of these nations may cooperate in building a socialist society, although in the end, one sector must prevail.[616]

Soviet writers were inconsistent in their appraisal of the need for industrialization in the underdeveloped areas. The Soviet Union, as well as other members of the socialist camp, stressed rapid industrialization as a basic component of its program of economic development and this seems to have influenced I. Tiul'panov who asserted:

> Without industrialization, these countries would be doomed to remain without economic rights as agrarian dependencies of the industrially developed countries. A one-crop agriculture, oriented almost entirely to a foreign market, and an extractive industry, producing even a very valuable raw material, cannot form the basis for the economic independence of a country or for the flowering of its people.[617]

Tiul'panov was citing the role of industrialization in de-

---

[614] Ponomarev, "Concerning the National Democratic State," *op. cit.,* p. 42.

[615] O. Ul'rikh, "The State Economic Policy in the Underdeveloped Countries," *Mirovaia Ekonomika i Mezhdunarodnye Otnosheniia,* No. 4 (April, 1962). See JPRS 14607 (September, 1962), pp. 84–85.

[616] Grishechkin, *op. cit.,* p. 8.

[617] Tiul'panov, "The Problem of State Capitalism in Underdeveloped Countries," *op. cit.,* p. 7.

creasing the amount of the underdeveloped nations' dependence on the imperialist powers but other relevant arguments were that industrialization leads to a growth of the working class and creates a situation in which the Soviet model of development may be easily imitated.

Ul'ianovskii, speaking at the 1964 Moscow conference on the underdeveloped nations, took exception to the view that these nations should necessarily build heavy industry:

> The effectiveness of any underdeveloped country's economic policy depends on how far it succeeds in strengthening and broadening the national bases of the economy as a whole. Reactionary bourgeois economists slanderously assert that Soviet economists insist on the development of heavy industry for every economically backward country at whatever cost. Soviet experience has shown the key importance of the development of heavy industry; but that does not mean that Soviet experience must be copied everywhere.[618]

Ul'ianovskii's approach was rather liberal and recognized national differences and the inapplicability of dogmatic views to the dynamic social developments manifested throughout Asia and Africa. His flexibility included a belief that the Soviet model of development need not be followed.

THE ROLE OF AGRICULTURAL COOPERATIVES

Soviet spokesmen maintained that the communal and cooperative agricultural systems practiced in Africa, which feature the absence of private landholding, are capable of aiding the transition of the African nations to socialism. On this point, they appear to have had a theoretical basis in the works of Marx and Engels, who also recognized the importance of the type of landholding prevalent in the underdeveloped areas. In a letter to Engels dated June 2, 1853, Karl Marx stated: "Bernier rightly considered the basis of all phenomena

---

[618] "The U.S.S.R. and the Developing Countries,"*op. cit.,* p. 5.

in the East—he refers to Turkey, Persia, Hindustan—to be the absence of private property in land. This is the real key, even to the Oriental heaven."[619] In his reply of June 6, 1853, Engels declared: "The absence of property in land is indeed the key to the whole of the East."[620]

During the nineteenth century, Russia was a backward agrarian country and the comments of Engels on the system of communal agriculture practiced there are therefore relevant to his views on underdeveloped areas. In his "On Social Conditions in Russia," he asserted:

> It is clear that communal ownership in Russia is long past its flourishing period and to all appearances is moving towards its dissolution. Nevertheless, the possibility undeniably exists of transforming this social form into a higher one, if it should last until circumstances are ripe for that, and if it shows itself capable of development in such a way that the peasants no longer cultivate the land separately, but collectively; and to transform it into this higher form, without it being necessary for the Russian peasants to go through the intermediate stage of bourgeois small ownership. This, however, can happen only if, before the complete breakup of communal ownership, a proletarian revolution is successfully carried out in Western Europe, creating for the Russian peasant the pre-conditions necessary for such a transformation, in particular, the material conditions which he needs in order to carry through the reconstruction of his whole agricultural system, thereby necessarily involved.[621]

Engels was contending that communal agriculture can be converted to "a higher form" and that landholding of the capitalist type can be by-passed. However, a successful proletarian revolution must first be carried out in Western Europe.

---

[619] Letter from Marx to Engels, London, June 2, 1853 in Karl Marx and Friedrich Engels, *On Colonialism* (Moscow, Foreign Languages Publishing House, 1961), p. 277.
[620] Letter from Engels to Marx, Manchester, June 6, 1853 in *Ibid.*, p. 278.
[621] See Feuer, *op. cit.*, p. 472.

The Soviet position during the Khrushchevian era was quite similar as the Russian Revolution and the victorious Soviet proletariat were substituted for the historic events which Engels expected to take place in the advanced countries of Western Europe and the underdeveloped nations of Asia and Africa took the place of pre-revolutionary Russia.

L. Aleksandrovskaia maintained that the colonialists used the cooperative movement as an instrument of economic control and that the African bourgeoisie was aided but placed in a position subordinate to the foreign monopolies.[622] The bourgeoisie tries to develop capitalism within the cooperatives but revolutionary democrats, like those in Ghana, Guinea, and Mali, use the cooperatives to further economic advancement.[623] In listing the number of members of agricultural cooperatives in the African countries, Aleksandrovskaia cited the U.A.R., Algeria, Morocco, Uganda, Kenya, Tanganyika, the Congo (Leopoldville), Nigeria, Ghana, and the Sudan as the leaders in this respect while Guinea and Mali were not included.[624] However Guinea and Mali, as well as Ghana, were singled out for praise by the author and she asserted that they were taking the non-capitalist path. Foreign policy, rather than domestic African, considerations therefore appear to have been paramount in the mind of the author.

Aleksandrovskaia affirmed that conditions are favorable for the development of producers' cooperatives in Africa and that the preservation of the communal structure facilitates the transition to cooperative agriculture. However, the communes cannot carry out this transition alone and direction must be given by the state authorities.[625] Potekhin concurred and

---

[622] L. Aleksandrovskaia, "Kooperativnoe dvizhenie v Afrike: problemy i perspektivy," *Mirovaia Ekonomika i Mezhdunarodnye Otnosheniia*, No. 3, 1963, pp. 39–40 and p. 51.

[623] *Ibid.*, p. 51.

[624] *Ibid.*, p. 42.

[625] *Ibid.*, p. 48. Also see Aleksandrovskaia, "Kooperativnoe dvizhenie," *op. cit.*, p. 17 and Potekhin, *Afrika smotrit v budushchee, op. cit.*, p. 44.

asserted: "The most progressive representatives of African society want the preservation of the commune, considering it as one of the means which will facilitate the transition to socialism."[626]

Soviet writers also discerned some negative aspects of communal agriculture in Africa. Potekhin averred that the communes are dualistic and have collective ownership of land but private production on it. The basic question is which aspects will come to the fore.[627] He then wrote:

If we examine the tendency in the development of African peasant farming on communal land during the last decade, we can reach a specific conclusion: the proprietary principle has gained the upper hand over the collective principle. This is demonstrated by the growth of social differentiation among the peasantry and the appearance of capitalist elements, in the development of mortgages and rent, and the involvement of land in commodity exchange.[628]

Another point made by Soviet authors was that the chiefs often control the communes under a feudal system of exploitation and that they receive payments from their tribesmen.[629] In a similar vein, it was claimed that the rich farmers benefit most when communes are converted into cooperatives. They exploit the poorer members and retain the right to dispose of land. Vladimir Iordanskii elicited the view from a Burundi student that maybe cooperatives should be comprised of peasants who have left the communes and who maintain their freedom from exploitation. Without explicitly stating so, Iordanskii seemed to concur.[630]

---

[626] Potekhin, "Nekotorye problemy Afrikanistiki v svete reshenii XXII s' 'ezda KPSS," *op. cit.,* p. 11.

[627] Potekhin, "Land Relationships in the Countries of Africa," *op. cit.,* p. 240.

[628] *Ibid.,* pp. 240–241.

[629] V. Ia. Katsman, "Krest'ianskoe zemlevladenie v nekotorykh stranakh Zapadnoi Afriki," *Sovetskaia Etnografiia,* No. 6 (November–December, 1963), p. 51.

[630] V. Iordanskii, "Burundi's Anxieties and Hopes," *New Times,* No. 2 (January 11, 1965), p. 26.

Discussing Mali, V. Tsoppi maintained that the cooperative movement avoids many of the pitfalls of capitalism and that the government of Mali hopes to acquire funds from the sale of agricultural products in order to aid other branches of the economy, especially industry.[631] He also affirmed: "Having declared the building of socialism their aim, the leaders of the new state came to the conclusion that co-operative farming was both necessary and inevitable, for no agricultural development to speak of could be expected as long as farming remained uncoordinated."[632]   However, A. B. Letnev contended that there are some shortcomings in Malian agriculture. He claimed that the transition to more progressive forms of cooperation does not always proceed smoothly and that there are mistakes in the organizing of labor in collective fields. Peasants evade work in the collective fields, the collective fields are developing too slowly, and the program of "investissement humain" is incorrectly identified with collective fieldwork. Despite these bad aspects, Letnev wrote that the Union Soudanaise, the press, and the radio are leading a campaign to overcome these shortcomings.[633] It was pointed out elsewhere that cooperatives are plagued by the lack of funds and qualified cadres.[634]

Soviet writers saw the African communes as a step toward the non-capitalist path of development.[635] The various types of cooperative movements (credit, producers', and consumers') were also believed to have "great social and economic significance" but the cooperatives were not yet considered to be "true mass democratic organizations."[636] However, Ivan Potekhin asserted that the producers' cooperatives

---

631 V. Tsoppi, "Mali: The Youth of an Ancient Country," *New Times,* No. 34 (August 22, 1962) , p. 28.
632 *Ibid.,* p. 28.
633 Letnev, *op. cit.,* p. 83.
634 Aleksandrovskaia, "Kooperativnoe dvizhenie," *op. cit.,* p. 17.
635 See *Ibid.,* p. 17 and I. Farizov, "The First Steps of the Cooperative Movement," *Kommunist,* No. 13 (September, 1962) . See *CDSP,* Vol. XIV, No. 41 (November 7, 1962) , p. 12.
636 Farizov, *Ibid.,* pp. 11–12.

in Ghana, Guinea, and Mali increase the possibilities for non-capitalist development.[637] Israeli cooperatives were roundly condemned as being capitalistic.[638]

In regard to the agricultural communes in Africa serving as a starting point for non-capitalist development, Potekhin believed that the main question is who wields the state power.[639] Potekhin discussed the history of the Russian communes and stated that although they passed through capitalism, this is not the only path and the African communes may bypass capitalism. This is possible with the aid of the proletariat of the advanced industrial countries and he cited Marx to support his point.[640] K. Ivanov even cited Chernyshevsky to support his contention that the communes can proceed to socialism, bypassing capitalism.[641]

When writing about African communes, Soviet analysts seemed to have in mind the African equivalent of the old Russian mirs, in which land was owned collectively but in which private initiative played a role since pieces of land were periodically distributed to families for their personal use. These analysts were probably not thinking about either the Chinese communes or the experimental communes set up in Russia during the Civil War.

The Soviet view of African agricultural systems was marked by a certain ambivalence but, in the main, a favorable attitude was taken toward communes and cooperatives. A weakness of the Soviet analysis was the failure to differentiate clearly between communes and cooperatives and to outline the roles of each in the transition to socialism.

---

[637] Ivan Potekhin, "Afrika: itogi i perspektivy antiimperialisticheskoi revoliutsii," part two, *Aziia i Afrika Segodnia,* No. 10 (October, 1961), p. 15.

[638] See Gavrilov, "Preobrazovanie Afrikanskoi derevni," *op. cit.,* pp. 13–15.

[639] Potekhin, *Afrika smotrit v budushchee, op. cit.,* pp. 24–25.

[640] *Ibid.,* pp. 20–24.

[641] Ivanov, "The National-Liberation Movement and Non-Capitalist Path of Development," part two, *op. cit.,* pp. 7–8.

6 Retrospect and Prospect

DURING THE KHRUSHCHEVIAN ERA, SOVIET WRITERS CAME TO recognize many positive aspects of African socialism and to believe that African socialism could evolve into scientific socialism. Cordial state relations with most African nations were accompanied by a coming to terms with African socialism on an ideological plane and the exigencies of *Realpolitik* therefore found their reflection in the analyses of the journalists and academicians. The Soviet approach toward Africa was marked by a fairly realistic assessment of the chances for communist influence in that continent and the rigid doctrinal tenets of the Stalinist period gave way to the realization that there are tremendous differences between the political and economic relationships in the various African countries. Being optimistic about the rise of socialism in Africa and about the anti-imperialist posture of the new African political regimes, Soviet theorists were nevertheless cautious and were careful to point out the dualistic nature of the national bourgeoisie, state capitalism, the peasantry, nationalism, and other forces at work in the African states.

Ideological erosion was a by-product of the new Khrushchevian outlook on Africa as the cherished theoretical concepts became tempered by their adjustment to the realities of life on the African continent. The basic precipitate of this doctrinal dilution was the realization that the underdeveloped

226

nations play a key role in the world revolutionary process and that the proletariat of most Asian and African states is not yet ready to establish its hegemony in the national-liberation movement and in the process of nation-building. Prospects for the advent of scientific socialism appeared brighter in the former colonial areas than in advanced industrial countries of the West and the tenets of Marxism-Leninism were revised to meet this changing situation.

Soviet political analysts realistically understood that the African nations were not ready for the Soviet brand of socialism (communism) and therefore sought to outline paths of development for these nations which could bring them to socialism in the near future. They also attempted to foster imitation of the Soviet model since such elements as collectivization, state ownership of the means of production, and centralized one-party regimes would tend to increase the chances for Soviet influence in these countries and at the same time advance them on the road to socialism. It is quite evident that most African leaders favor some variety of socialism but the Soviet model presents certain points for hesitation since, among other things, the Soviet Union's program of agricultural collectivization has not produced the expected results and since there is a fear that imitation of the Soviet system and increased economic ties with the Soviet Union may lead to Soviet political domination of the African states.[642] Emphasizing their independence of action, the African nations appear to be rather susceptible to Soviet economic influence but less willing to commit themselves politically to the Soviet cause. Richard Lowenthal has perceptively written: "It is, above all, as an engine for the forced modernization of an underdeveloped society that Communism is today admired

---

[642] Zbigniew Brzezinski has discussed a survey conducted under the auspices of *Jeune Afrique* (Tunis) which reveals the desire of French African students to build some variety of socialism in their countries. Of those interviewed, only 38% indicated that they wished to follow the Soviet model. See Brzezinski, *Africa and the Communist World, op. cit.*, p. 207.

by large sections of the intelligentsia of the new nations, while it is the peculiar price of using that engine—in ideology, in institutions of permanent totalitarian rule, and in subjection to Soviet imperialism—which repels many of them."[643] The African leaders assert their identity and, while accepting many aspects of the ideological and institutional premises of Marxism-Leninism, they strive to give them a uniquely African flavor.

John Kautsky has convincingly explained that the elements of the revolutions in the underdeveloped areas are similar to those manifested in the Soviet Union because the Russian Revolution was itself carried out in an underdeveloped country and was directed against the domination by both the domestic aristocracy and foreign interests. He believed that nationalism alone accounts for the policies adopted by the Asian and African leaders and that their resemblance to Soviet socialism (communism) is due to the similar paths taken by the Russian, Asian, and African revolutions.[644] Kautsky was quite correct in pointing out that certain features common to the revolutions in underdeveloped areas are usually discussed solely in terms of Marxism but he failed to realize that the programs carried out by numerous Asian and African leaders were not completely pragmatic nationalist responses to underdevelopment. Many of these leaders were indeed influenced by Marxist thought.

Adam Ulam has also discussed the relevance of Marxist ideas to the revolutions unfolding in the underdeveloped nations and has expressed the view that Marxism, in terms of its economic program, "is the natural ideology of underdeveloped societies in today's world."[645] Ulam maintained that the ap-

---

[643] Richard Lowenthal, "The Points of the Compass," in John Kautsky, ed., *Political Change in Underdeveloped Countries* (New York and London, John Wiley and Sons, 1962), p. 336.

[644] See John Kautsky, "An Essay in the Politics of Development," in Kautsky, *Ibid.*, p. 87.

[645] Adam Ulam, *The Unfinished Revolution* (New York, Random House, 1960), p. 285.

plicability of Karl Marx's views to the process of industrial revolution can now be seen quite clearly in the emerging areas of Asia and Africa and he then stated:

> Every society reaching for industrialization and modernization has its 'Marxist' period, when some of the ideas of Marx are relevant to its problems and are reflected in everyday sentiments of the masses of people, even though the name of Marx and his movement may be unknown to them. Hence the attraction for Marxism, and the quasi-Marxist character of social protest in many areas of the world—an attraction which would still exist, though perhaps in a different form, were Marxism not represented by one of the two greatest powers of the world.[646]

Although the Marxist and socialist views of the African leaders are partly a result of the tasks facing their underdeveloped nations, as Ulam has suggested, the views of these leaders did not gestate in a completely independent manner and appear to have been influenced by the teachings of Lenin and by contact with the Soviet Union and other socialist (communist) countries. Among the African leaders probably influenced in this way are Nkrumah, Touré, Babu, and Hanga, although these men were influenced to different extents and have adopted different programs of political action.

Closely related to this issue is the question of whether most African leaders have knowledge of Soviet and Marxist theoretical writings. Scholarly African leaders, such as Senghor and Nkrumah, are certainly familiar with the basic writings of Marx and Lenin but the majority of African leaders probably have not gone beyond Lenin's theory of imperialism, a theory which has helped shape the attitudes of many educated Africans toward the colonial and post-colonial policies of the Western powers. It has discredited capitalism by linking it with imperialism, it has created the illusion that the foreign policies of all capitalist countries are concerned only with the economic welfare of these countries, and it has helped spread

---

[646] *Ibid.,* p. 7.

the Marxist tenet that politics is only a reflection of the dynamic economic forces present in any society.

Although most African leaders are not Marxist scholars, they nevertheless are familiar with the foreign policy pronouncements of the Soviet Union and have accepted certain Soviet explanations of imperialism and neo-colonialism. In fact, Zbigniew Brzezinski has written: "Indeed, the concept of neocolonialism seems to be displacing Lenin's notions about imperialism as the most popular conceptual stereotype by which Africans can explain their view of the West's relationship to them."[647] Many of these leaders have also taken the Soviet side on many world issues such as opposition to the American actions in Vietnam and opposition to the Belgian-American paratroop drop in the Congo but this in no way implies that the African leaders were directly influenced by the Soviet Union. It is more likely that they reached their own independent conclusions which just happened to coincide with those of the Soviet leaders. However, there is one area in which Soviet pronouncements have had a direct effect: vocabulary. The simple slogans and repetitive phrases amply evident in Soviet speeches and writings have found their way into the speeches and writings of many African leaders. Therefore, when an African leader is in accord with the Soviet position on an issue, his declaration often has a quasi-Soviet tone in regard to its choice of words. This does not necessarily mean that this leader has fallen under Soviet influence, in fact this is rarely the case, but it may lead to an increasingly rigid adherence to ideological phraseology which is similar to that expressed in the Soviet Union and this in turn may lead, through a process of ideological feedback, to actions which are increasingly in accord with the expressed ideology. The phrases may become dogmas and freedom of action will therefore be somewhat limited by the need to adhere to them

---

[647] Zbigniew Brzezinski, "The African Challenge" in Zbigniew Brzezinski, ed., *Africa and the Communist World, op. cit.,* p. 206.

in regard to policy, or at least rationalize actions in terms of them.

This whole process has been described by Zbigniew Brzezinski.[648] Although he was analyzing the ideological feedback present in the Soviet Union during the Stalinist era, his comments have great relevance to the role of ideology in the developing nations. Brzezinski claimed that when the language of a leader is permeated with ideological concepts, "the processes of communications and information" are affected. A chain reaction reaching down to the lower levels is the result as people repeat the ideological phrases to which they have been conditioned. They become so ideologically orthodox that the leader is put in a position where it is difficult for him to act in defiance of the ideology or where he must at least justify his actions in terms of it. He is therefore somewhat bound by the ideological phrases which he himself introduced to his people.

It should also be mentioned at this point that although most African leaders are familiar with Soviet foreign policy pronouncements, they are probably relatively unfamiliar with Soviet writings on Africa. Their own writings and statements do not seem to be influenced by Soviet sources and, of course, almost all of these leaders are unable to read Russian.

The socialist methods used in the Soviet Union appeal to many African leaders because they promise a revolutionary approach to overcoming backwardness in a short period of time. On the other hand, the capitalist and parliamentary democratic system of the Western nations seems too slow in responding to urgent needs and, besides that, it is associated with the colonial powers. Another reason for the appeal of socialist programs similar to those in the Soviet Union is that the African elites are often divorced from the people and seek to set themselves up as a new favored class. The Marxist-

---

[648] Zbigniew Brzezinski, *The Soviet Bloc,* revised edition (New York, Praeger, 1961), p. 389.

Leninist type of political organization permits such control from the top and, at the same time, allows this elitist group to serve the masses by guiding them along the path which it has adopted in accordance with its self-appointed status as the vanguard.[649]

Nationalist movements in Africa have much in common with the countries of the socialist camp since both strive to develop industry and agriculture at a rapid pace and this realization led George Padmore to contend that dynamic nationalism is the only bulwark against the spread of communism in Africa as both present solutions to the same problems.[650] He therefore advocated Pan-Africanism, which he believed could "fulfil the socio-economic mission of Communism under a libertarian political system."[651] Padmore correctly analyzed this issue and even the communists realized the revolutionary potential of nationalism, such as in China. The Chinese communists used nationalism as one of their basic platforms so that they themselves would not become submerged in the nationalist tide and so that they could attract people to the communist side through the use of nationalist slogans. Dan Kurzman called this strategy "the Yenan Way" and defined it as "the art of disguising communism in the mask of a legitimate national movement, such as anti-imperialism or agrarian reform."[652] Considering the power of African nationalism and the desire among Africans not to be dominated by foreign communist countries, there is a good possibility that African communists will emphasize nationalism. In fact, Soviet writers expected the African communists to work within the nationalist movements in an effort to convert them into Marxist-Leninist parties.[653] As Walter La-

---

[649] For a discussion of this idea, see Hugh Seton-Watson, "The Communist Powers and Afro-Asian Nationalism," in Kurt London, ed., *Unity and Contradiction* (New York, 1962), p. 204.
[650] George Padmore, *Pan Africanism or Communism?* (London, Dennis Dobson, 1956), p. 339.
[651] *Ibid.*, pp. 21–22.
[652] Kurzman, *op. cit.*, p. 7.
[653] See above, p. 199.

queur has pointed out, the creation of African communist parties at the present time may be a liability since Africans value their independence and national identity and are reluctant to join international movements.[654] On the other hand, African communist parties may possibly seize power in the future and they have therefore been created to serve as alternatives to the hoped for infiltration of the nationalist parties.

Laqueur emphasized that the communist leaders in Africa are generally young and have not had ties with the Comintern and extensive Marxist training. They are activists rather than theorists and are strongly influenced by nationalism, Pan-Africanism, and racialism. He suggested that the Afro-Communists may become real communists in the Soviet sense or, on the contrary, the real communists may become national communists. Present developments point to the latter course.[655]

The years of the Khrushchevian era witnessed the fragmentation of the Soviet bloc as various communist regimes exercised an increasing amount of independence vis-à-vis the Soviet Union. The Sino-Soviet dispute has further accelerated these centrifugal tendencies and the example of the Cuban revolution has shown that there are indeed diverse ways of building socialism and of gaining membership in the socialist camp. While some members of the camp are attempting to maintain a precarious balance between the Soviet and Chinese factions and while Rumania is exhibiting a great deal of national independence, the prospects for the development of national communism are becoming more evident. The concept of national democracy may also contribute to this tendency, especially if it is really modeled in accord with the Cuban experience.

There is a possibility that national communist regimes may be established in some African countries. They could con-

[654] Walter Laqueur, "Communism and Nationalism in Tropical Africa," *Foreign Affairs,* Vol. XXXIX, No. 4 (July, 1961), p. 611.
[655] *Ibid.,* pp. 611–614.

ceivably join the socialist camp but would most likely exercise a great deal of independence, as Cuba now does. Ben Bella's Algeria may have been heading in this direction and there were indications that Nkrumah''s Ghana was steering a course to the left. The Congo (Brazzaville) and Zanzibar are other areas which deserve mention in this respect. Although this possibility exists, it is more probable that the leftist nations of Africa will increase their ties to the socialist camp but avoid direct membership. In addition, the brand of communism which may be practised in Africa will probably be removed from the Soviet and Chinese understandings of Marxism-Leninism as it will include many elements uniquely relevant to the African continent. Alexander Dallin has pithily summed up the prospects for communism in Africa: "African nationalists may adapt Communism but they will not adopt it. Communism could perhaps become 'nativized' in Africa, but Communism africanized would not yield a Muscovite Africa. The prospect therefore seems to be: Soviet appeal, yes; Soviet control, no."[656]

It should be noted that Soviet sources dismiss the possibility for national communism since all communists are supposedly united in accordance with proletarian internationalism. A *Kommunist* editorial of January, 1957 stated: "The very expression 'national communism' is a logical absurdity. Communism is itself really international and cannot be conceived of in any other way."[657]

The Sino-Soviet conflict has shown that the socialist camp is not monolithic and this has probably reduced fears among African socialists that close ties to the socialist (communist) countries brings political subjugation. In addition, the formerly sacred tenets of Marxism-Leninism have been torn asunder and have been subjected to conflicting interpretations

---

[656] Alexander Dallin, "The Soviet Union: Political Activity," in Brzezinski, *Africa and the Communist World, op. cit.,* p. 47.
[657] "Vyshe znamia Marksistko-Leninskoi ideologii," *Kommunist* editorial, No. 1 (January, 1957), p. 9.

and this has most likely reinforced the view of African leaders that the teachings of Marx and Lenin must be adapted to specific national conditions. If any African nation should desire to join the socialist camp, it will probably insist on its own national interpretation of Marxism-Leninism. Walter Laqueur has accordingly pointed out the paradoxical situation in which the world socialist movement finds itself:

> Under a veneer of Marxist-Leninist ideology, of anti-imperialist slogans, state control of the economy and one-party rule, influences are at work which have very little to do with Marxism or even Leninism. Communism is Africanised and Asianised even faster and more thoroughly than Christianity, because it is a secular movement and therefore in greater need of adaptation. The outcome is a mixture of communist elements and components alien to it. This, from the point of view of communist unity, is highly regrettable, but the irony of it is that any progress by world communism can now be achieved only by strengthening the centrifugal trends and thus weakening the movement from within.[658]

Herbert Dinerstein has raised some penetrating questions in regard to the fragmentation of the socialist camp and to the erosion manifested in the Soviet ideology. He asserted:

> Every movement that aspires to universality faces the problem of the dilution of faith. When the early Christian church consented to absorb various elements of paganism it spread rapidly, because converts, at least in the first generation, had to make few important accommodations. Are the Soviet leaders prepared to accept as Communist a large number of local parties with policies that diverge in important aspects from those of traditional Communism or conflict with current Soviet aims? If Communism is diluted, it may be easier to swallow, but are Soviet leaders prepared to spread the faith at the cost of political control?[659]

Viewing the actions taken by Khrushchev in regard to Cuba and the invitations extended to the ruling parties of Ghana,

---

[658] Walter Laqueur, "The Schism," in Laqueur and Leopold Labedz, eds., *Polycentrism* (New York, Praeger, 1962), p. 5.
[659] Dinerstein, *op. cit.*, p. 89.

Guinea, and Mali to attend the Twenty-second Congress of the C.P.S.U., both of Dinerstein's questions could most likely be answered in the affirmative. Khrushchev's successors apparently are following a similar course.

There appears to be a strong interrelationship between Soviet theory and practice but the causality is often difficult to determine. During the period 1955–1964, foreign policy considerations seem to have been predominant and theoretical pronouncements followed close behind. The new Soviet foreign-policy approach to the Asian and African nations brought forth innovations on the doctrinal plane and changing circumstances within the underdeveloped countries also contributed to theoretical change, such as the Cuban experience leading to the concept of national democracy. However, it must be taken into account that the ideological precepts, which themselves evolved in accord with Soviet policies and actual situations in the underdeveloped countries, had a pronounced effect upon later Soviet policies and political analyses. For example, the concept of national democracy was probably formulated as a result of events in Cuba but once adopted, it served as a basis for Soviet policies toward Ghana and for analyses of the roads to socialism and the roles of communists and revolutionary democrats in the purportedly progressive nations of Asia and Africa. Hugh Seton-Watson has supplied what is perhaps the best description of the complex kinship between theory and practice. He wrote: "Theory influences political action. Political action is, however, also influenced by the facts of international politics. When a new policy is adopted for empirical reasons, a new theoretical justification has to be found for it. The new theory, in turn, has its effect on policy"[660]

The Soviet Union did not pressure countries, such as Ghana, to join the socialist camp and immediately follow the Soviet pattern of development but instead maintained cordial relations with these countries and bided its time in the ex-

---

[660] Seton-Watson, *op. cit.*, p. 188.

pectation that they would eventually turn socialist (communist) in accordance with the development of the national democratic state. In addition, Soviet theorists stressed the point that certain Asian and African leaders could come over to Marxist-Leninist positions and the role of the communist parties in these areas was therefore not particularly significant. The fact that communist parties are now outlawed in all Arab states has not greatly affected state relations between the Soviet Union and these Arab states.

One way to view the interaction between Soviet theory and practice is to distinguish between long-term and short-term foreign policy objectives. Ideology generally plays a more significant role in regard to basic aims than it does in regard to everyday tactical manoeuvres. Another distinction of great relevance has been made by Zbigniew Brzezinski.[661] He differentiates between doctrines and action programs and considers both to be facets of ideology. Doctrines are basic beliefs which shape one's concept of history and the dynamic forces in the world while action programs are specifically related to the short-term policies through which change is initiated in any given situation. Doctrines rarely change while action programs must change to keep abreast of reality. "Without the doctrine, ideology would be just a static dogma. Doctrine linked with action program gives modern ideology its religious fervor, its sense of constant direction, as well as its freedom of manoeuvre in the use of political power to achieve that which must be."[662]

In their long-term view of history, Soviet foreign policy analysts adhere to certain fundamental doctrines: there is a definite progression of historical stages and the advent of both socialism and communism is inevitable, economic forces are at the base of society and they determine the prevalent polit-

---

[661] Brzezinski, *The Soviet Bloc, op. cit.,* p. 387 and Zbigniew Brzezinski and Samuel Huntington, *Political Power: U.S.A./U.S.S.R.* (New York, Viking Press, 1964), p. 21.
[662] Brzezinski, *The Soviet Bloc, Ibid.,* p. 387.

ical structure, the evolution of history is directly related to the conflicts between various socio-economic classes, imperialism and capitalism will always be fundamental enemies of the Soviet regime. However, doctrine is often relegated to a minor role in the formulation of short-term action programs, as evidenced by the facts that the Soviet Union first made a pact with Nazi Germany, then joined the capitalistic Allies during the Second World War and, years later, failed to take the Chinese side in the Sino-Indian border conflict. Soviet policy-makers therefore have a fairly good comprehension of power politics and when strategic power positions are at stake, doctrine must take a back seat. The expressed justification for any moves which may seem to run counter to Marxist-Leninist doctrinal tenets is that anything which strengthens the power of the Soviet Union hastens the advent of world communism.

Although basic doctrinal precepts are often subordinated to the need for quick, short-term action, they nevertheless do have some effect upon policy decisions since the views of Soviet political analysts tend to be shaped by underlying doctrinal assumptions. Soviet foreign aid almost always goes to the state sector of a nation's economy; socialist leaders in the underdeveloped countries are considered to be friends of the Soviet Union even though these leaders, such as Nasser, often suppress local communists; strong, highly disciplined leftist parties, such as those in Guinea and Mali, are considered to be on the threshold of becoming Marxist-Leninist parties and are therefore favored by the Soviet Union as the Soviet leaders seem oblivious to the idea that this type of dynamic nationalist party may serve as an alternative to the rise of communism in these countries; and, of course, the greatest example of Soviet doctrinal blindness was the incorrect assessment given to the historical significance of the rise of Adolf Hitler.

During the Khrushchevian era, Soviet foreign policy toward Africa was apparently influenced by certain doctrinal assumptions which helped distort the true picture of African politics. Soviet analysts saw events on the African continent within the framework of a world-wide struggle between imperialism and socialism and they failed to see that African leaders often think only about the welfare of their own countries when they adopt certain programs and policies. These leaders do not necessarily place all decisions within the context of the imperialist-socialist struggle nor within the context of East-West relations. Therefore, Soviet observers attached too much relevance to the foreign policy postures of some African states, to the programs of rapid industrialization, to the creation of agricultural cooperatives, and to the Marxist ideologies expressed by certain African leaders. These observers had too much faith in the view that history is on the side of socialism and that the African countries must eventually adopt the Marxist-Leninist variety of socialism. They failed to see that Africans may solve their own problems in their own way and they therefore overreacted to changes within Africa and developed a bloated sense of optimism. Inviting delegates from the ruling parties of Ghana, Guinea, and Mali to the Twenty-second Congress of the C.P.S.U. was probably the result of an overly optimistic assessment of the evolution of these organizations toward Marxist-Leninist parties modeled on the C.P.S.U. Soviet analysts may have mistaken form for content.

In the foreign policy field, this ideologically conditioned view that the African nationalist parties will become Marxist-Leninist parties led to Soviet support for most African nationalist regimes. Communist parties in Africa were relegated to a minor role and, for the sake of maintaining cordial state relations with the African governments, the Soviet leaders were even willing to overlook the suppression of African communists. Although it is still too early to tell, this may have been a major tactical blunder on the part of the Soviet Union since it seems unlikely that the African governments will ever voluntarily place themselves in the Soviet camp. They may become allies of the Soviet Union but they will not become satellites. The coming to power of an African communist party may have produced a Soviet satellite but the improbability of this ever happening, the fissiparous tendencies evident within international communism, and the possibility that the Soviet leaders no longer even had hopes of acquiring a true satellite must certainly be taken into account.

The Soviet doctrine that economic forces determine the political structure had a direct effect upon the Soviet foreign aid and trade programs in Africa. Soviet analysts saw the aid and trade programs of the Western powers as aspects of neo-colonialism and they believed that the Western powers were trying to direct the political evolution of the African nations by acting through the economic systems of these nations (Although partly true, this interpretation was much too simplified.) This view was accompanied by a Soviet desire to compete economically with the West for the African political spoils and led to the mistaken assumption that the Soviet Union could gain friends and accelerate the advent of socialism in this manner. During the Khrushchevian era, the Soviet Union greatly stepped up its economic offensive in Africa but many millions of rubles later, it finally realized that the financial strain upon the Soviet economy was not worth the price of trying to influence African governments. Leaders like Nasser and Touré, who had accepted Soviet aid and goods, were not falling under the political control of the Soviet Union and Soviet leaders decided to reduce the intensity of their economic forays into Africa.

Did the foreign policy positions of the African nations accord with the Soviet image of these positions? This question must be answered in the negative since Soviet theory often led to a distorted perception of reality. Although Lenin's' theory of imperialism and the concept of neo-colonialism influenced most African leaders, these men nevertheless sought Western aid; although the African nations joined with the socialist camp in condemning colonialism, imperialism, and many acts of Western foreign policy, there was not really a world revolutionary process, as envisioned by Soviet analysts;

and these analysts often made the mistake of confusing anti-Westernism with communism. The ideas that any move away from Western imperialism is toward socialism and that historical inevitability is on the side of socialism led Soviet observers into a false sense of optimism.

In the long-range Soviet view, Africa was only one battleground on which the forces of imperialism fight those of socialism. It was believed that Africa will move into the socialist orbit when the time and conditions are appropriate as the forces of Marxist-Leninism must eventually triumph. Since time supposedly favored the Soviet cause, the short-range objective of the Khrushchevian regime was to turn the African nations against the West (That is why Soviet writers advocated four-class, anti-imperialist alliances for the African countries rather than three-class, anti-capitalist alliances); the long term objective was to win these nations over to the Soviet camp. The former objective was largely realized, although Soviet overtures had little to do with molding the views of the African leaders, while the Soviet Union met with little success in regard to its latter objective.

Ideology did not always serve as an obstacle to the correct understanding of African political events. The Soviet leaders realized that Ghana, Guinea, and Mali were friends of the socialist camp even though these states did not have large working classes and they also realized that non-proletarian leaders may have viewpoints similar to those of the Soviet leadership. The Soviet Union even had cordial state relations with monarchical and feudal Ethiopia and, after a short period of coolness, it catered the friendship of Boumedienne, a military man who had over-thrown one of the Soviet Union's closest friends, Ben Bella. Some issues therefore became divorced from primarily ideological considerations and moved into the realm of strategic politics. Zbigniew Brzezinski and Samuel Huntington have perceptively written: "On balance, therefore, Soviet ideology cannot be viewed merely as a liability. Ideology is not incompatible with national behavior, once the basic assumptions are granted. While these assumptions may or may not be rational, they are at least so far removed from immediate concerns that they do not produce a conflict between the ideological commitment and a rational approach to reality."[663] Brzezinski has even asserted that ideology sometimes plays a positive role:

> Ideology as a method of organizing the perception of reality provides certain categories for determining the meaning of an era, the nature of the era's dominant forces—it distinguishes between broad trends and mere passing episodes. It helps to clarify the various observable contradictions and conflicts, and through this provides a sense of purpose and a clarity of direction which involve a long-range commitment transcending the short-range crises. In this respect it is a source of confidence, even blind confidence.[664]

Ideology may have helped Soviet theoreticians understand the influences of Western economic policies upon the African political structures and may also have helped them arrive at the conclusion that those African countries, such as Ghana, Guinea, and Mali, which had embarked upon programs of radical economic and political reform, tended to be the countries most liable to seek the friendship of the Soviet Union. However, ideology generally tended to obfuscate rather than elucidate and the "blind confidence" which it instilled among Soviet analysts had a basically negative effect.

During the Khrushchevian era, the Soviet Union was quite successful in increasing its influence in Africa, although no African country has yet joined the socialist camp. Of course, the Soviet Union's prestige in Africa as of 1955 was almost non-existent so it could not fail to rise when the U.S.S.R. began a concerted effort to gain the good will of the African peoples and governments. Since the Soviet Union has never colonized Africa and has consistently opposed the colonial policies of the Western powers, it has a strong asset in terms

---

[663] Brzezinski and Huntington, *op. cit.*, p. 66.
[664] Brzezinski, *The Soviet Bloc, op. cit.*, p. 388.

of competing for influence in Africa with these powers. It also is able to maintain that it has overcome economic backwardness in a relatively short period of time, while another relevant theme is the purportedly harmonious relationship between the various nationalities of the Soviet Union. On the negative side, it has difficulty competing financially with the Western powers, has to contend with the outflanking tactics of Communist China, and is a newcomer to the vagaries of African politics.

Thomas Thornton raised the issue of the relationship between the Soviet scholarly writings on the underdeveloped areas and Soviet policies toward these areas.[665] He maintained that they are closely correlated and claimed that the appearance of numerous articles on the underdeveloped nations at the time that the Soviet Union began to curry favor with these nations was no mere accident. It showed that research is responsive to policy. On the question of whether research influences policy, Thornton generally answered in the affirmative. He asserted that since researchers are permitted to function, their writings must be considered significant by the Soviet leadership and, since the Soviet leaders probably are deficient in their knowledge of Asian and African affairs, they look to the scholarly journals as sources of information. Thornton's interpretation appears reasonable and Uri Ra'anan has cited many facts which lend corroborating evidence.[666]

During the years of Khrushchev's rule, the Soviet writers shed many of their previous misconceptions about Africa. The preoccupation with rigid class differentiations gave way to new, flexible, more realistic, and almost trans-class categories such as revolutionary democrats and progressive intelligentsia and the idea that only the proletariat can secure complete independence and build socialism was replaced by a new analysis which recognized the significant role of the national

[665] Thornton, *op. cit.,* p. x.
[666] Ra'anan, *op. cit.*

bourgeoisie. National peculiarities in socialist construction also came to be tolerated, and even advocated, by Soviet theorists. However, many misconceptions about the African situation were nevertheless prevalent during the Khrushchevian era. Soviet observers based their analyses on the assumption that the African nations must follow either the capitalist or the socialist path and failed to realize that these nations may adopt a path unique to the African continent. The Marxist concept of historical stages was adhered to in too rigid a manner and this contributed to the over-optimistic belief that the African socialist leaders will eventually become Marxist-Leninists. Another important misconception was the view that state capitalism and agricultural cooperatives may be positive steps toward scientific socialism. It is more likely that these programs were devised as African responses to economic backwardness, not as byways to the construction of a communist society.

Soviet writers analyzed almost all political events in Africa in terms of class struggle and therefore failed to understand the roles of racialism, tribalism, regionalism, and personal charisma. Their reluctance to attribute an important role to racialism was obviously related to the facts that the Soviet Union was generally considered to be a "white" power and that the Chinese were trying to use the racial theme to unite the peoples of Asia, Africa, and Latin America. Tribalism and regionalism were almost completely ignored as Soviet scholars did not recognize that differences between politicians and political parties were based more on tribal and regional animosities than on ideological differences brought about by contrasting class backgrounds. The role of tribalism in countries such as Nigeria, Uganda, and Kenya was hardly mentioned, nor was the role of regionalism in Nigeria, the Congo (Kinshasa) or Dahomey. With such a gap in their theoretical framework, it is not surprising that Soviet writers often proffered analyses greatly divorced from reality. Another great impediment to their comprehension of African politics was their failure to take into account the role of personal charisma or the personalization of power. The ascendancy of African leaders and the popularity of these men among the masses were seen as the products of class forces and the magnetism of men like Nkrumah, Kenyatta, Banda, Touré, and Lumumba was not recognized. Related to this was the fact that the concept of national democracy was interpreted in terms of class structure. If this concept was truly based upon the Cuban experience, Soviet theorists should have realized that Cuba's transition to socialism was not primarily the result of changing class forces but was the result of personal power and the dynamic image presented by Fidel Castro. Castro was the force, not the object. Another greatly distorted view held by Soviet writers was that the nature of African governments could most effectively be determined by assessing the relationships of various classes to the seat of state power. The state was seen as the instrument of certain class forces and such a view was really ridiculous when related to countries like Kenya, Nigeria, the Congo (Kinshasa), and Somalia.

Soviet theorists constantly discussed the role of the African proletariat, despite the fact that this class was minuscule in almost all African countries. While recognizing that the proletariat was not then capable of dominating African politics, Soviet articles nevertheless discussed the size of the proletariat in various countries, its class consciousness, its influence upon the political process, and its task during the existence of a national democratic state. This preoccupation with the proletariat was completely unrealistic because of the weakness of this class and because a class evaluation of African society sheds little light upon its true mechanics.

Another Soviet misconception concerned the doctrine that there are objective laws of historical development which are applicable to all continents. This was a rather dogmatic approach and it led Soviet writers to place all African events into neat historical compartments. While recognizing that Africa may have its own road to socialism, these writers unrealisti-

cally maintained that Africa was not unique in most respects.
The course of African development was therefore squeezed
into a rigid doctrinal framework and the peculiarities of
African life were bent and twisted so they would fit in.

Thus, the Soviet analysis of African politics was marred by
numerous misconceptions. Africa was often seen in the Soviet
image while, at the same time, Soviet leaders were laying the
groundwork for eventually seeing her in the Soviet shadow.

Soviet writers of the Khrushchevian era also became deeply
enmeshed in many ideological inconsistencies but it is extremely difficult to determine whether these writers were
aware of their predicament. While maintaining that capitalism may be bypassed, they stressed that socialism may not;
while maintaining that class determines consciousness, they
claimed that national bourgeois leaders may become Marxist-
Leninists; while maintaining that socialism arises out of the
industrial process and the growth of the proletariat, they
looked toward Africa for its growing pains, rather than toward the technologically advanced states of Western Europe.
Their usual approach to the problem of ideological inconsistency was to avoid discussing it. However, there was one
noteworthy instance when Ivan Potekhin made a concerted
effort to explain the Soviet claim that the non-capitalist path
may be traversed even by those countries which have rudimentary capitalist relations. He analyzed Karl Marx's dictum
that a social order is not replaced until all of its productive
forces have been fully utilized and sought to convince the
reader that there was no contradiction between this Marxian
view and the later Soviet contention. Potekhin failed miser-
ably at this task.[667]

When compared with the Africanist writings of the Stalin
period, those produced during the years of Khrushchev's rule
were, to some extent, marked by a realism which was partly
conditioned by the exigencies of the Soviet Union's foreign

---

[667] Potekhin, *Africa: Ways of Development, op. cit.,* p. 37. Also see
above, p. 202.

policy. Ideology responded to the dynamic stimuli produced by African (and Cuban) political events and therefore became eroded as these events unfurled at a rapid pace. Zbigniew Brzezinski has described such a process in these words: "That erosion might ultimately occur through a continuing confrontation of ideology with reality. Unlike religion where the ultimate sanction is supernatural, material reality is said to validate the ideological assumptions of Communism."[668] However, this process of ideological erosion is not necessarily part of a historical continuum leading inexorably to the decomposition of all theoretical tenets but is possibly just a phase of Soviet development peculiar to the Khrushchevian era. It is quite conceivable that a new Stalinist or sectarian interpretation of the basic Marxist-Leninist dictums will arise and that Soviet ideology will therefore take a new turn or revert to its form during Stalin's later years in power. However, this possibility is rather unlikely.

*   *   *

Marxism of some sort appears to be a fundamental part of the programs of nation-building throughout Africa since it is highly pertinent to the problems of underdevelopment and the initiation of radical economic and political reform. However, most African leaders will probably continue to adapt the teachings of Marx and Lenin to the specific needs of the African peoples and will avoid political alliance and ideological conformity with the Soviet Union. The Africans value their independence too much to turn from one master to another and they also try to assert their identity, long suppressed by the colonial powers, through their ideological pronouncements. Therefore, the prospect for the African nations appears to be development along a socialist path, possibly leading to some variety of national communism in some nations such as Guinea. Since the socialist camp is itself disintegrating into nationalistic communist entities, the world of the

---

[668] Brzezinski, *The Soviet Bloc, op. cit.,* p. 407.

future may present a plethora of states purportedly based upon Marxism which, although conceivably channeling their political energies toward the same goals, will almost certainly maintain an enormous amount of ideological independence. The political leaders of Africa will not become Soviet satraps but may join the Soviet leaders in pointing to Marx and Lenin as their philosophical forebears and sources of socio-economic knowledge.

Bibliography

SOVIET BOOKS USED AS PRIMARY SOURCES

Afrika: entsiklopedicheskii spravochnik (two volumes). Moscow: Gosudarstvennoe Nauchnoe Izdatel'stvo "Sovetskaia Entsiklopcdiia," 1963.

Brutents, Karen. *Protiv ideologii sovremennogo kolonializma.* Moscow: Izdatel'stvo Sotsial'no-Eknomicheskoi Literatury, 1961.

Datlin, S. *Raspad kolonial'noi sistemy imperializma.* Moscow: Gosudarstvennoe Izdatel'stvo Politicheskoi Literatury, 1956.

Dzhunusov, M. S. *O zakonomernostiakh perekhoda narodov ranee otstalykh stran k sotsializmu.* Alma-Ata: Akademiia Nauk Kazakhskoi SSR, Institut Filosofii i Prava, Izdatel'stvo Akademii Nauk Kazakhskoi SSR, 1961.

Fundamentals of Marxism-Leninism. Moscow: Foreign Languages Publishing House, 1960.

Fundamentals of Marxism-Leninism. Second revised edition. Moscow: Foreign Languages Publishing House, 1963.

Gavrilov, Nikolai. *Gvineiskaia Respublika.* Moscow: Akademiia Nauk SSSR, Institut Afriki, Izdatel'stvo Vostochnoi Literatury, 1960.

Glukhov, A. M. *Keniia: ul'timatum kolonializmu.* Moscow: Izdatel'stvo Mezhdunarodnye Otnosheniia, 1964.

Mirskii, Georgii and Lev Stepanov. *Asia and Africa: A New Era.* Moscow: Foreign Languages Publishing House, 1960.

Ol'derogge, D. A. and Ivan Potekhin. *Narody Afrika.* Moscow: Izdatel'stvo Akademii Nauk SSSR, 1954.

Potekhin, Ivan. *Africa: Ways of Development,* Moscow: Nauka Publishing House, 1964.
————, *Afrika, 1956–1961.* Moscow: Akademiia Nauk SSSR, Institut Afriki, Izdatel'stvo Vostochnoi Literatury, 1961.
————, *Afrika smotrit v budushchee.* Moscow: Akademiia Nauk SSSR, Institut Afriki, Izdatel'stvo Vostochnoi Literatury, 1960.
————, *Formirovanie natsional'noi obshchnosti iuzhnoafrikanskikh bantu.* Moscow: Akademiia Nauk SSSR, Izdatel'stvo Akademii Nauk SSSR, 1955.
Program of the Communist Party of the Soviet Union. Moscow: Foreign Languages Publishing House, 1961.
Sivolobov, A. M. *The National-Liberation Movement in Africa.* Moscow: Znanie Publishing House, 1961 (JPRS 10683, October 24, 1961).
Sovetskii Soiuz-iskrennii drug narodov Afriki. Moscow: Gosudarstvennoe Izdatel'stvo Politicheskoi Literatury, 1961.
Suslov, M. A. *O bor'be KPSS za splochennost' mezhdunarodnogo kommunisticheskogo dvizheniia.* Moscow: Izdatel'stvo Politicheskoi Literatury, 1964.
Turchaninov, D. I. *Vseafrikanskaia Federatsiia Profsoiuzov.* Moscow: Izdatel'stvo VTsPS Profizdat, 1962.
Uvachan, V. *Peoples of the Soviet North.* Moscow: Foreign Languages Publishing House, 1960.
————, *Perekhod k sotsializmu malykh narodov severa.* Moscow: Gosizpolit, 1958.
Vadeev, O., ed. *Vstrecha s Afrikoi.* Moscow: Izdatel'stvo Politicheskoi Literatury, 1964.
Verin, V. P. *Prezidentskie respubliki v Afrike.* Moscow: Izdatel'stvo Instituta Mezhdunarodnykh Otnoshenii, 1963.
Zorin, V., ed. *Liudi i politika, 1964.* Moscow: Izdatel'stvo "Pravda," 1964.

ARTICLES FROM SOVIET PERIODICALS USED AS PRIMARY SOURCES

Abet, Ia., "Federatsiia Mali," *Mirovaia Ekonomika i Mezhdunarodnye Otnosheniia,* No. 5 (May, 1960), pp. 105–108.
Aleksandrovskaia, L., "Kooperativnoe dvizhenie," *Aziia i Afrika Segodnia,* No. 10 (October, 1963), pp. 16–17.
————, "Kooperativnoe dvizhenie v Afrike: problemy i perspektivy," *Mirovaia Ekonomika i Mezhdunarodnye Otnosheniia,* No. 3, 1963, pp. 39–51.

Avakov, R. and R. Andreasian, "The Progressive Role of the State Sector," *Kommunist*, No. 13 (September, 1962), pp. 92–96 (*CDSP*, Vol. XIV, No. 41, November 7, 1962, pp. 9–11, complete text).

Avakov, R. and G. Mirskii, "Class Structure in the Underdeveloped Countries," *Mirovaia Ekonomika i Mezhdunarodnye Otnosheniia*, No. 4, 1962, pp. 68–82 (complete text translated in Thomas Thornton, ed. *The Third World in Soviet Perspective*. Princeton: Princeton University Press, 1964, pp. 276–304).

Avakov, R. and L. Stepanov, "Sotsial'nye problemy natsional'-no-osvoboditel'noi revoliutsii," *Mirovaia Ekonomika i Mezhdunarodnye Otnosheniia*, No. 5, 1963, pp. 46–54.

Azembski, Miroslaw, "Report on the Ivory Coast," *New Times*, No. 40 (October 4, 1961), pp. 26–28.

Beliaev, I., "From Bamako to Timbuktu," *Pravda*, April 21, 1964, p. 4. (*CDSP*, Vol. XIV, No. 16, May 13, 1964, pp. 28–29, complete text).

Bochkarev, Iu., "Communists are Doughtiest Fighters for National Independence," *Kommunist*, No. 5 (March, 1963), pp. 105–113 (JPRS 18768, U.S. Government Publication Number 10469, June, 1963, pp. 13–26).

———, "The Guinean Experiment," *New Times*, No. 24 (June, 1960), pp. 23–26; No. 25 (June, 1960), pp. 21–25; and No. 29 (July, 1960) pp. 27–30.

———, "New Paths for New States," *New Times*, No. 41 (October 11, 1961) pp. 14–16.

———, "The Soviet Union and the National-Liberation Movement," *New Times*, No. 26 (July 3, 1963), pp. 5–8.

Bragina, E., "Planning as a Method for Developing the National Economy," *Kommunist*, No. 13 (September, 1962), pp. 99–101 (*CDSP*, Vol. XIV, No. 41, November 7, 1962, pp. 12–13).

Braginskii, M. I., "O polozhenii rabochego klassa i profsoiuznom dvizhenii v kolonial'nykh stranakh Afriki," *Problemy Vostokovedeniia*, No. 5, 1959, pp. 104–111.

———, "Sotsial'nye sdvigi v tropicheskoi Afrike posle Vtoroi Mirovoi Voiny," *Sovetskaia Etnografiia*, No. 6, 1960, pp. 31–43.

Bruk, S. I. and N. N. Cheboksarov, "Sovremennyi etap natsional'nogo razvitiia narodov Azii i Afriki," *Sovetskaia Etnografiia*, No. 4, 1961, pp. 74–99.

Brutents, Karen, "Integral Part of the World Revolutionary Process," *International Affairs,* No. 2 (February, 1964), pp. 30–37.

———, "The October Revolution and Africa," *New Times,* No. 45 (November 7, 1962), pp. 7–10.

Commentator, "The National-Liberation Movement," *International Affairs,* No. 4 (April, 1955), pp. 14–21.

Davidson, A., "The Gold Coast," *New Times,* No. 34 (August, 1956), pp. 29–30.

Dement'ev, Iu., "Kooperirovanie v Maliiskoi derevne," *Mirovaia Ekonomika i Mezhdunarodnye Otnosheniia,* No. 7 (July, 1961), pp. 109–111.

Dmitriev, V., "Kontinent bor'by i nadezhd," *Aziia i Afrika Segodnia,* No. 4 (April, 1963), pp. 11–13.

Dolgopolov, E., "National-Liberation Wars in the Present Epoch," *International Affairs,* No. 2 (February, 1962), pp. 17–21.

"XXI S"ezd KPSS i zadachi Vostokovedeniia," *Problemy Vostokovedeniia* editorial, No. 1, 1959, pp. 18–25.

Dzhunusov, M. S., "O zakonomernostiakh nekapitalisticheskogo puti razvitii otstalykh stran k sotsializmu," *Voprosy Filosofii,* No. 2, 1962, pp. 14–24.

Farizov, I., "The First Steps of the Cooperative Movement," *Kommunist,* No. 13 (September, 1962), pp. 96–99 (*CDSP,* Vol. XIV, No. 41, November 7, 1962, pp. 11–12).

Gafurov, B. G., "O perspektivakh razvitiia Sovetskogo Vostokovedeniia," *Sovetskoe Vostokovedenie,* No. 3, 1957, pp. 7–16.

Gatsoiev, A., F. Politkin and P. Khmylov, "Two System Competition and the Young States," *International Affairs,* No. 9, 1964, pp. 78–82.

Gavrilov, Nikolai, "O migratsii rabochei sily v Zapadnoi Afrike," *Problemy Vostokovedeniia,* No. 3, 1959, pp. 82–90.

———, "Preobrazovanie Afrikanskoi derevni," *Aziia i Afrika Segodnia,* No. 12 (December, 1962), pp. 13–15.

———, "Respublika Mali—molodoe nezavisimoe gosudarstvo Afriki," *Narody Azii i Afriki,* No. 4, 1961, pp. 29–36.

———, "Splitters at Work in Africa," *New Times,* No. 6 (February 7, 1962), pp. 17–19.

Glezerman, G. E., "Obshchie zakonomernosti i svoeobraznye formy sotsialisticheskoi revoliutsii," in I. A. Khliabich, ed., *Obshchie zakonomernosti perekhoda k sotsializmu i osobennosti ikh proiavleniia v raznykh stranakh.* Moscow: Akademiia Obshchestvennykh Nauk pri Ts. K. KPSS, Izdatel'stvo VPSh i AON pri Ts. K. KPSS, 1960.

Gordon, L. A. and L. A. Fridman, "Nekotorye osobennosti sotsial'noi struktury razvivaiuschikhsia stran," *Narody Azii i Afriki,* No. 6, 1964, pp. 3–18.

Grishechkin, K., "African Prospects," *New Times,* No. 41 (October 16, 1963), pp. 7–9.

Guber, A. A., "Distinctive Features of the National-Liberation Movement in the Eastern Colonial and Dependent Countries," *International Affairs,* No. 3 (March, 1959), pp. 71–75.

———, "Gluboko i vsestoronne izuchat' krizis i raspad kolonial'noi sistemy imperializma," *Sovetskoe Vostokovedenie,* No. 3, 1956, pp. 3–14.

Gudlak, Bakhab, "Nigeriia nakanune vseobshchikh vyborov," *Pravda,* November 21, 1964, p. 3.

Guzevaty, Iu., "'Third Way' or Genuine Freedom?," *International Affairs,* No. 4 (April, 1963), pp. 43–49.

Iordanskii, Vladimir, "Burundi's Anxieties and Hopes," *New Times,* No. 2 (January 11, 1965), pp. 24–26.

Iskenderov, A., "Rabochii klass i natsional'no-osvoboditel'nye revoliutsii," *Aziia i Afrika Segodnia,* No. 5 (May, 1962), pp. 6–8.

Ismagilova, R. N. and L. D. Iablochkov, "Koordinatsionnoe soveshchanie sovetskikh Afrikanistov," *Sovetskaia Etnografiia,* No. 3, 1957, pp. 184–186.

Iudin, I. A., "Some Problems of the Establishment of National States in the Independent African Countries," *Sovetskoe Gosudarstvo i Pravo,* No. 2, 1961, pp. 35–47 (complete text translated in Thomas Thornton, ed., *The Third World in Soviet Perspective.* Princeton: Princeton University Press, 1964, pp. 252–275).

Ivanov, K., "The National-Liberation Movement and Non-Capitalist Path of Development," *International Affairs,* No. 9, 1964, pp. 34–43 and No. 12, 1964, pp. 7–16.

———, "Present-Day Colonialism and International Relations," *International Affairs,* No. 4 (April, 1962), pp. 36–44.

———, "Present-Day Colonialism: Its Socio-Economic Aspect," (part two), *International Affairs,* No. 6 (June,

1960), pp. 27–34 and (part three), No. 10 (October, 1960), pp. 13–22.

Katsman, V. Ia., "Krest'ianskoe zemlevladenie v nekotorykh stranakh Zapadnoi Afriki," *Sovetskaia Etnografiia,* No. 6 (November–December, 1963), pp. 46–56.

———, "Rost imushchestvennoi differentsiatsii sredi Afrikanskogo krest'ianstva Tangan'iki posle Vtoroi Mirovoi Voiny," *Sovetskaia Etnografiia,* No. 1, 1961, pp. 83–93.

Katsman, V. Ia. and P. I. Kuprianov, "O meste i roli vozhdei v Afrikanskom obshchestve," *Sovetskaia Etnografiia,* No. 3, 1962, pp. 149–159.

Keita, Madeira, "Madeira Keita on the New Mali," *New Times,* No. 35 (September 2, 1964), pp. 14–15.

Keita, Modibo, "Speech in Moscow," *Pravda,* May 23, 1962, p. 1 (*CDSP,* Vol. XIV, No. 21 June 20, 1962, p. 21).

Khrushchev, Nikita, "Report of the Central Committee of the Communist Party of the Soviet Union to the Twentieth Party Congress, *Pravda,* February 15, 1956, pp. 1–11 (*CDSP,* Vol. VIII, No. 4, March 7, 1956, pp. 3–15, complete text).

———, "Speech in Sofia," *Pravda,* May 20, 1962, pp. 1–3 (*CDSP,* Vol. XIV, No. 20, June 13, 1962 p. 7).

———, "Speech to Twenty-first Congress," *Pravda,* January 28, 1959, pp. 2–10 (*CDSP,* Vol. XI, No. 4, March 4, 1959, pp. 17–25 and Vol. XI, No. 5, March 11, 1959, pp. 13–20).

———, "Za novye pobedy mirovogo kommunisticheskogo dvizheniia," *Kommunist,* No. 1 (January, 1961), pp. 3–37.

Kim, G. F., "O gosudarstve natsional'noi demokratii," *Aziia i Afrika Segodnia,* No. 10 (October, 1962), pp. 2–5.

———, "Soiuz rabochego klassa i krest'ianstva v natsional'no-osvoboditel'nykh revoliutsiakh," *Narody Azii i Afriki,* No. 5, 1962, pp. 3–12.

———, "Sorevnovanie dvukh sistem i ekonomicheski slabo razvitye strany Vostoka," *Sovremennyi Vostok,* No. 11 (November, 1959), pp. 13–16.

Kirichenko, M. G., "O nezavisimom gosudarstve natsional'noi demokratii," *Kommunist,* No. 11 (November, 1961), pp. 104–115.

Kiselev, V., "Rabochii klass i natsional'no-osvoboditel'nye revoliutsii," *Mirovaia Ekonomika i Mezhdunarodnye Otnosheniia,* No. 10 (October, 1963), pp. 93–98.

Kolesnichenko, T., "Novaia zhizn' Gany," *Pravda,* July 1, 1964, p. 3.

Korionov, V., "Velichaishaia sila sovremennosti," *Kommunist*, No. 14 (September, 1961), pp. 37–47.

Krasin, Iu. A. and V. F. Li, "O zakonomernostiakh nekapitalisticheskogo razvitiia osvobodivshikhsia stran," *Voprosy Filosofii*, No. 18, 1964, pp. 29–40.

Kudriavtsev, V., "Africa in One Formation," *Izvestiia*, October 10, 1963, p. 2 (*CDSP*, Vol. XV, No. 41 November 6, 1963, pp. 20–21).

———, "Africa's Hopes and Anxieties," *International Affairs*, No. 11 (November, 1963), pp. 40–45.

———, "Fighting Africa's Daily Round," *International Affairs*, No. 10 (October, 1962), pp. 51–57.

Letnev, A. B., "Novoe v Maliiskoi derevne," *Sovetskaia Etnografiia*, No. 1 (January–February, 1964), pp. 81–88.

Li, V., "Dva litsa odnogo klassa," *Aziia i Afrika Segodnia*, No. 3 (March, 1962), pp. 6–9 and No. 4 (April, 1962), pp. 6–9.

———, "O nekapitalisticheskom puti razvitiia," *Aziia i Afrika Segodnia*, No. 11 (November, 1961), pp. 10–13.

Melikian, O., "Review of Kwame Nkrumah's 'I Speak of Freedom'," *Narody Azii i Afriki*, No. 6, 1962, pp. 154–157.

Mikhailov, V., "Republic of Mali," *New Times*, No. 22 (May 30, 1962), pp. 16–17.

Mikoyan, Anastas, "Speech to the Eighth Congress of the Communist Party of China," *Pravda*, September 18, 1956, pp. 2–3 (*CDSP*, Vol. VIII, No. 38, October 31, 1956, pp. 6–10).

Mirskii, Georgii, "Creative Marxism and Problems of the National-Liberation Movement," *Mirovaia Ekonomika i Mezhdunarodnye Otnosheniia*, No. 2 (March–April, 1963), pp. 63–68 (JPRS 19821, U.S. Government Publication No. 14223, August, 1963, pp. 9–18).

———, "O nekapitalisticheskom puti razvitiia byvshikh kolonii," *Pravda*, January 31, 1965, p. 5.

———, "The Proletariat and National Liberation," *New Times*, No. 18 (May 1, 1964), pp. 6–9.

Mirskii, Georgii and V. Tiagunenko, "Tendentsii i perspektivy natsional'no-osvobodital'nykh revoliutsii," *Mirovaia Ekonomika i Mezhdunarodnye Otnosheniia*, No. 11 (November, 1961), pp. 21–33.

"The National-Liberation Movement at the Present Stage," *Kommunist*, No. 13 (September, 1962), pp. 89–109

(*CDSP,* Vol. XIV, No. 41, November 7, 1962, pp. 8–15, complete text).

"The National-Liberation Movement is an Integral Part of the World Revolutionary Process," *Kommunist,* No. 2 (January, 1962), pp. 15–20 (*CDSP,* Vol. XIV, No. 6, March 7, 1962, pp. 3–5).

"Obmen pis'mami mezhdu tt. Brezhnevym, L. I. i Modibo Keita," *Pravda,* January 26, 1965, p. 3.

Ogurtsov, S., "The Developing Countries and Social Progress," *Aziia i Afrika Segodnia,* No. 7 (July, 1963), pp. 2–4 (*CDSP,* Vol. XV, No. 37, October 9, 1963, pp. 10–12, complete text).

"Okonchatel'noe krushenie kolonializma neizbezhno," *Pravda* editorial, January 5, 1965, p. 1.

Orlova, A. S., "O meste i roli traditsionnykh vlastei Afrikanskogo obshchestva v proshlom i nastoiashchem," *Sovetskaia Etnografiia,* No. 6, 1960, pp. 92–105.

Osmanova, Z., "Vsesoiuznaia nauchnaia sessiia 'Zakonomernosti Perekhoda Ranee Otstalykh Narodov k Sotsializmu i Kommunizmu, Minuia Stadiiu Kapitalizma'," *Narody Azii i Afriki,* No. 1, 1963, pp. 237–240.

Ostrovitianov, Iu., "Sotsialisticheskie doktriny razvivaiushchikhsia stran: formy i sotsial'noe soderzhanie," *Mirovaia Ekonomika i Mezhdunarodnye Otnosheniia,* No. 6, 1964, pp. 82–91.

Pavlov, V. I., "Soiuz rabochego klassa i krest'ianstva i sotsial'nye preobrazovaniia na Vostoke," *Aziia i Afrika Segodnia,* No. 10 (October, 1961), pp. 10–13.

Pavlov, V. I. and I. B. Red'ko, "Gosudarstvo natsional'noi demokratii i perekhod k nekapitalisticheskomu razvitiiu," *Narody Azii i Afriki,* No. 1, 1963, pp. 29–40.

————, "Leninskii soiuz mirovogo sotsializma s natsional'no-osvoboditel'nym dvizheniem," *Narody Azii i Afriki,* No. 5, 1963, pp. 10–22.

Ponomarev, B., "Concerning the National-Democratic State," *Kommunist,* No. 8 (May, 1961), pp. 33–48 (*CDSP,* Vol. XIII, No. 22, June 28, 1961, pp. 3–7).

————, "Mezhdunarodnoe kommunisticheskoe dvizhenie na novom etape," *Kommunist,* No. 15 (October, 1958), pp. 12–30.

Popov, Iu., "O nekotorykh chertakh rabochego dvizheniia v Afrike (Iuzhnee Sakhary)," *Narody Azii i Afriki,* No. 5, 1961, pp. 46–56.

——, "Rabochii klass Afriki," *Aziia i Afrika Segodnia,* No. 5 (May, 1963), pp. 3–6.

——, "Zhizn' oprovergaet," *Aziia i Afrika Segodnia,* No. 12 (December, 1961), pp. 11 and 21.

Pospelova, N. G., "Ekonomicheskie, klassovye i politicheskie osnovy gosudarstva natsional'noi demokratii i ego funktsii," *Vestnik Leningradskogo Universiteta* (Seriia Ekonomiki, Filosofii i Prava), No. 23, 1962, pp. 131–135.

Potekhin, Ivan, "Africa Shakes Off Colonial Slavery," *International Affairs,* No. 2 (February, 1959), pp. 84–90.

——, "The African Peoples Forge Unity," *International Affairs,* No. 6 (June, 1961), pp. 80–84.

——, "Afrika: itogi i perspektivy antiimperialisticheskoi revoliutsii," (part two), *Aziia i Afrika Segodnia,* No. 10 (October, 1961), pp. 14–15.

——, "Etnicheskii i klassovoi sostav naseleniia Zolotogo Berega," *Sovetskaia Etnografiia,* No. 3, 1953, pp. 112–133.

——, "Etnograficheskie nabliudeniia v Gane," *Sovetskaia Etnografiia,* No. 3, 1958, pp. 142–153.

——, "Kharakternye cherty raspada kolonial'noi sistemy imperializma v Afrike," *Problemy Vostokovedeniia,* No. 1, 1960, pp. 12–29.

——, "Land Relationships in the Countries of Afrika," *Narody Azii i Afriki,* No. 3, 1962, pp. 16–31 (complete text translated in Thomas Thornton, ed., *The Third World in Soviet Perspective.* Princeton: Princeton University Press, 1964, pp. 224–251).

——, "Legacy of Colonialism," *International Affairs,* No. 3, 1964, pp. 15–20.

——, "Nekotorye problemy Afrikanistiki v svete reshenii XXII s' 'ezda KPSS," *Narody Azii i Afriki,* No. 1, 1962, pp. 6–16.

——, "O feudalizme u Ashanti," *Sovetskaia Etnografiia,* No. 6, 1960, pp. 86–91.

——, "On 'African Socialism'," *International Affairs,* No. 1 (January, 1963), pp. 71–79.

——, "Osnovnye problemy istorii narodov Afriki," *Kommunist,* No. 12 (August, 1961), pp. 99–109.

——, "Pan-Africanism and the Struggle of the Two Ideologies," *International Affairs,* No. 4, 1964, pp. 48–54.

——, "Politicheskoe polozhenie v stranakh Afriki," *Sovetskoe Vostokovedenie,* No. 1, 1956, pp. 22–36.

————, "Raspad kolonial'noi sistemy v Afrike," *Kommunist,* No. 17 (December, 1958), pp. 99–112.

————, "Stalin's Theory of Colonial Revolution and the National Liberation Movement in Tropical and South Africa," *Sovetskaia Etnografiia,* No. 1, 1950, pp. 24–40 (complete text translated in Thomas Thornton, ed., *The Third World in Soviet Perspective.* Princeton: Princeton University Press, 1964, pp. 24–40).

————, "1960 god—reshaiushchii god natsional'noi revoliutsii v Afrike," *Sovremennyi Vostok,* No. 12 (December, 1960), pp. 2–5.

————, "Zadachi izucheniia etnicheskogo sostava Afriki v sviazi s raspadom kolonial'noi sistemy," *Sovetskaia Etnografiia,* No. 4, 1957, pp. 103–110.

Pribytkoskii, L. and L. Fridman, "The Choice Before Nigeria," *International Affairs,* No. 2 (February, 1963), pp. 75–80.

————, "The Future of the African Continent," *International Affairs,* No. 3, 1964, pp. 98–100.

"Proekt programmy KPSS i nekotorye problemy natsional'noosvoboditel'nogo dvizheniia narodov Azii i Afriki," *Narody Azii i Afriki* editorial, No. 5, 1961, pp. 3–14.

Rasulov, D. R. and S. Radzhabov, "Respubliki Sovetskogo Vostoka—obrazets perekhoda ranee otstalykh stran k sotsialisticheskomu obshchestvennomu i gosudarstvennomu stroiu," *Kommunist,* No. 7 (July, 1961), pp. 26–35.

"Razvivaetsia sotrudnichestvo mezhdu SSSR i Senegalom," *Pravda,* November 3, 1964, p. 3.

"Replies of N. S. Khrushchev to Questions of Editors of Ghanaian Times, Alger Républicain, Le Peuple and Botataung," *Pravda* and *Izvestiia,* December 22, 1963, pp. 1–2 (*CDSP,* Vol. XV, No. 51, January 15, 1964, pp. 11–16, complete text).

"Respublika Mali na puti sotsial'nykh preobrazovanii," *Narody Azii i Afriki,* No. 2, 1963, pp. 23–36.

Rostovskii, S. N., "Leninskoe uchenie o nekapitalisticheskom puti razvitiia," *Problemy Vostokovedeniia,* No. 2, 1960, pp. 21–28.

Rozaliev, I., "State Capitalism in Asia and Africa," *International Affairs,* No. 2 (February, 1963), pp. 33–38.

Savel'ev, Iu. and I. Sanovich, "Polozhenie i bor'ba rabochego klassa Azii i Afriki," *Aziia i Afrika Segodnia,* No. 5 (May, 1962), pp. 9–13.

Savel'ev, N., "O roli burzhuazii v natsional'no-osvoboditel'nom dvizhenii," *Mirovaia Ekonomika i Mezhdunarodnye Otnosheniia*, No. 5 (May, 1962), pp. 97–102.

Sektor Rabochego Dvizheniia Instituta Narodov Azii AN SSSR, "Pod' 'em rabochego dvizheniia v stranakh Azii i Afriki," *Kommunist*, No. 6 (April, 1962), pp. 103–111.

Shepilov, D. T., "Speech by Comrade D. T. Shepilov to the Twentieth Party Congress," *Pravda*, February 17, 1956, pp. 3–5 (*CDSP*, Vol. VIII, No. 7, March 28, 1956, pp. 16–21).

Shimmel, N., "From Feudalism to Socialism," *New Times*, No. 28 (July 12, 1961), pp. 9–10.

Shirendyb, B., "Uspekhi stroitel'stva sotsializma v Mongol'skoi Narodnoi Respublike," *Sovetskoe Vosokovedenie*, No. 5, 1958, pp. 52–54.

Skorov, G., "Torzhestvo Leninizma i narody Vostoka," *Mirovaia Ekonomika i Mezhdunarodnye Otnosheniia*, No. 4 (April, 1960), pp. 22–35.

"Soiuz sil sotsializma i natsional'no-osvoboditel'nogo dvizheniia," *Kommunist* editorial, No. 8 (May, 1964), pp. 3–10.

Sokolov, I., "The Principle Problems of the Present Age," *Mirovaia Ekonomika i Mezhdunarodnye Otnosheniia*, No. 2 (March–April, 1963), pp. 15–26 (JPRS 19821, U.S. Government Publication No. 14223, August, 1963, pp. 1–8).

Solodovnikov, V., "Africa on the Path of Freedom," *Pravda*, December 1, 1964, p. 5 (*CDSP*, Vol. XVI, No. 48, December 23, 1964, pp. 18–19).

Solonitskii, A., "Nezavisimaia Gvineiskaia Respublika," *Mirovaia Ekonomika i Mezhdunarodnye Otnosheniia*, No. 1 (January, 1959), pp. 99–101.

"Speeches by Khrushchev and Bulganin During Trip to India, Burma and Afghanistan, November–December, 1955," Supplement to *International Affairs*, No. 1, 1956, pp. 171–248.

Starushenko, G., "O gosudarstve natsional'noi demokratii," *Pravda*, January 25, 1963, p. 3.

———, "Socialism and the National Liberation Movement," *Mirovaia Ekonomika i Mezhdunarodnye Otnosheniia*, No. 2 (March–April, 1963), pp. 155–157 (JPRS 19821, U.S. Government Publication No. 14223, August, 1963, pp. 19–23).

———, "Through General Democratic Transformations to Socialist Transformation," *Kommunist*, No. 13 (September, 1962), pp. 104–109 (*CDSP*, Vol. XIV, No. 41, November 7, 1962, pp. 14–15 and 25).

Suret-Canale, J., "The French Community at the Hour of African Independence," *International Affairs*, No. 2 (February, 1961), pp. 23–30.

Suslov, V. M., "Speech by Comrade V. M. Suslov at the Twentieth Party Congress," *Pravda*, February 18, 1956, p. 7 (*CDSP*, Vol. VIII, No. 8, April 4, 1956, pp. 22–26).

Tiagunenko V., "Aktual'nye voprosy nekapitalisticheskogo puti razvitiia," *Mirovaia Ekonomika i Mezhdunarodnye Otnosheniia*, No. 10, 1964, pp. 13–25 and No. 11, 1964, pp. 15–28.

———, "Na glavnuiu revoliutsionnuiu magistral," *Krasnaia Zvezda*, November 11, 1964, pp. 2–3.

———, "Tendentsii obshchestvennogo razvitiia osvobodivshikhsia stran v sovremennuiu epokhu," *Mirovaia Ekonomika i Mezhdunarodnye Otnosheniia*, No. 3 (March, 1962), pp. 20–33.

Tiul'panov, S. I., "Nekotorye teoreticheskie voprosy raspada kolonial'noi sistemy imperializma," *Vestnik Leningradskogo Universiteta* (Seriia Ekonomiki, Filosofii i Prava), No. 11, 1959, pp. 5–25.

———, "The Problem of State Capitalism in Underdeveloped Countries," *Vestnik Leningradskogo Universiteta* (Seriia Ekonomiki, Filosofii i Prava), Vol. XVI, No. 1 (March, 1961), pp. 5–22 (JPRS 8370, U.S. Government Publication No. 13265, August, 1961, pp. 1–20).

Tomilin, Iu., "East Africa Chooses the Way," *International Affairs*, No. 1 (January, 1964), pp. 41–47.

———, "East Africa Will Be Free," *International Affairs*, No. 5 (May, 1961), pp. 46–51.

Touré, Sékou, "Speech by Sékou Touré," *Pravda*, February 13, 1961, pp. 5–6 (*CDSP*, Vol. XIII, No. 7, March 15, 1961, pp. 26–27).

Tretiakov, P., "The Mali Peasant," *New Times*, No. 13 (March 28, 1962), pp. 26–28.

Tsedenbal, Yumjagiyn, "Mongolia's Path," *New Times*, No. 47 (November 25, 1964), pp. 8–10.

Tsoppi, Victor, "Mali: The Youth of an Ancient Country," *New Times*, No. 34 (August 22, 1962), pp. 27–29.

Tumur-Ochir, D., "Mongol'skaia Narodnaia Respublika na puti k sotsializmu," *Sovetskoe Vostokovedenie*, No. 2, 1956, pp. 15–28.

———, "O nekapitalisticheskom puti razvitiia otstalykh stran k sotsializmu," *Voprosy Filosofii*, No. 1, 1956, pp. 47–62.

"The Twentieth Congress of the C.P.S.U. and the Problems of Studying the Contemporary East," *Sovetskoe Vostokovedenie* editorial, No. 1, 1956, pp. 3–12 (an abridged translation appears in Thomas Thornton, ed., *The Third World in Soviet Perspective*. Princeton: Princeton University Press, 1964, pp. 78–87).

Ul'rikh, O., "Osnova industrializatsii," *Aziia i Afrika Segodnia*, No. 10 (October, 1963), pp. 13–14.

———, "The State Economic Policy in the Underdeveloped Countries," *Mirovaia Ekonomika i Mezhdunarodnye Otnosheniia*, No. 4 (April, 1962), pp. 95–98 (JPRS 14607, U.S. Government Publication No. 17880, September, 1962, pp. 84–90).

"Usilit' bor'bu protiv burzhuaznoi i reformistskoi ideologii," *Kommunist* editorial, No. 2 (February, 1958), pp. 3–13.

Usov, G., "Gosudarstvennyi sektor v ekonomike stran Vostochnoi Afriki," *Mirovaia Ekonomika i Mezhdunarodnye Otnosheniia*, No. 2, 1963, pp. 52–62.

———, "The National Bourgeoisie and the Liberation Movement in East Africa," *Mirovaia Ekonomika i Mezhdunarodnye Otnosheniia*, No. 4 (April, 1962), pp. 82–87 (JPRS 14607, U.S. Government Publication No. 17880, September, 1962, pp. 53–64).

———, "Rabochii klass Afriki v bor'be protiv imperializma," *Mirovaia Ekonomika i Mezhdunarodnye Otnosheniia*, No. 6 (June, 1961), pp. 127–130.

Valiev, S., "Maliiskii frank," *Aziia i Afrika Segodnia*, No. 2 (February, 1963), pp. 20–21.

Vasil'ev, I., "Gvineia: proshloe i budushchee," *Aziia i Afrika Segodnia*, No. 10 (October, 1963), pp. 8–10.

"Velikaia Oktiabr'skaia Sotsialisticheskaia Revoliutsiia i sovremennyi Vostok," *Sovetskoe Votokovedenie*, No. 5, 1956, pp. 3–10.

Vol'skii, D., "Profsoiuzy Afriki," *Sovremennyi Vostok*, No. 1 (January, 1959), pp. 23–26.

"Vsepobezhdaiushchie idei kommunizma," *Sovremennyi Vostok*, No. 11 (November, 1958), pp. 5–6.

"Vyshe znamia Marksistsko-Leninskoi ideologii," *Kommunist* editorial, No. 1 (January, 1957), pp. 3–14.

Wolk, S., "The Mali Coup," *New Times,* No. 36 (September, 1960), pp. 18–19.

Zhukov, E. M., "The Bandung Conference of African and Asian Countries and its Historic Significance," *International Affairs,* No. 5 (May, 1955), pp. 18–32.

————, "The Bankruptcy of the Imperialist Colonial System and International Relations," *International Affairs,* No. 3 (March, 1959), pp. 64–68.

————, "The October Revolution and the Rise of the National-Liberation Movement," *International Affairs,* No. 9 (September, 1957), pp. 39–44.

————, "Pol'nyi krakh kolonializma neminuet," *Pravda,* January 5, 1961, pp. 3–4.

————, "Significant Factor of Our Times," *Pravda,* August 26, 1960, pp. 3–4 (*CDSP,* Vol. XII, No. 34, September 21, 1960, pp. 18–19, condensed text).

————, "Velikaia Oktiabr'skaia Revoliutsiia i natsional'no-osvoboditel'naia bor'ba narodov," *Pravda,* November 5, 1964, p. 3.

Zhukov, Iu., "Vstrecha s Afrikoi," *Pravda,* May 19, 1964, p. 4.

Zusmanovich, A., "Proletariat Afriki boretsia protiv imperializma," *Sovremennyi Vostok,* No. 5 (May, 1958), pp. 30–32.

ARTICLES WHICH APPEARED IN THE
WORLD MARXIST REVIEW

Kremnev, Mikhail, "Africa in Search of New Paths," *World Marxist Review,* Vol. VI, No. 8 (August, 1963), pp. 72–76.

Potekhin, Ivan, "Some Aspects of the National Question in Africa," *World Marxist Review,* Vol. IV, No. 11 (November, 1961), pp. 41–46.

Sobolev, A., "National Democracy—The Way to Social Progress," *World Marxist Review,* Vol. VI, No. 2 (February, 1963), pp. 39–48.

Tsedenbal, Yumjagiyn, "From Feudalism to Socialism," *World Marxist Review,* Vol. IV, No. 3 (March, 1961), pp. 11–18.

Zakharia, Ibrahim and Cuthbert Magigwana, "The Trade Unions and the Political Scene in Africa," *World Marxist Review,* Vol. VII, No. 12 (December, 1964), pp. 19–24.

BOOKS WRITTEN BY NON-SOVIET AUTHORS

Black, Cyril and Thomas Thornton, eds. *Communism and Revolution*. Princeton: Princeton University Press, 1964.

Brockway, Fenner. *African Socialism*. Chester Springs (Pennsylvania): Dufour Editions, 1963.

Brzezinski, Zbigniew, ed. *Africa and the Communist World*. Stanford: Stanford University Press, 1963.

Brzezinski, Zbigniew. *The Soviet Bloc*. Revised edition, New York: Praeger, 1961.

Brzezinski, Zbigniew and Samuel Huntington. *Political Power: USA/USSR*. New York: Viking Press, 1964.

Dia, Mamadou. *The African Nations and World Solidarity*. New York: Praeger, 1961.

Feuer, Lewis, ed. *Marx and Engels: Basic Writings on Politics and Philosophy*. Garden City: Doubleday, 1959.

Friedland, William and Carl Rosberg, Jr., eds. *African Socialism*. Stanford: Stanford University Press, 1964.

Hamrell, Sven and Carl Gosta Widstrand, eds. *The Soviet Bloc, China and Africa*. Uppsala: Scandinavian Institute of African Studies, 1964.

Heilbroner, Robert. *The Great Ascent*. New York, Evanston and London: Harper and Row, 1963.

Jacobs, Dan, ed. *The New Communist Manifesto and Related Documents*. Evanston and Elmsford (New York): Row, Peterson, 1961.

Kautsky, John, ed. *Political Change in Underdeveloped Countries*. New York and London: John Wiley and Sons, 1962.

Kolarz, Walter. *Communism and Colonialism*. London: Macmillan and New York: St. Martin's Press, 1964.

Kurzman, Dan. *Subversion of the Innocents*. New York: Random House, 1963.

Laqueur, Walter and Leopold Labedz, eds. *Polycentrism*. New York: Praeger, 1962.

Legum, Colin. *Pan-Africanism: A Short Political Guide*. London and Dunmow: Pall Mall Press, 1962.

Leonhard, Wolfgang. *The Kremlin Since Stalin*. New York: Praeger, 1962.

London, Kurt, ed. *New Nations in a Divided World*. New York and London: Praeger, 1963.

————, ed. *Unity and Contradiction*. New York: Praeger, 1962.

Marx, Karl and Friedrich Engels. *The Communist Manifesto.* New York: International Publishers, 1948.

————, *On Colonialism.* Moscow: Foreign Languages Publishing House, 1960.

Mboya, Tom. *Freedom and After.* Boston: Little, Brown and Co., 1963.

Morison, David. *The U.S.S.R. and Africa.* London: Institute of Race Relations and Central Asian Research Centre, and New York and London: Oxford University Press, 1964.

Nkrumah, Kwame. *Consciencism.* London: Heinemann, 1964.

————, *Ghana: The Autobiography of Kwame Nkrumah.* New York: Thomas Nelson and Sons, 1957.

————, *I Speak of Freedom.* New York: Praeger, 1961.

Padmore, George. *Pan-Africanism or Communism?* London: Dennis Dobson, 1956.

Russia Looks at Africa. London: Central Asian Research Centre and Soviet Affairs Study Group of St. Antony's College, Oxford, 1960.

Schapiro, Leonard, ed. *The U.S.S.R. and the Future.* New York and London: Praeger, 1962.

Senghor, Léopold. *On African Socialism.* New York and London: Praeger, 1964.

Sigmund, Paul, Jr., ed. *The Ideologies of the Developing Nations.* New York and London: Praeger, 1963.

Thornton, Thomas, ed. *The Third World in Soviet Perspective.* Princeton: Princeton University Press, 1964.

Touré, Sékou. *Expérience Guinéenne et Unité Africaine.* Paris: Présence Africaine, 1961.

Ulam, Adam. *The Unfinished Revolution.* New York: Random House, 1960.

World Strength of Communist Party Organizations. Sixteenth Annual Report. U.S. Department of State, Bureau of Research and Intelligence, January, 1964.

SOURCES FROM NON-SOVIET PERIODICALS AND BOOKS

Africa Report, "Special Issue on African Socialism," Vol. VIII, No. 5, May, 1963.

"Africa's Future: The Soviet View," Supplement to *Mizan Newsletter,* No. 4, April, 1961.

Andrain, Charles, "Guinea and Senegal: Contrasting Types of

African Socialism," in William Friedland and Carl Rosberg, Jr., eds. *African Socialism*. Stanford: Stanford University Press, 1964, pp. 160–174.

Ansprenger, Franz, "Communism in Tropical Africa," in Sven Hamrell and Carl Gosta Widstrand, eds. *The Soviet Bloc, China and Africa*. Uppsala: Scandinavian Institute of African Studies, 1964, pp. 75–100.

Brzezinski, Zbigniew, "The Politics of Underdevelopment," *World Politics*, Vol. IX, No. 1 (October, 1956), pp. 55–75.

Bourke, Fred, "Tanganyika: The Search for Ujamaa," in William Friedland and Carl Rosberg, Jr., eds. *African Socialism*. Stanford: Stanford University Press, 1964, pp. 194–219.

Césaire, Aimé, "The Political Thought of Sékou Touré," *Présence Africaine* (English edition), Vol. I, 1960, pp. 63–72.

Dallin, Alexander, "The Soviet Union: Political Activity," in Zbigniew Brzezinski, ed. *Africa and the Communist World*. Stanford: Stanford University Press, 1963, pp. 7–48.

Dinerstein, Herbert, "Soviet Doctrines on Developing Countries: Some Divergent Views," in Kurt London, ed. *New Nations in a Divided World*. New York and London: Praeger, 1963, pp. 75–89.

Erlich, Alexander and Christian Sonne, "The Soviet Union: Economic Activity," in Zbigniew Brzezinski, ed. *Africa and the Communist World*. Stanford: Stanford University Press, 1963, pp. 49–83.

Friedland, William, "Four Sociological Trends in African Socialism," *Africa Report*, Vol. VIII, No. 5 (May, 1963), pp. 7–10.

Gasteyger, Curt, "The Soviet Union and the Tiers Monde," *Survey*. No. 43 (August, 1962), pp. 10–22.

Griffith, William, "Communist Polycentrism and the Underdeveloped Areas," in Kurt London, ed. *New Nations in a Divided World*. New York and London: Praeger, 1963, pp. 274–286.

——, "Yugoslavia," in Zbigniew Brzezinski, ed. *Africa and the Communist World*. Stanford: Stanford University Press, 1963, pp. 116–141.

Grundy, Kenneth, "The 'Class Struggle' in Africa: An Examination of Conflicting Theories," *Journal of Modern*

African Studies, Vol. II, No. 3 (November, 1964), pp. 379–393.

———, "Mali: The Prospects of 'Planned Socialism,' " in William Friedland and Carl Rosberg, Jr., eds. *African Socialism.* Stanford: Stanford University Press, 1964, pp. 175–193.

———, "Marxism-Leninism and African Underdevelopment," *International Journal,* Vol. XVII, No. 3 (summer, 1962), pp. 300–304.

Kautsky, John, "Russia, China and Nationalist Movements," *Survey,* No. 43 (August, 1962), pp. 119–129.

Kolarz, Walter, "The Impact of Communism on West Africa," *International Affairs* (London), Vol. XXXVIII, No. 2 (April, 1962), pp. 156–169.

———, "The West African Scene," *Problems of Communism,* Vol. X, No. 6 (November–December, 1961), pp. 15–23.

Labedz, Leopold, "Introduction," *Survey,* No. 43 (August, 1962), pp. 3–9.

Laqueur, Walter, "Communism and Nationalism in Tropical Africa," *Foreign Affairs,* Vol. XXXIX, No. 4 (July, 1961), pp. 610–621.

Lewis, William, "Sub-Saharan Africa," in Cyril Black and Thomas Thornton, eds. *Communism and Revolution.* Princeton: Princeton University Press, 1964, pp. 367–390.

Lowenthal, Richard, "China," in Zbigniew Brzezinski, ed. *Africa and the Communist World.* Stanford: Stanford University Press, 1963, pp. 142–203.

———, "On National Democracy: Its Function in Communist Policy," *Survey,* No. 47 (April, 1963), pp. 119–133.

———, "The Points of the Compass," in John Kautsky, ed. *Political Change in Underdeveloped Countries.* New York and London: John Wiley and Sons, 1962, pp. 335–347.

———, "The Prospects for Pluralistic Communism," *Dissent.* Vol. XII, No. 1 (winter, 1965), pp. 103–143.

———, "The Sino-Soviet Split and its Repercussions in Africa," in Sven Hamrell and Carl Gosta Widstrand, eds. *The Soviet Bloc, China and Africa.* Uppsala: Scandinavian Institute of African Studies, 1964, pp. 131–145.

Mboya, Tom, "African Socialism," in William Friedland and Carl Rosberg, Jr., eds. *African Socialism.* Stanford: Stanford University Press, 1964, pp. 250–258.

Morgenthau, Ruth Schachter, "African Socialism: Declaration of Ideological Independence," *Africa Report*, Vol. VIII, No. 5 (May, 1963), pp. 3–6.

Morison, David, "Moscow's First Steps," *Problems of Communism*, Vol. X, No. 6 (November–December, 1961), pp. 8–15.

————, "Soviet Policy Towards Africa," in Sven Hamrell and Carl Gosta Widstrand, eds. *The Soviet Bloc, China and Africa*. Uppsala: Scandinavian Institute of African Studies, 1964, pp. 30–42.

Nkrumah, Kwame, "Some Aspects of Socialism in Africa," in William Friedland and Carl Rosberg, Jr., eds. *African Socialism*. Stanford: Stanford University Press, 1964, pp. 259–263.

Nove, Alec, "The Soviet Model and Underdeveloped Countries," *International Affairs* (London), Vol. XXXVII, No. 1 (January, 1961), pp. 29–38.

Nyerere, Julius, "Ujamaa: The Basis of African Socialism," in William Friedland and Carl Rosberg, Jr., eds. *African Socialism*. Stanford: Stanford University Press, 1964, pp. 238–247.

Pipes, Richard, "Nationalism and Nationality," in Leonard Schapiro, ed. *The U.S.S.R. and the Future*. New York and London: Praeger, 1962, pp. 69–85.

Pistrak, Lazar, "Soviet Views on Africa," *Problems of Communism*. Vol. XI, No. 2 (March–April, 1962), pp. 24–31.

Potekhin, Ivan, "De quelques questions méthodologiques pour l'étude de la formation des nations en Afrique au Sud du Sahara," *Présence Africaine*, No. 17 (December, 1957–January, 1958), pp. 60–75.

————, "Ethnographic Observations in Ghana," *West Africa*, November 8, 1958, pp. 1061–1062.

Ra'anan, Uri, "Moscow and the 'Third World,' " *Problems of Communism*. Vol. XIV, No. 1 (January–February, 1965), pp. 22–31.

Schatten, Fritz, "Africa: Nationalism and Communism," in Walter Laqueur and Leopold Labedz, eds. *Polycentrism*. New York: Praeger, 1962, pp. 235–246.

Senghor, Léopold, "African-Style Socialism," in William Friedland and Carl Rosberg, Jr., eds. *African Socialism*. Stanford: Stanford University Press, 1964, pp. 264–266.

Seton-Watson, Hugh, "The Communist Powers and Afro-

Asian Nationalism," in Kurt London, ed. *Unity and Contradiction*. New York: Praeger, 1962, pp. 187–206.

Shinn, William, Jr., "The National Democratic State: A Communist Program for Less-Developed Areas," *World Politics*, Vol. XV, No. 3 (April, 1963) , pp. 377–389.

Sonnenfeldt, Helmut, "Soviet Strategy in Africa," *Africa Report*. Vol. V, No. 11 (November, 1960), pp. 5–6, 10, 14–15.

"The U.S.S.R. and the Developing Countries," *Mizan Newsletter* special issue, Vol. VI, No. 10, November, 1964.

Yakobson, Sergius, "Russia and Africa," in Ivo Lederer, ed. *Russian Foreign Policy: Essays in Historical Perspective*. New Haven and London: Yale University Press, 1962, pp. 453–488.

Zartman, William, "Communism in Africa," in Jeane Kirkpatrick, ed. *The Strategy of Deception: A Study in World-Wide Communist Tactics*. New York: Farrar, Straus and Co., 1963, pp. 165–192.

Index

BIOGRAPHICAL AND GEOGRAPHICAL INDEX

Abet, Ia., 84, 75
Abidjan, 135
Accra (Ghana), 77, 93, 135
Afghanistan, 48
Akopian, 100
Aleksandrovskaia, L., 153, 193, 222, 224
Algeria, 68, 84, 153, 173, 193, 198, 222, 234
Andreasian, R., 103, 105, 184, 215, 218
Angola, 139, 140
Ataturk, Kemal, 176
Australia, 182
Avakov, R., 89, 91, 92, 100, 101, 102, 103, 105, 121, 123, 124, 127, 130, 133, 135, 143, 148, 149, 151, 154, 155, 184, 193, 215, 218
Azembski, Miroslaw, 113, 114
Azikiwe, Nnamdi, 18

Baako, Kofi, 31
Babu, Adbul Rahman Mohammed, 17, 229, 231
Bamako (Mali), 31
Banda, Hastings, 18, 245
Basutoland, 198
Belgium, 53

Beliaev, I., 81, 115
Ben Bella, Ahmed, 15, 75, 234, 241
Bochkarev, Iurii, 76, 107, 115, 116, 143, 160, 174, 188
Boumedienne, Houari, 241
Braginskii, M., 124, 139, 141
Brazil, 66
Brezhnev, Leonid, 34
Bruk, S. I., 191, 211
Brutents, Karen, 83, 99, 100, 156, 174, 178, 179, 184, 186, 189, 190
Brzezinski, Zbigniew, 38, 227, 230, 237, 241, 242, 247
Bulganin, Nikolai, 44, 48, 49
Bulgaria, 127
Burma, 48, 84, 98, 173

Cameroun, 17
Canada, 182
Castro, Fidel, 64, 166, 167, 187, 188, 245
Chad, 116
Cheboksarov, N. N., 191, 211
Chernyshevsky, Nikolai, 225
Chiang Kai-shek, 176
China, 51, 66, 67, 72, 169, 180, 198, 202, 208, 210, 232, 233, 234, 243, 244

269

Congo (Brazzaville), 16, 103, 166, 234
Congo (Kinshasa), 17, 53, 222, 230, 244, 245
Cuba, 53, 63, 166, 167, 187, 188, 189, 196, 212, 213, 233, 235, 236, 245, 247

Dahomey, 244
Dallin, Alexander, 191, 192, 234
Davidson, A., 105
DeGaulle, Charles, 21, 106
Dement'ev, Iu., 111
Denmark, 66
Dinerstein, Herbert, 156, 235, 236
Djilas, Milovan, 129
Dmitriev, V., 89, 90
Dolgopolov, E., 157
Dzhunusov, M. S., 204

Engels, Friedrich, 22, 54, 55, 80, 181, 182, 183, 201, 220, 221, 222
Ethiopia, 134, 241

Farizov, I., 224
Feuer, Lewis, 182, 221
France, 18, 73, 74, 109
Fridman, L. A., 152
Friedland, William, 18, 22
Friedrich, Carl, 38

Gabon, 17
Gatsoiev, A., 184
Gavrilov, N. I., 107, 110, 115, 138, 139, 140, 141, 145, 225
Gbenye, Christophe, 17
Germany, 54, 238
Ghana, 16, 27, 31, 37, 38, 53, 63, 64, 65, 68, 77, 93, 94, 96, 97, 103, 104, 105, 108, 116, 117, 131, 132, 134, 135, 136, 139, 140, 152, 153, 164, 174, 187, 193, 198, 212, 216, 218, 222, 225, 234, 235, 236, 238, 239, 241, 242, 247
Glukhov, A. M., 94

Gold Coast (now Ghana), 44
Gordon, L. A., 152, 242
Great Britain, 18, 76
Griffith, William, 14, 200
Grishechkin, K., 81, 89, 103, 126, 191, 193, 194, 214
Grundy, Kenneth, 128, 129
Guber, A. A., 90, 167
Guinea, 16, 21, 22, 23, 31, 33, 53, 63, 65, 96, 102, 103, 104, 105, 106, 107, 108, 109, 111, 113, 115, 116, 117, 118, 134, 135, 136, 140, 145, 152, 153, 167, 193, 198, 212, 214, 216, 218, 222, 225, 236, 238, 239, 241, 242, 247
Guzevaty, Iu., 82

Hanga, Abdullah Kassim, 17, 229
Hitler, Adolf, 238
Holdsworth, Mary, 209
Houphouët-Boigny, Félix, 113
Huntington, Samuel, 241, 242

India, 48, 49, 56, 58, 165, 202
Indonesia, 212
Iordanskii, Vladimir, 223
Israel, 63, 114, 115, 225
Iudin, Iu., 50
Ivanov, K., 46, 52, 146, 149, 150, 153, 163, 168, 170, 171, 173, 185, 186, 204, 225
Ivory Coast, 113, 114

Jacobs, Dan, 67, 88, 161, 210

Kankan (Guinea), 22
Katsman, V. Ia., 123, 125, 143, 144, 146, 223
Kaunda, Kenneth, 17
Kautsky, Karl, 18, 182, 228
Kazakh Soviet Socialist Republic, 204
Keita, Modibo, 16, 31, 35, 53, 78, 81, 84, 85, 97, 108, 109, 111, 112, 134
Kenya, 17, 34, 68, 139, 193, 222, 244, 245

Kenyatta, Jomo, 17, 18, 19, 34, 149, 245

Khmylov, P., 184

Khrushchev, Nikita, 6, 40, 41, 44, 47, 48, 49, 50, 52, 53, 54, 55, 57, 58, 59, 60, 61, 62, 64, 65, 66, 67, 68, 69, 77, 85, 87, 88, 92, 102, 103, 105, 106, 118, 120, 125, 127, 128, 135, 142, 151, 157, 162, 163, 165, 175, 178, 180, 183, 185, 187, 189, 190, 194, 202, 203, 210, 218, 222, 226, 233, 235, 236, 238, 240, 241, 243, 244, 246, 247

Kim, G. F., 128, 159, 161, 162, 169, 171, 172, 173, 191, 197, 201, 213

Kirichenko, S. N., 208

Kirkpatrick, Jeanne, 198

Kiselev, V., 136, 146

Kolarz, Walter, 198

Kolesnichenko, T., 93

Korionov, V., 212, 213

Kouyate, Seydou Badian, 20

Krasin, Iu., 187

Kremnev, Mikhail, 112, 196, 199

Kudriavtsev, V., 75, 85, 116, 117, 169, 170, 175

Kuprianov, P., 123, 125

Kurzman, Dan, 232

Lagos (Nigeria), 135

Laqueur, Walter, 232, 233, 235

Lenin, Vladimir (and Leninism), 19, 22, 32, 37, 51, 53, 54, 55, 56, 57, 58, 59, 69, 97, 108, 156, 157, 159, 171, 173, 179, 183, 202, 229, 235, 240, 247, 248

Leonhard, Wolfgang, 65

Letnev, A. B., 141, 224

Lewis, William, 97, 209

Li, V., 187, 216

Liberia, 17

Libya, 198

London (England), 18, 199, 200

Lowenthal, Richard, 41, 57, 199, 200, 210, 211, 227

Lumumba, Patrice, 245

Madagascar, 198

Malaya, 66

Malenkov, Georgii, 44

Mali, 16, 20, 23, 31, 33, 35, 37, 53, 63, 65, 81, 84, 85, 93, 96, 102, 103, 104, 105, 106, 109, 110, 111, 112, 115, 116, 127, 134, 139, 140, 141, 145, 153, 187, 193, 198, 212, 216, 218, 222, 224, 225, 236, 238, 239, 241, 242

Manchester (England), 18

Mao Tse-tung, 54, 55, 56, 57, 58, 187

Marx, Karl (and Marxism), 15, 22, 24, 25, 26, 27, 30, 32, 36, 54, 55, 56, 57, 59, 66, 70, 75, 80, 82, 85, 88, 91, 95, 96, 97, 99, 122, 126, 128, 129, 132, 133, 151, 153, 173, 182, 183, 186, 187, 188, 201, 202, 220, 225, 228, 229, 230, 233, 235, 239, 244, 246, 247, 248

M'ba, Leon, 17

Mboya, Tom, 17, 20, 21, 25, 27, 29

Melikian, O., 96

Mikhailov, V., 110

Mikoyan, Anastas, 7, 66, 96, 97, 102, 108, 183, 214, 216

Mirskii, Georgii, 7, 71, 72, 89, 96, 121, 123, 124, 130, 133, 135, 143, 147, 148, 149, 151, 153, 154, 155, 163, 168, 169, 187, 189, 193, 194, 196, 198, 199, 202, 216

Mongolia, 117, 181, 196, 205, 206, 207

Morgenthau, Ruth Schachter, 28

Morison, David, 128, 129, 217

Morocco, 198, 222

Moscow (U.S.S.R.), 25, 35, 48, 64, 73, 84, 100, 102, 133, 155, 163, 166, 175, 193, 198, 199, 200, 208, 220

Mulele, Pierre, 17

Nasser, Gamal Abdel, 15, 58, 230, 240
Nehru, Jawaharlal, 48, 97
Ne Win, 97
Nigeria, 133, 139, 143, 222, 244, 245
Nikolaiev, V., 115
Nkrumah, Kwame, 18, 19, 20, 21, 22, 25, 27, 28, 29, 30, 31, 32, 35, 38, 44, 53, 58, 64, 65, 74, 78, 93, 94, 96, 97, 104, 105, 108, 109, 134, 164, 229, 234, 245
North Korea, 208
Kyerere, Julius, 19, 20, 27, 28, 29, 34, 114

Ogurtsov, S., 90, 98, 99, 192, 213, 214
Orlova, A. S., 120
Osmanova, Z., 201
Ostrovitianov, Iu., 91, 97, 109, 130
Overstreet, Gene, 56

Padmore, George, 232
Paris (France), 18, 73
Pavlov, V. I., 159, 210, 212, 214, 217
Peking, 64, 211
Pipes, Richard, 176
Politkin, F., 184
Ponomarev, Boris, 94, 95, 98, 212, 218, 219
Popov, Iu., 126, 127, 136, 139, 140
Pospelova, N., 6, 197
Potekhin, Ivan, 7, 42, 43, 44, 45, 46, 53, 60, 61, 68, 69, 70, 71, 72, 73, 74, 77, 78, 79, 80, 81, 82, 83, 86, 87, 88, 89, 92, 93, 104, 105, 111, 112, 113, 114, 120, 121, 122, 123, 124, 125, 129, 130, 131, 132, 134, 135, 138, 143, 144, 145, 146, 147, 149, 150, 155, 156, 157, 161, 164, 166, 168, 174, 175, 183, 184, 185, 186, 189, 191, 201,

202, 203, 204, 208, 209, 216, 218, 222, 223, 224, 225, 246
Prague, 100, 143

Ra'anan, Uri, 6, 148, 154, 197, 243
Red'ko, I. B., 210, 212, 214
Republic of South Africa, 5, 53, 139, 146, 198
Rhodesia, 139
Rosberg, Jr., Carl, 18
Rostovskii, S. N., 208
Rousseau, Jean Jacques, 31
Roy, M. N., 54
Rumania, 233
Rybakov, 189

Sanovich, I., 142
Savel'ev, N., 142, 147
Schram, Stuart, 57
Senegal, 17, 35, 92, 110, 112, 113, 198
Senghor, Léopold, 15, 17, 19, 21, 24, 25, 28, 30, 31, 33, 35, 73, 74, 84, 97, 110, 112, 113, 114
Seton-Watson, Hugh, 232, 236
Shapiro, Leonard, 176
Shepilov, Dmitri, 66, 95
Shimmel, N., 205
Shinn, William, 209, 213
Shirendyb, B., 205
Sivolobov, A. M., 135, 136, 139, 144, 147
Skorov, G., 170, 171
Sobolev, A., 101, 102, 130, 188, 190, 204, 214, 215
Sofia (Bulgaria), 151
Sokolov, I., 50
Solod, Daniel, 108
Solodovnikov, V., 50, 68, 90
Solonitskii, A., 106, 107
Somalia, 245
Stalin, Iosif (and Stalinism), 40, 41, 42, 43, 45, 47, 51, 52, 54, 55, 57, 58, 62, 64, 88, 122, 125, 301
Starushenko, G., 100, 192, 193

Stepanov, Lev, 71, 72, 89, 91, 92, 154, 155, 168
Sudan, 81, 198, 222
Sukarno, 58, 65, 97
Suret-Canale, J., 113
Suslov, V. M., 66

Tanganyika, 139, 143, 146, 222
Tanzania, 114
Thornton, Thomas, 243
Tiagunenko, V., 84, 89, 103, 104, 106, 115, 116, 154, 157, 162, 184, 189, 190, 202, 214, 216
Tiul'panov, S. I., 177, 216, 129
Tomilin, Iu., 114, 132, 141, 144, 193
Touré, Sékou, 16, 21, 25, 26, 28, 31, 32, 34, 53, 77, 93, 102, 104, 107, 108, 109, 229, 240, 245
Tubman, William, 17
Tsedenbal, Yumjagiyn, 205, 206, 207
Tsoppi, V., 224
Tumur-Ochir, D., 203
Tunisia, 198
Turchaninov, D. I., 136, 138
Turkey, 221

Uganda, 143, 221, 244
Ulam, Adam, 228, 229
Ul'ianovskii, 48, 220
Ul'rikh, O., 218, 219
Union of Soviet Socialist Republics (Soviet Union), 6, 24, 34, 35, 37, 40, 41, 44, 48, 49, 53, 54, 57, 58, 62, 63, 64, 65, 66, 67, 70, 75, 77, 83, 84, 90,

91, 93, 94, 95, 97, 98, 99, 102, 103, 108, 109, 114, 117, 118, 129, 141, 145, 153, 155, 167, 168, 169, 170, 172, 175, 176, 178, 183, 184, 186, 189, 191, 193, 196, 198, 199, 200, 201, 203, 204, 205, 207, 217, 219, 227, 228, 230, 231, 238, 239, 241, 242, 243
United Arab Republic, 53, 84, 153, 154, 173, 198, 222
United States, 53, 57, 79, 166
Uppsala (Sweden), 128
Usov, G., 104, 114, 136, 139, 140, 149, 161, 218
Uvachan, V., 210

Vadeev, O., 73
Varga, Eugene, 57
Vasil'ev, I., 108, 109
Verin, V. P., 85, 86, 132, 190
Vietnam, 53, 208, 230
Vol'skii, D., 139

Wolk, S., 110, 112

Youlou, Fulbert, 116
Yugoslavia, 65, 114

Zambia, 17, 139, 198
Zanzibar, 17, 198, 234
Zartman, William, 198
Zhukov, E. M., 45, 98, 117, 150, 158, 159, 162, 163, 167, 169, 186, 189, 208, 217
Zhukov, Iu., 126
Zusmanovich, A., 137

SUBJECT INDEX

Afro-Malgash Union, 132
"Afro-Marxists," 16
African personality, 21, 37, 74
All-African People's Conference, 77

Baku Congress (1920), 55
Bandung Conference, 40, 44
Bolsheviks, 54
Bourgeois-democratic revolution, 43, 55, 56, 82, 162, 164, 215

Bypassing capitalism, 56, 62, 80, 195, 196, 197, 200–208, 225, 246

Casablanca powers, 103
Christianity, 29, 31
Comintern, 54
Communist parties, 41, 117, 128, 138, 157, 166, 176, 179, 181, 186, 195, 197, 198, 199, 203, 207, 212, 214, 232, 233, 237, 238, 239
Convention People's Party (Ghana), 16, 22, 32, 44, 93, 96, 97, 104, 105, 106, 187
Creative Marxism, 41, 47, 48, 59

Democratic centralism, 22, 37
Different roads to socialism, 66, 67

Eighty-one Party Statement, 88, 161, 208, 210

Fifth Pan-African Congress, 18
French Community, 106
Fundamentals of Marxism-Leninism, 48, 68, 69, 79, 91, 122, 136, 138, 160, 179, 184, 203, 216

Groupes d'Études Communistes, 18

Humanistic socialists, 16, 24

Investissement humain, 33, 224
Islam, 29, 31, 75, 76, 107, 126

Jews, 122

Lenin Peace Prizes, 53, 85, 108

Marxism-Leninism, 16, 22, 23, 26, 35, 45, 48, 59, 60, 61, 64, 65, 66, 72, 75, 78, 81, 82, 87, 90, 93, 94, 101, 102, 113, 162, 167, 179, 185, 187, 188, 193,

195, 197, 198, 199, 200, 203, 206, 228, 231, 232, 234, 235, 238, 239, 244, 246, 247
Mensheviks, 55
"Militant extremists," 17
"Moderate socialists," 17
Mongolian People's Revolutionary Party, 117, 206, 207

National bourgeoisie, 41, 43, 44, 45, 52, 58, 61, 64, 65, 81, 98, 105, 119, 134, 135, 137, 147–151, 153, 156, 157, 158, 160–162, 167, 188, 191, 192, 211, 218, 226, 243, 244, 246
National democracy, 61, 63, 101, 102, 104, 108, 110, 187, 197, 208–215, 236, 237, 245
National-liberation movement, 44, 45, 47, 51, 96, 99, 101, 110, 123, 144, 155, 156–168, 169, 171, 172, 173, 174, 176, 177, 197, 218, 227
National-type socialism, 82, 89, 91, 99, 100, 101, 102, 177
Negritude, 21, 72, 73, 74
Negro democrats, 153, 155
Neo-colonialism, 47
New democracy, 56
Non-capitalist path, 41, 104, 105, 106, 108, 116, 117, 133, 134, 135, 142, 152, 153, 181–200, 201, 202, 205, 207, 208, 211, 214

Pan-Africanism, 16, 18, 19, 23, 39, 76, 77, 78, 112, 232, 233
Parti Africain de l'Indépendance (Senegal), 17, 93, 113, 198
Parti Démocratique Guineen (Guinea), 22, 31, 34, 93, 104, 106, 107, 108, 115, 187
Peasantry, 43, 55, 79, 105, 113, 114, 123, 125, 128, 137, 141, 142–147, 155, 156, 159, 160, 171, 172, 190, 192, 200, 206, 207, 208, 210, 211, 212, 217, 218, 221, 223, 226

Petty bourgeoisie, 43, 79, 82, 85, 86, 90, 95, 131, 137, 149, 154, 155, 160, 177, 189, 190, 212, 217

Positive neutralism, 16

Program of the Communist Party of the Soviet Union (1961), 47, 160, 177, 194, 195

Proletariat (working class), 40, 42, 43, 44, 45, 46, 54, 55, 56, 59, 61, 67, 79, 82, 84, 88, 95, 119, 123, 128, 130, 133, 134–142, 147, 151, 152, 155, 156, 157, 158, 159, 160, 163, 165, 167, 170–174, 177, 182, 188, 189, 190, 191–195, 197, 199, 200, 201, 203, 204, 206, 207, 208, 210, 211, 212, 213, 214, 215, 217, 218, 220, 227, 243, 245, 246

"Radical socialists," 16

Rassemblement Démocratique Africain (RDA), 18, 113

Revolutionary democrats, 63, 84, 96, 149, 154, 155, 187, 188, 193, 194, 212, 213, 236, 243

Second Comintern Congress (1920), 54

Seventh Comintern Congress (1935), 57

Sixth Comintern Congress (1928), 57

"Social democrats," 17

Socialist revolution, 43

Twelve Party Declaration, 67

Twentieth Congress of the Communist Party of the Soviet Union (1956), 40, 45, 51, 65, 95

Twenty-first Congress of the Communist Party of the Soviet Union (1959), 53, 202

Twenty-second Congress of the Communist Party of the Soviet Union (1961), 53, 108, 236, 239

Ujamaa, 28, 30

Union des Populations Camerounaises (Cameroun), 17

Union Progressiste Sénégalaise, 112, 113

Union Soudanaise (Mali), 75, 81, 93, 110, 115, 187

World War II, 18, 42, 113, 238

PERIODICAL REFERENCE INDEX

African Report, 16, 20, 22, 25, 28, 31, 108, 138, 198

The African Communist, 166, 199, 200

Aziia i Afrika Segodnia, 7, 47, 51, 90, 91, 97, 99, 108, 115, 127, 136, 142, 159, 171, 172, 191, 192, 193, 197, 211, 213, 214, 216, 217, 218, 224, 225,

Dissent, 41

Foreign Affairs, 233

International Affairs (London), 198

International Affairs (Moscow), 7, 45, 47, 49, 52, 69, 70, 71, 73, 74, 75, 77, 78, 79, 81, 82, 83, 85, 87, 89, 92, 93, 99, 100, 113, 114, 115, 116, 117, 118, 124, 129, 130, 131, 132, 135, 141, 144, 146, 149, 150, 153, 155, 156, 159, 160, 161, 163, 164, 167, 168, 171, 173, 175, 184, 185, 186, 193, 202, 204, 217, 225

Izvestiia, 68, 87, 169, 170, 174, 185, 194, 218

Jeune Afrique, 227
Journal of Modern African Studies, 128

Kommunist, 71, 76, 95, 103, 105, 160, 168, 174, 180, 183, 184, 188, 192, 193, 208, 210, 211, 212, 213, 215, 218, 219, 224, 234
Krasnaia Zvezda, 154, 158, 162, 193, 214

Mirovaia Ekonomika i Mezhdunarodnye Otnosheniia, 7, 84, 85, 89, 92, 96, 100, 103, 104, 106, 107, 108, 111, 114, 116, 121, 124, 130, 133, 134, 135, 136, 137, 139, 140, 143, 147, 148, 149, 151, 153, 154, 155, 159, 161, 170, 184, 187, 189, 190, 199, 202, 203, 216, 218, 219, 222
Mizan Newsletter, 6, 48, 84, 91, 100, 102, 127, 130, 133, 153, 163, 187, 191, 196, 217, 220

Narody Azii i Afriki, 7, 51, 53, 75, 78, 96, 98, 99, 110, 124, 125, 128, 130, 131, 136, 140, 144, 145, 146, 147, 152, 162, 171, 172, 175, 186, 189, 201, 210, 212, 214, 223
New Times, 7, 81, 83, 89, 105, 107, 108, 110, 112, 114, 115, 126, 138, 139, 143, 169, 174, 189, 191, 193, 194, 205, 207, 223, 224
New York Times, 35

Pravda, 26, 35, 36, 65, 66, 67, 68, 81, 87, 90, 93, 94, 95, 96, 97, 98, 102, 107, 108, 115, 126, 127, 128, 151, 158, 166, 167, 169, 174, 183, 185, 186, 190, 193, 194, 203, 208, 214, 216, 218
Présence Africaine, 26, 121, 122
Problems of Communism, 6, 148, 154, 243
Problemy Vostokovedeniia, 51, 139, 141, 157, 186, 208

Sovetskaia Etnografiia, 7, 42, 43, 44, 111, 120, 121, 123, 124, 125, 131, 132, 141, 144, 145, 146, 156, 191, 211, 223, 224
Sovetskoe Gosudarstvo i Pravo, 50, 183
Sovetskoe Vostokovedenie, 45, 46, 52, 98, 150, 174, 205
Sovremennyi Vostok, 46, 51, 137, 139, 169, 173
Survey, 211

Vestnik Leningradskogo Universiteta, 177, 197, 216, 219
Voprosy Filosofii, 187, 203

West Africa, 131, 132
World Marxist Review, 101, 112, 138, 143, 188, 190, 196, 199, 204, 206, 215
World Politics, 209, 213